nst 8.95

BEER ADVERTISING OPENERS

A Pictorial Guide

by

Donald Bull

Trumbull, Connecticut
1978

Library of Congress Catalogue Card Number 77-94261

ISBN 0-9601190-4-3

Printed in the United States of America

Printed by Ampco, Stamford, CT

Cover design by Bonnie Bull

Typesetting by Type Plus Graphics, Inc., Stamford, CT

Published by Donald Bull, ~~21 Frelma Drive~~, Trumbull, CT 06611
Box 106

also by the author ...

THE REGISTER OF UNITED STATES BREWERIES 1876 — 1976 (with Manfred Friedrich)

THE REGISTER OF UNITED STATES BREWERIES 1876 — 1976, Volume II, An Alphabetical Index (with Manfred Friedrich)

CONTENTS

just for openers...

"Budweiser means moderation." That was the inscription on the first opener to come into my possession. Since then I have immoderately "gathered" (as fellow collector Richard Wilkey so aptly puts it) many more. Too many more if you were to ask my wife. I found that Budweiser opener several years ago while rummaging through a small "junk" box in a South Windsor antique shop. Here, I decided, was something to collect which I could not imagine anyone else collecting. Within a very short time I learned this was indeed not the case. There are a great many collectors and as the years have passed I have found openers harder and harder to come by with more and more collectors taking up the search.

I started out by collecting all types of openers : beer advertising, soda advertising, hotel combination spoon and cap lifters, combination cap lifter and paint can lid lifters, hair coloring advertising, motor oil advertising, etc. I was amazed at the number of companies using this form of advertising and the variety of combinations of multi-purpose openers devised. There were openers in combination with lighters, shoe horns, ladles, spatulas, knives, cigar cutters, belt buckles, and even whisk brooms. I was overwhelmed and soon began to concentrate solely on beer advertising openers.

What better place for a brewery to advertise its product than on an opener? A beer brand could be advertised on a coaster, tray, foam scraper, glass, or mirror. Those would get the message across when seen in the taproom, but the opener's presence was always felt. Prior to the introduction of twist off tops and pull tabs, a person had to have an opener to get the contents of the beer bottle or can. What 1957 Chevy did not have an opener in the glove compartment? Who would go fishing without putting an opener in his tackle box? Openers went to work in tool boxes and lunch boxes. They hung on strings and chains from work benches and bartops. And there was always an opener in the kitchen drawer. They were indispensable. Although they may not be the most attractive form of brewery advertising, for me, they are the most fascinating.

The first bottle opener was the corkscrew. With the introduction of the crown top in the late 1800's bottle cap lifters and cap pullers entered the market as another advertising medium. In the thirties the beer can was introduced and with it, the can piercer. During the fifties the annual production of openers was over two hundred million. The small brewers would order one quarter to one half million of the combination can piercer — cap lifter. Orders from the large conglomerates ran as high as 5 to 10 million. In the sixties the twist off cap and the pull tab were introduced. By 1963 the bottom had fallen out of the "opener" market. According to Elliot Baritz of the Handy Walden Co. over 90% of the openers produced by his firm prior to 1963 were sold to breweries. In 1963 they introduced the "Ro-Loc Process" which is shown in this book. Sample openers were made — none were ever sold.

My intention in the following pages is to establish a ready identification system for collectors for ease in buying, selling, and trading openers. The first section contains actual size photographs of over 200 different types and varieties of openers. Only the obvious variations of types have been included. To incorporate minor variations in dimensions, combination cap lifter-can piercers with ends reversed, openers with and without hanger holes, differences in sharpness and angle of point on can piercers, etc. would be a monumental task and, in the end, far too confusing for the average collector.

The second section is a catalog of openers. This is not intended to be a complete list, rather it is a compilation of the openers in the collections of a number of devoted collectors who went to considerable efforts to supply their lists in order to make this book possible. With the exception of patent numbers, directions for use, and manufacturers' names, the complete inscription on each opener is given. If there is an inscription on the reverse as well as on the obverse of the opener, the information is separated by a diagonal line. A few foreign, soda, and other advertising openers have been included.

In the third section, the reader will find an interesting study of the development of the can piercer by John Burroughs, a look at the openers of the Cleveland & Sandusky Brewing Co. by Glenn Kuebeler, notes on some special openers, The Handy Walden Co. catalog, and photographs of some foreign beer advertising openers.

I thank the following collectors who helped make this work possible by supplying information about their collections: Will Anderson, Paul Auburn, Richard Barnes, Leon Beebe, John Bernhard, Paul Brady, Robert Brockmann, John Burroughs, Bruce Clark, George Clarkson, Walter and Mark Colditz, Fred Davie, Duane Dummer, Donald Fehr, Jack Ford, Phil Fouch, William Frederick, Jim Freeman, John Gaskell, Leon Geller, John Germann, Ray Geyer, Bob Gottschalk, Ron Griffith, Andy Growe, William Hartmann, Linda Haskins, Herbert Haydock, Ed Hayes, Ray Heet, Harry Horn, Bob and Marilou Kay, Ed Kaye, Orville Kramer, Glenn Kuebeler, Don Kurtz, Tom Labeska, Jean Laughlin, Tom Lothridge, Stan Loula, Pete Lundell, Herb Lyngass, John Mathot, Midge Melchoir, Carl Meyer, Hamp and Sue Miller, Patrick Miller, John Morra, Dennis Murphy, Bob Novak, R. Ojala, Jeffrey Pepperman, Chris and Carl Peters, Edward Pollock, R.W. Post, Don Reed, Curt Reinik, Harry Richards, Charles Robinson, Donald Salyers, Don Sarver, Al Schafer, Jerry Schele, Alex Schwertner, Danny Sellenthin, Larry Sherk, William Spencer, Bob Taylor, Lewis Thornburg, Dale Van Wieren, Bernie Wallace, Richard Wilkey, and J.H. Wilson.

Thanks yous also to the following individuals who supplied specific notes on a few openers: Grace Ellis of Pabst Brewing Co., Willett Foster of The Edlund Company, Joan Hanselman of Anheuser Busch, Don Lee of Olympia Brewing, John Schneider of Carling National, and John Strommer of Schmidt's of Philadelphia.

Special thanks to the following: Elliot Baritz of The Handy Walden Company who was so helpful in contributing notes to the photographs, allowed me to take pictures in the Walden plant, and permitted the reproduction of the Walden catalog. John Burroughs for the section on the "Quick and Easy" opener. Glenn Kuebeler for the section on the openers of The Cleveland & Sandusky Brewing Co. Andy Badinsky of Trumbull for his instruction in the photographic and darkroom arts.

If you have any beer advertising openers not included in this book, I would appreciate hearing from you.

Donald Bull
~~21 Frelma Drive~~ Box 106
Trumbull, CT 06611

SECTION I
OPENER CLASSIFICATION

Indian openers from the Iroquois Beverage Corp., Buffalo, New York

TYPE A FIGURAL OPENERS

A-1 Girl wading in water. "Old Style Beer" Pat'd.

A-2 Nude Girl. "Sweet Adeline's Bar, Ashland, Wis."

A-3 Girl in bathing suit. "Compliments of Indestro Mfg. Co., Chicago, Ill."

A-4 Female figure, dressed. "Leisy Beer, Peoria, Ill." C T & O Co., Chicago, Pat'd.

A-4 Female figure, nude. "The Crockery City Brew. Co., E. Liverpool, Ohio" C T & O Co., Chicago, Pt'd.

A-5 Female figure, nude. "Drink Golden Ribbon Beer"

A-6 Boot. "Compt's West End Brg. Co." / "It's in the taste — Pilsener, Utica Club, Wuerzburger — Ginger Ale"

A-7 Boot. "White Bock Beer" Pat'd Mar. 12, 1912

A-8 Knickerbocker. "In your home use Jacob Ruppert Knickerbocker"

A-9 Baseball player. "The Hoster-Columbus A.B. Co., Drink Gold Top — That's the beer"

A-10 Eagle. "Drink Muehlebach's Pilsener Beer" C T & O Co. (from the collection of Don Reed)

A-11 Shoe. "Drink Wooden Shoe Beer" (from the collection of Duane Dummer)

A-12 Sword. "Pointer Brewing Co., Clinton, Iowa"

A-13 Auto. "Drink Star Beer brewed by Star Brewery, Lomira, Wis. (from the collection of Duane Dummer)

A-14 Bridge. "Rainier Beer" / same on reverse (from the collection of Harry Horn)

Female figural openers were available in various stages and varieties of dress and undress.

Several varieties of A and B type openers were available with a square hole which was used as a wrench to open a valve on carbide tanks on the running boards of autos. When the valve was opened, it furnished gas for the headlights.

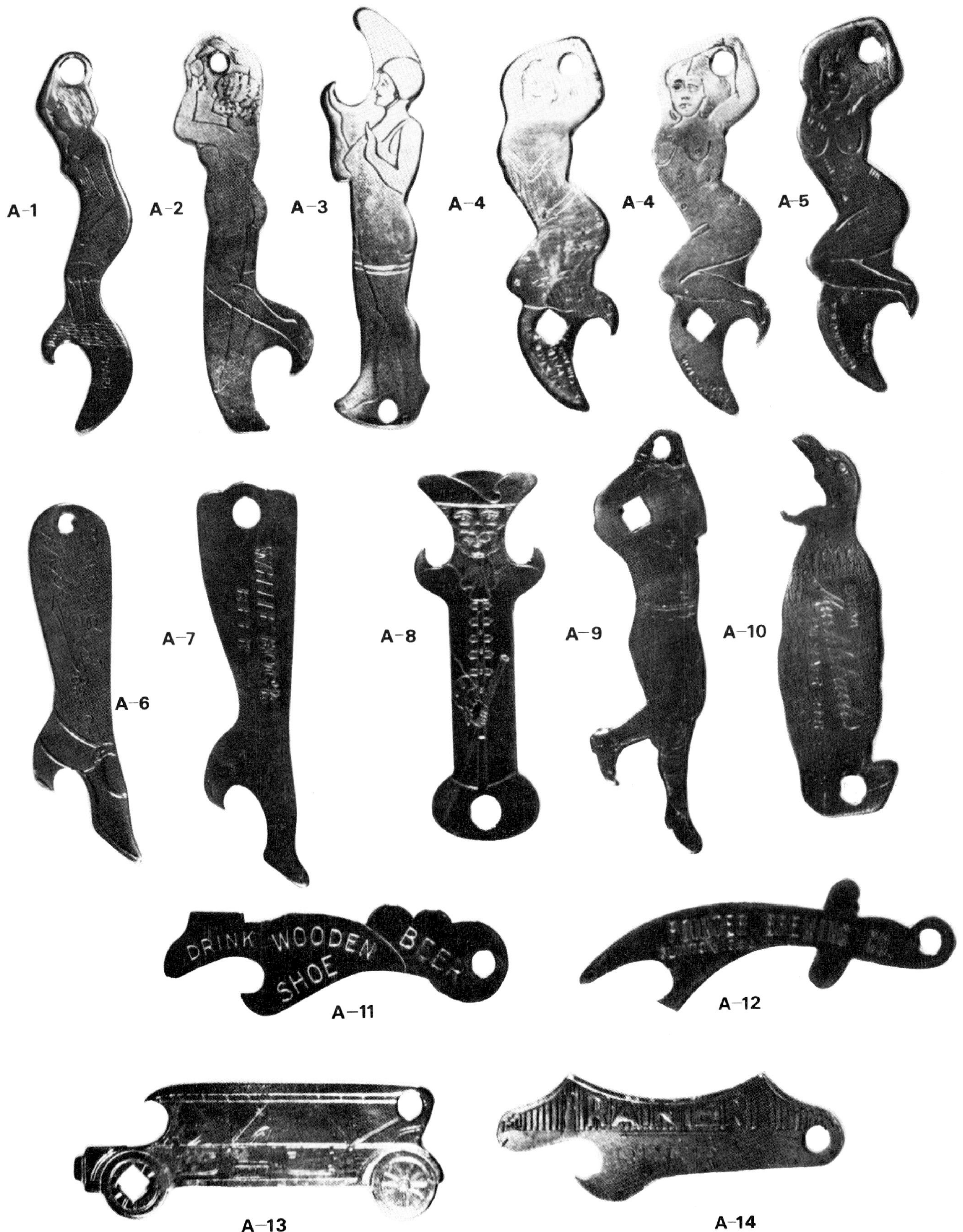

A-1 A-2 A-3 A-4 A-4 A-5

A-6 A-7 A-8 A-9 A-10

A-11 A-12

A-13 A-14

TYPE A FIGURAL OPENERS

A-15 Eagle. Square hole. "Drink Neuweiler's Purity, Allentown, Pa." C T & O Co., Chgo., Pat'd 4.30.12

A-15 Eagle. No square hole. "Cook's, Evansville, Ind."

A-16 Moose Head. "Blakeslee Brothers Beverages" C T & O Co., Chicago. Patented

A-17 Lion. "The Kamm & Schellinger Brg. Co., Mishawaka, Ind." Crown T & Co. /"Our Brands — Private Stock Export, K & S Standard"

A-18 Fish."Buck & Century Beer" / "Phone 3-6176" Nov. 1, 1911

A-19 Alligator. "The Goebel Brewing Co., Detroit, Mich. The Pure Food Beer" (from the collection of Phil Fouch)

A-20 Hand. Spinner. "You Pay" "Wehle Ale, Lager" / "spin to see who wins"

A-21 Hand. Spinner. "You Pay" "Beck's, Buffalo's best beer" / "spin to see who pays." B & B made in U.S.A.

A-22 Bottle. "Ballantine Export Beer" / "Ballantine Breweries, Newark, New Jersey" (from the collection of Phil Fouch)

A-23 "Blackhawk Beer" / Dow, St. Paul

A-24 Bottle. "High Life Beer, Miller Brewing Co., Milwaukee, Wis., U.S.A." (from the collection of Al Schafer)

A-25 Bottle. "Hamm's Famous Beer, Hamm's St. Paul." (from the collection of Al Kroeger)

A-26 Bottle. "Empire State Lager Beer — Empire State Brewing Corp., Olean, N.Y." (from the collection of Don Reed)

A-27 Bottle. "First Prize Beer — Peter Doelger First Prize Brewery, N.Y." / "Peter Doelger first prize bottled beer, Best Beer Brewed" (from the collection of Don Reed)

A-28 Bottle. "Consumers Products Co., Brooklyn, N.Y." Pat'd Mar. 12, 1912 / "Use Pilser Brand Malt & Hops"

A-29 Bottle. "Maier Beer"

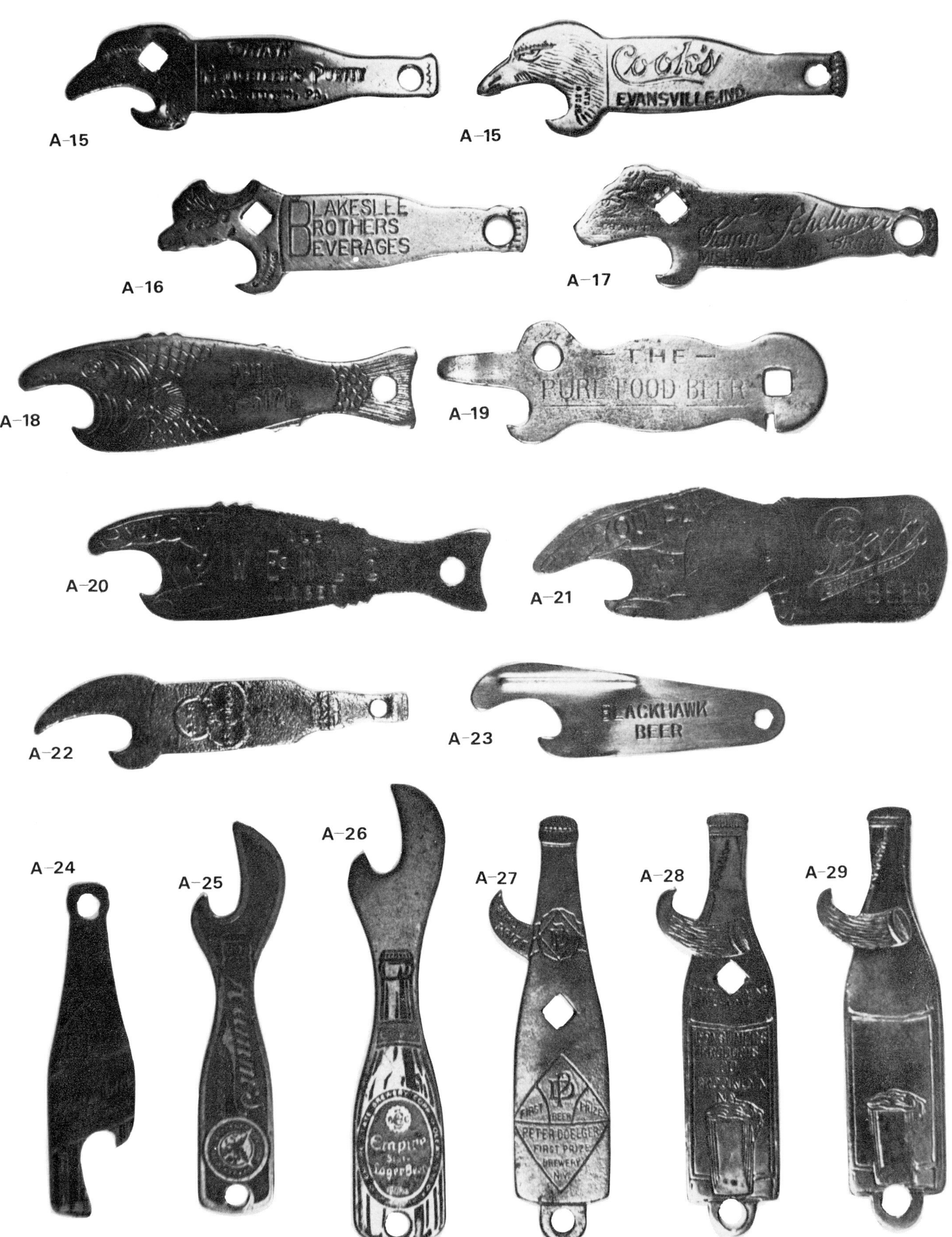

A–15 A–15

A–16 A–17

A–18 A–19

A–20 A–21

A–22 A–23

A–24 A–25 A–26 A–27 A–28 A–29

TYPE B KEY SHAPED OPENERS

B-1 "Drink Ben Brew, absolutely pure beer, Columbus, Ohio, U.S.A."

B-2 "Old Mission Lager, traditionally good, made in San Diego"

B-3 "Drink Edelweiss Beer"

B-4 "Scheidt's Valley Forge Beer"

B-5 "Storz Triumph Beer, the delicious artesian brew, Storz Br'g Co., Omaha, Neb." / "Storz Malt Extract — the best liquid and tonic" (from the collection of Don Reed)

B-6 "Drink Canada Dry, Pale Ginger Ale," The W & H Co., Newark, N.J.

B-7 "Key to Hauenstein's Beer, New Ulm, Minn." Handy pocket companion. Ruler. Patented Nov. 28, 1905. (from the collection of Al Kroeger)

B-8 "National Brewing Co., Steelton, Pa." / same on reverse. Pat. applied for. (from the collection of Ray Geyer)

B-9 "Compliments of Centennial Brewing Co., Butte, Mont." Pat. appl. for / "We make a specialty of bottle beer for family trade" (from the collection of Andy Growe)

B-10 "Congress Beer" / "Congress Beer" Pat. appl'd for. (from the collection of Don Reed)

B-11 "Key to Rainier Beer" (from the collection of Andy Growe)

B-12 "Fink's Beer, Harrisburg, U.S.A." Vaughan, Pat'd, Chicago. Button Hook. (from the collection of Don Reed)

B-13 "Iron City Lager" Made & Pat'd in U.S.A. / "Tech Dry Ginger Ale" Corkscrew.

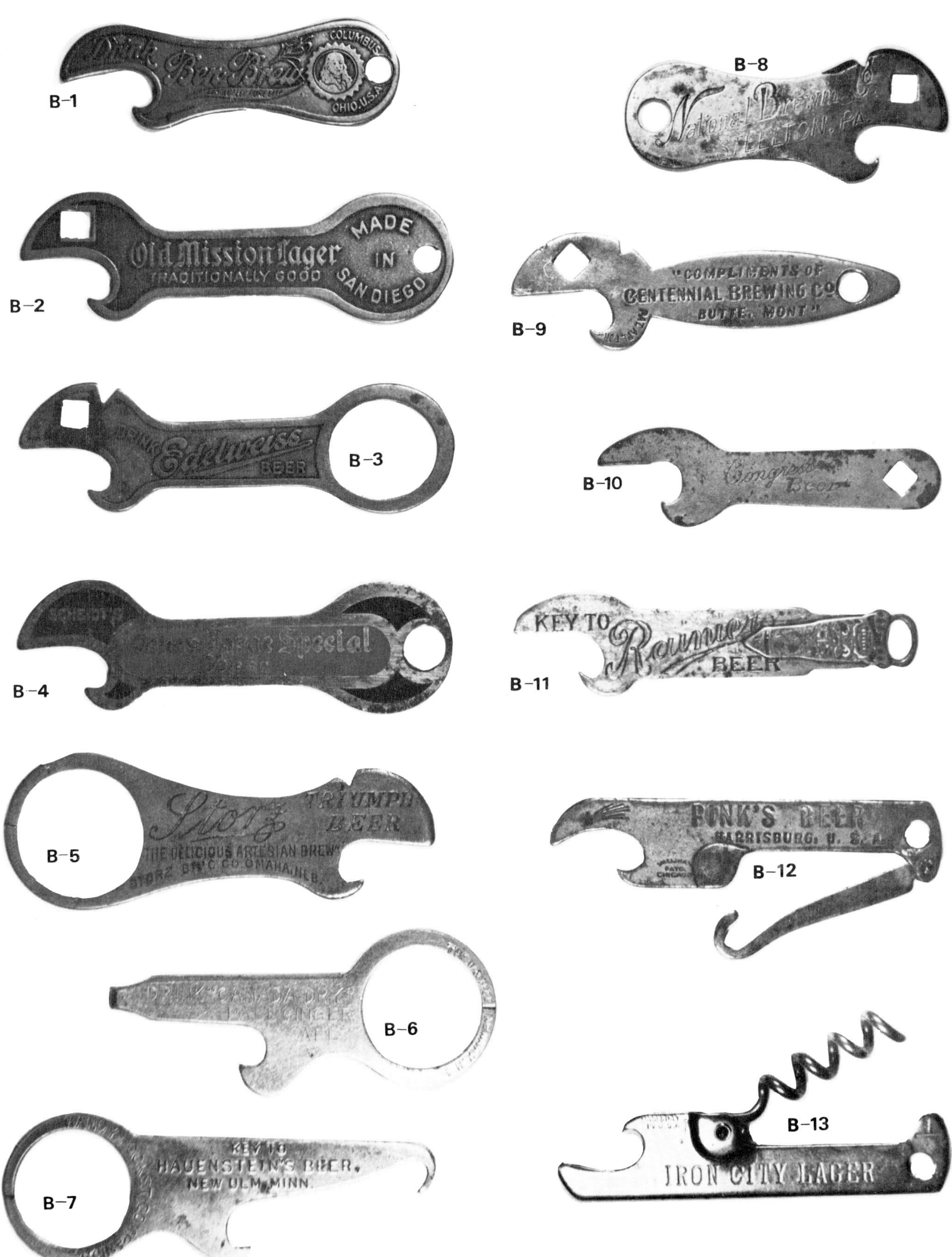
B-1
COLUMBUS
OHIO, U.S.A.
B-2
Old Mission Lager
TRADITIONALLY GOOD
MADE IN SAN DIEGO
B-3
Edelweiss
BEER
B-4
B-5
Storz
TRIUMPH BEER
THE DELICIOUS ARTESIAN BREW
STORZ BRG CO. OMAHA, NEB.
B-6
B-7
KEY TO
HAUENSTEIN'S BEER.
NEW ULM, MINN.
B-8
National Brewing Co.
STEELTON, PA.
B-9
"COMPLIMENTS OF
CENTENNIAL BREWING CO.
BUTTE, MONT"
B-10
Congress Beer
B-11
KEY TO
Rainier
BEER
B-12
BINK'S BEER
HARRISBURG, U. S. A.
B-13
IRON CITY LAGER

TYPE B KEY SHAPED OPENERS

B-14 ''The Franklin Brewing Co., Columbus, Ohio'' / ''Ask for 'Bennie' ''

B-15 ''Demand the Brown Label, Old German Lager'' (from the collection of Andy Growe)

B-16 ''Gold Label Beer, Menasha, Wis.'' (from the collection of Duane Dummer)

B-17 ''Stroh's Bohemian Beer'' / ''America's Favorite'' The Greenduck Co., Chicago. (from the collection of Phil Fouch)

B-18 ''Enterprise Brewing Co., Ale—Lager, Fall River, Mass.''

B-19 ''Drink Dick Bros' Pilsener Beer, Quincy, Ill.''

B-20 ''King's Bohemian Beer''

B-21 ''Call for the Brew from Kalamazoo, Kalamazoo Brewing Co., Kalamazoo, Mich.'' Picnic, trademark reg. U.S. Pat. Off. / A.W. Stephens Mfg. Co., Waltham, Mass., Pat. Feb. 19, 1901. (from the collection of Phil Fouch)

B-22 ''Falstaff Bottled Beer'' Outing. / ''Falstaff Bottled Beer''

B-23 ''Try Ehret's Extra'' / Ehret logo and trademark

B-24 ''Burkhardt's Beer'' / ''Mug Ale'' Vaughan, Chicago, Pat. U.S.A.

B-25 ''Elfenbrau'' / ''C & J Michel Brewing Co., LaCrosse, Wis.'' (from the collection of Stan Taylor)

B-14

B-15

B-16

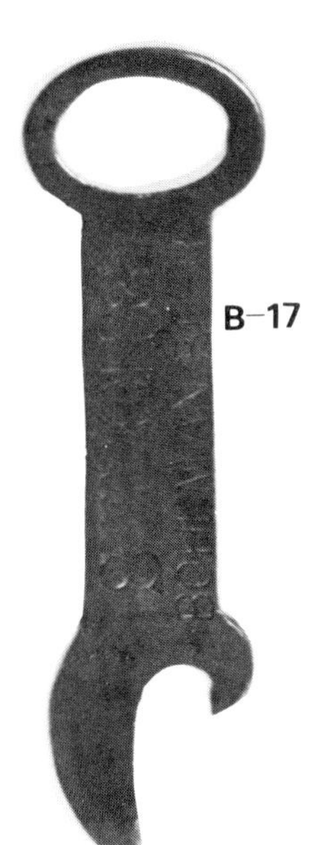
B-17

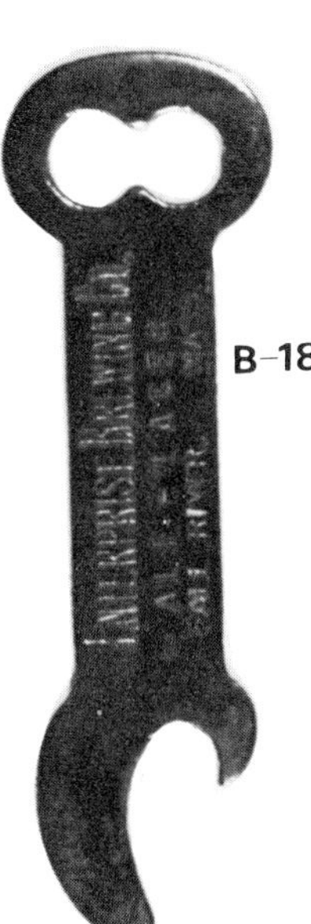
B-18

B-19

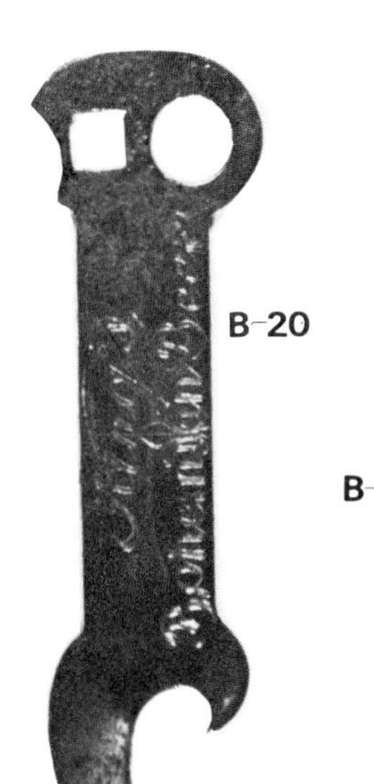
B-20

B-21

B-22

B-23

B-24

B-25

TYPE C FLAT METAL CAP LIFTERS

C-1 ‘‘Peter Doelger First Prize Quality Beer’’ (from the collection of Don Reed)

C-2 ‘‘Tech Beer, Pittsburgh Brewing Co.’’ Patented Feb. 15, 1916. Bottle and eagle.

C-3 ‘‘Don’t say beer, say Schlitz’’ (from the collection of Bob Brockmann)

C-4 ‘‘Pabst Blue Ribbon’’ / ‘‘The Beer of Quality’’ Square hole. Pabst 1916 promotional opener. (Grace Ellis, Pabst Brewing Co.)

C-5 ‘‘Pabst Blue Ribbon’’ / ‘‘The Beer of Quality’’ No square hole. (from the collection of Al Kroeger)

C-6 ‘‘Falls City Lager Beer’’

C-7 ‘‘Utica Club, Pilsener — Wuerzburger, it’s in the taste, pale dry ginger ale.’’ / same on reverse

C-8 ‘‘Drink Grain Belt’’ Caps off. 63-502 / Lift up.

C-1
Peter Doelger
FIRST PRIZE
QUALITY BEER
C-2
Tech Beer
C-3
DON'T SAY BEER
SAY Schlitz
C-4
Pabst Blue Ribbon
C-5
The Beer of Quality
C-6
Falls City
C-7
Utica Club
ITS IN THE TASTE
C-8

TYPE C FLAT METAL CAP LIFTERS

C-9 "Storz Beer — Omaha"

C-10 "Drink Dotterwyck Beers & Ale"

C-11 "Independent Milwaukee Brewery, Phone Mitchell 0880" / "Bill's Braumeister, the brew with that old time flavor" (from the collection of Duane Dummer)

C-12 "From the Cypress casks of Goebel" Eagle.

C-13 "Eldredge Portsmouth Ale" Bottle.

C-14 "Satisfying Stoney's, Jones Brewing Co., Smithton, Pa." Waiter.

C-15 "Camden Beer, tastes as good as it looks!" / Handy Walden, N.Y., U.S.A. 61.

C-16 "Schaefer, America's oldest lager beer" / same on reverse. Vaughan, Chicago.

C-17 "Moore & Quinn Ale"

Types C-12 through C-15 openers exist with and without hanger hole.

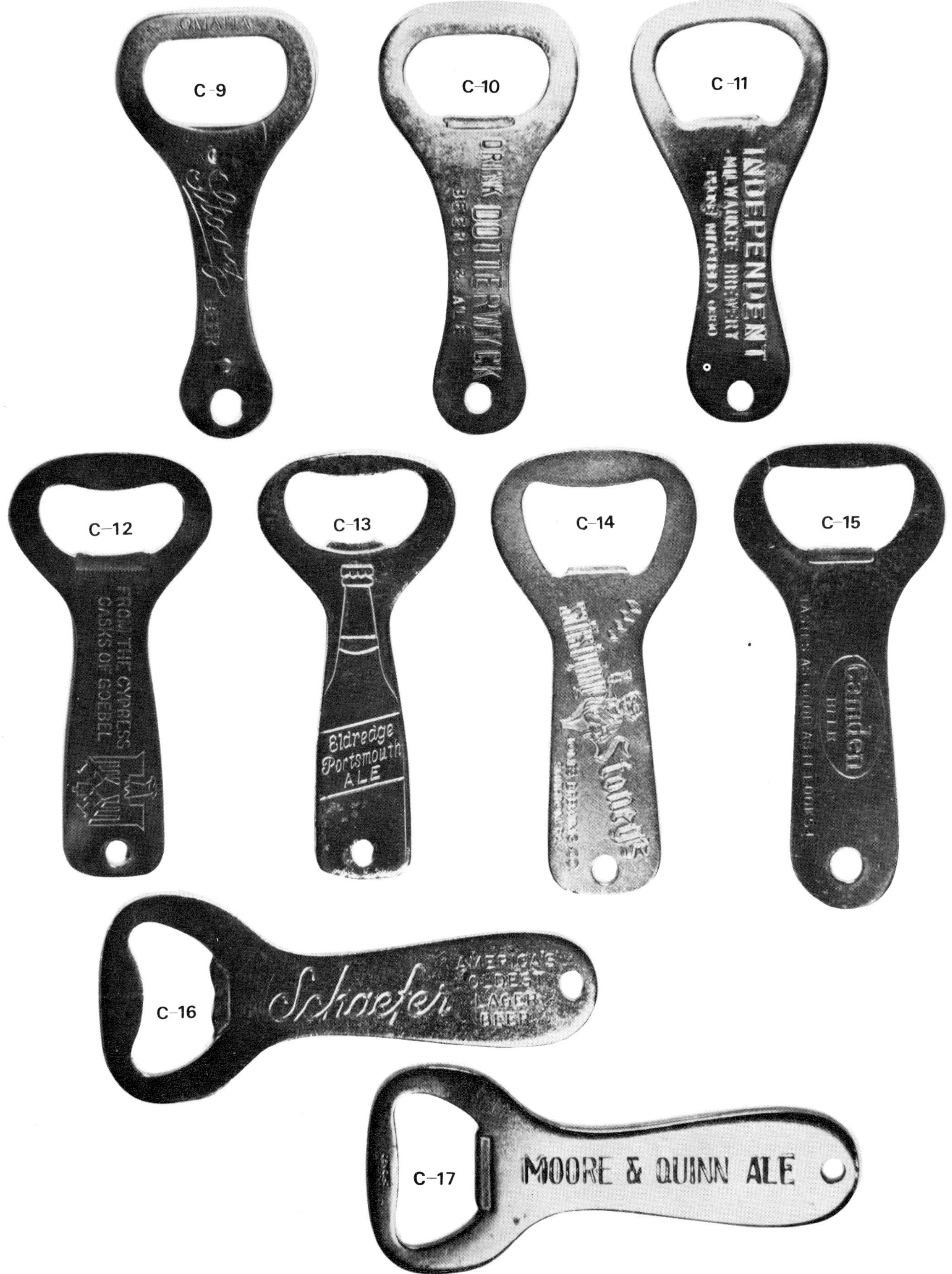
C–9
OMAHA
BEER
C–10
C–11
INDEPENDENT
MILWAUKEE BREWERY
C–12
FROM THE CYPRESS
CASKS OF GOEBEL
C–13
Eldredge
Portsmouth
ALE
C–14
C–15
Camden
BEER
C–16
Schaefer
AMERICA'S
OLDEST
LAGER
BEER
C–17
MOORE & QUINN ALE

TYPE C FLAT METAL CAP LIFTERS

C-18 ''Trommer's Beer''

C-19 ''Cremo Ale & Beer''

C-20 ''Betz — Ales — Beer — Porter''

C-21 ''The Wm. Peter Brewing Corp.'' (from the collection of Don Reed)

C-22 ''Jacob Ruppert, Brewer, New York'' Pat. No. 91635 / ''Save this opener, Order by the case, Knickerbocker, the brew that satisfies''

C-23 ''Drink Jax, best beer in town, Jackson Brewing Co., N.O., La.'' / same on reverse. (from the collection of Andy Growe)

C-24 Not shown. Type is similar to Type C-20 except ends are flat.

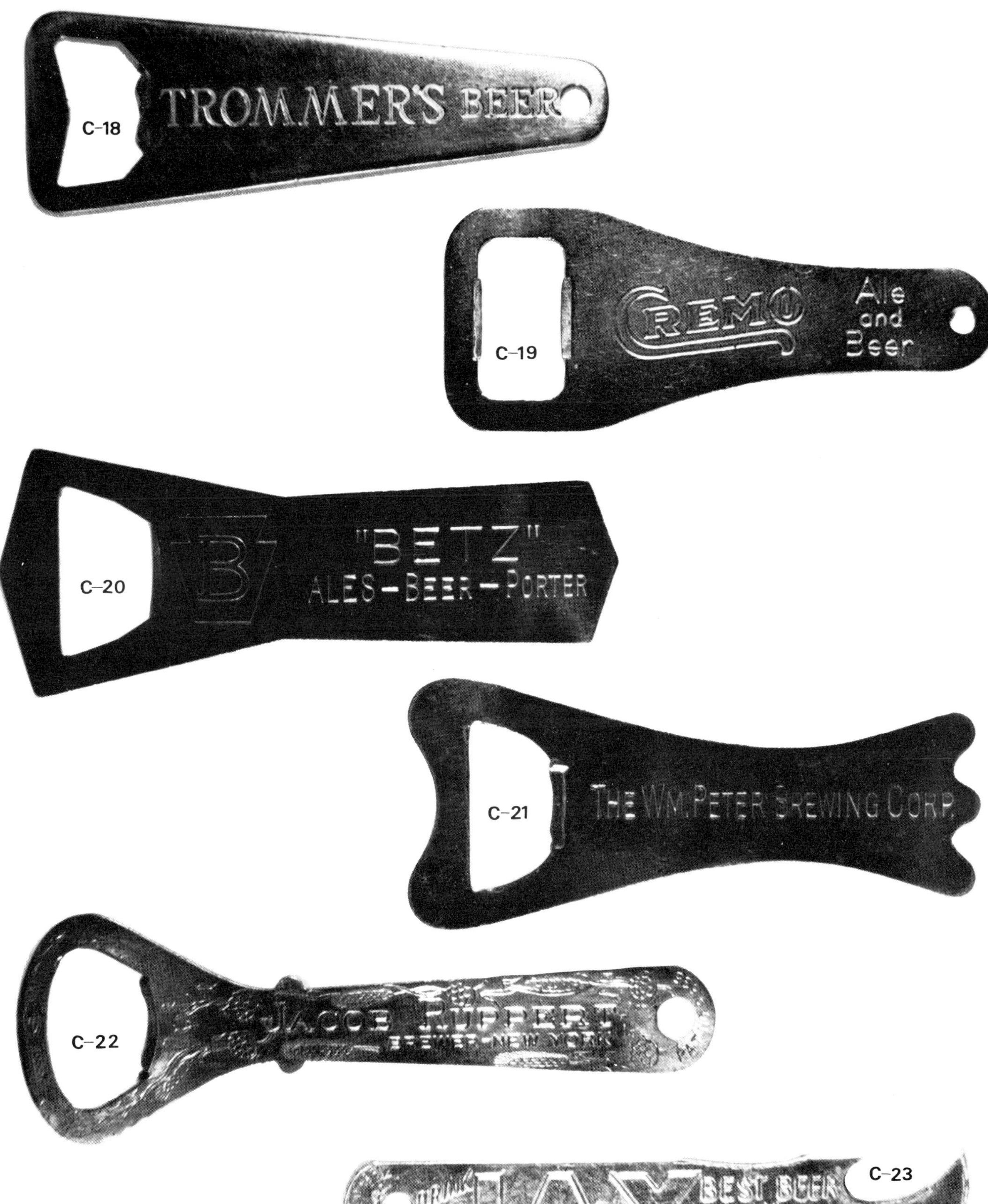
C–18
TROMMER'S BEER
C–19
CREMO
Ale and Beer
C–20
B
"BETZ"
ALES—BEER—PORTER
C–21
THE WM. PETER BREWING CORP.
C–22
JACOB RUPPERT
BREWER NEW YORK
C–23
DRINK
JAX
BEST BEER IN TOWN

TYPE D CAST IRON CAP LIFTERS

D-1 ‘‘Stroh’s Beer’’ / same

D-2 ‘‘Schlitz’’ / same

D-3 ‘‘Velvet’’ / ‘‘Terre Haute’’

D-4 ‘‘Leisy’s’’ / same

D-5 ‘‘Pointer Beer’’

D-6 ‘‘Fehr’s’’ / ‘‘Louisvlle’’ (note no letter ‘‘i’’) Bottle Stopper (from the collection of Jerry Schele)

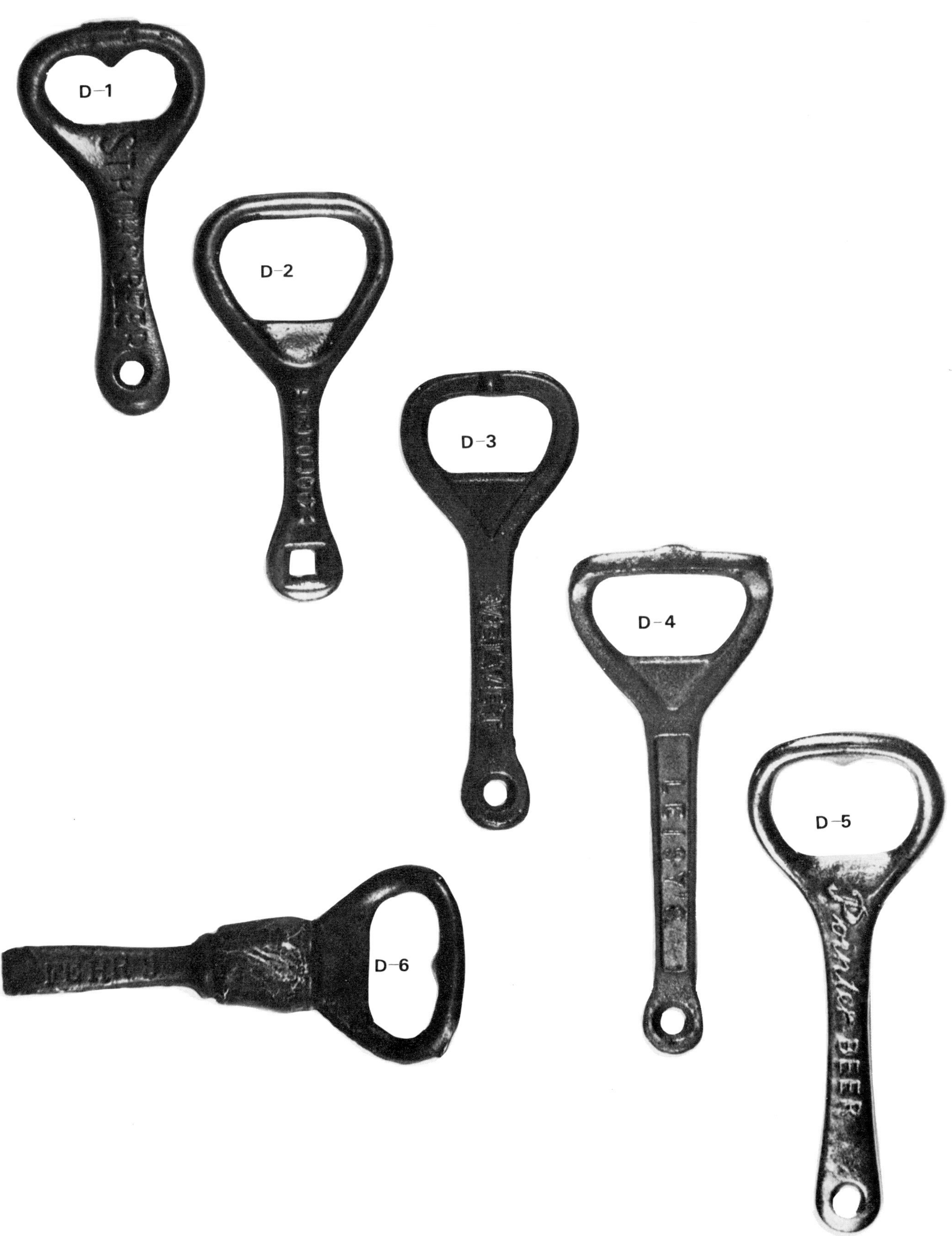
D–1
D–2
D–3
D–4
D–5
D–6

TYPE E WIRE FORMED OPENERS

E-1 "Hull Brewing Co., New Haven, Conn." / "Hull's Cream Ale & Lager"

E-2 "Adam Scheidt Brewing Co." / "Valley Forge Beer"

E-3 "Fisher Beer since 1884" / "Fisher Beer since 1884" Vaughan, Chicago

E-4 "Jacob Ruppert, Brewer — New York" / "Order Knickerbocker by the case"

E-4 "Cataract Cream Ale, Cataract Brewing Co., Inc." Pat. Pending / "Canandaigua High Hopped Ale, Cataract Brewing Co., Inc."

E-4 "Drink Heurich's Beer" / "Famous for quality since 1873"

E-5 "Esslinger's Beer and Ale, Philadelphila, Pa." Plastic Handle. Esslinger's Little Man.

Types E-1 to E-3: Sometimes called "Wide wire hoop."

Type E-4: Sometimes called "Single handle wire hoop." Varieties include single fret (or tab) at top of hoop, two frets at base of hoop, three frets; rounded tops, flat tops, dipped tops; screwdriver end.

Type E-5: Plastic handles vary in length.

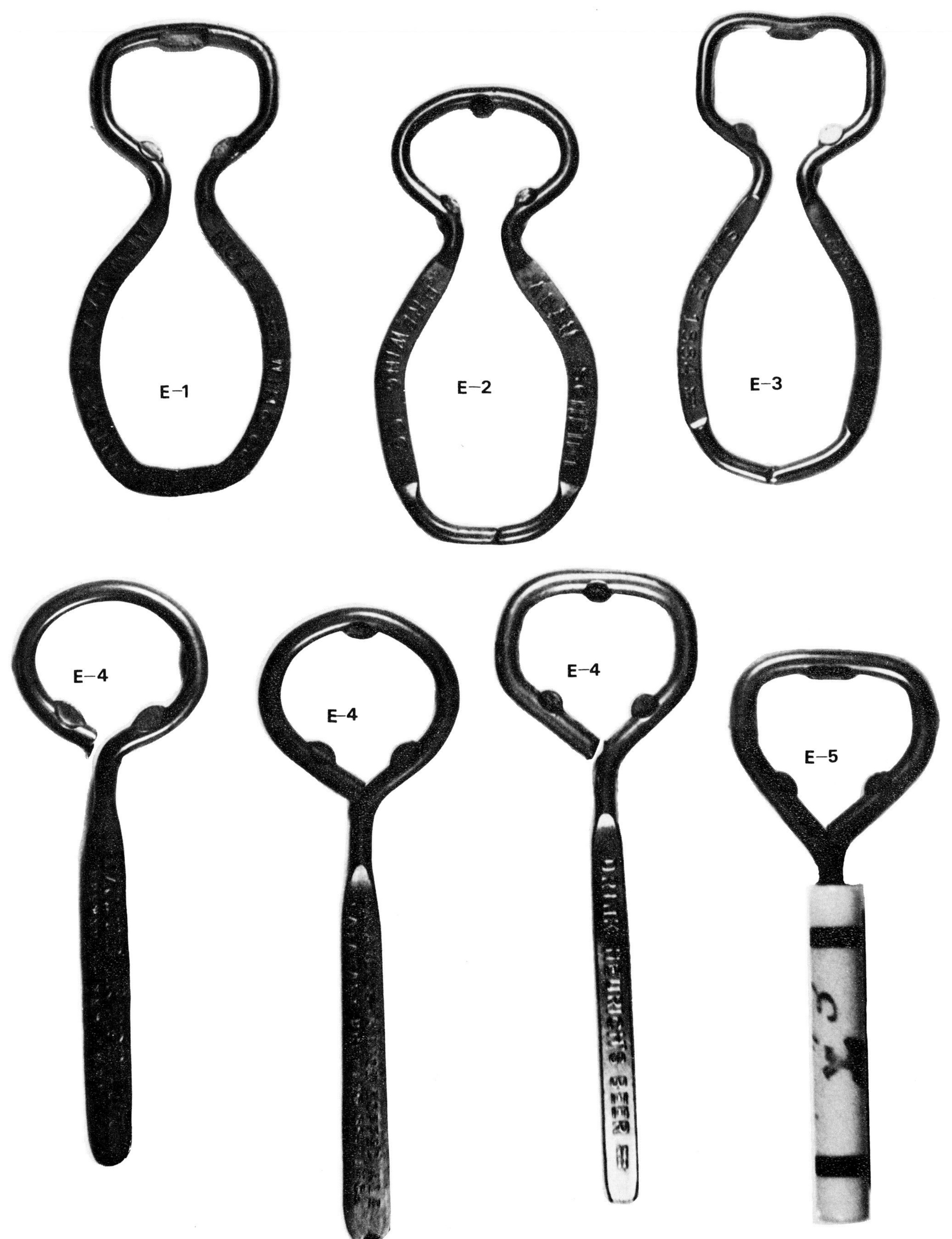
E–1
E–2
E–3
E–4
E–4
E–4
E–5

TYPE E WIRE FORMED OPENERS

E-6 "Flock's Beer — it stands on top"
E-7 "Burkhardt Brewing Co., Boston, Mass."
E-8 "Stegmaier, Wilkes-Barre, Pa." / same on reverse
E-9 "Anheuser-Busch, St. Louis, Mo." / "Budweiser means moderation"
E-10 "Hazleton Pilsener Beer, Hazleton Pilsener Beer" / same on reverse
E-10 "Cooper's Beer, Phila., Pa." / "Namar Premium Beer"
E-11 "Old Dutch Beer — Pennsylvania's Best" / Chevron design. Vaughan, Chicago
E-12 "Stoney's Pilsener" / Chevrons
E-13 "Eckert's Beer, Tel. Capitol 6111" / "Wins any test of taste"
E-14 "Monterey Brewing Co." / "Monterey Beer" Vaughan, Chicago.

Variations of these openers include rounded tops, dipped tops, and flat tops.

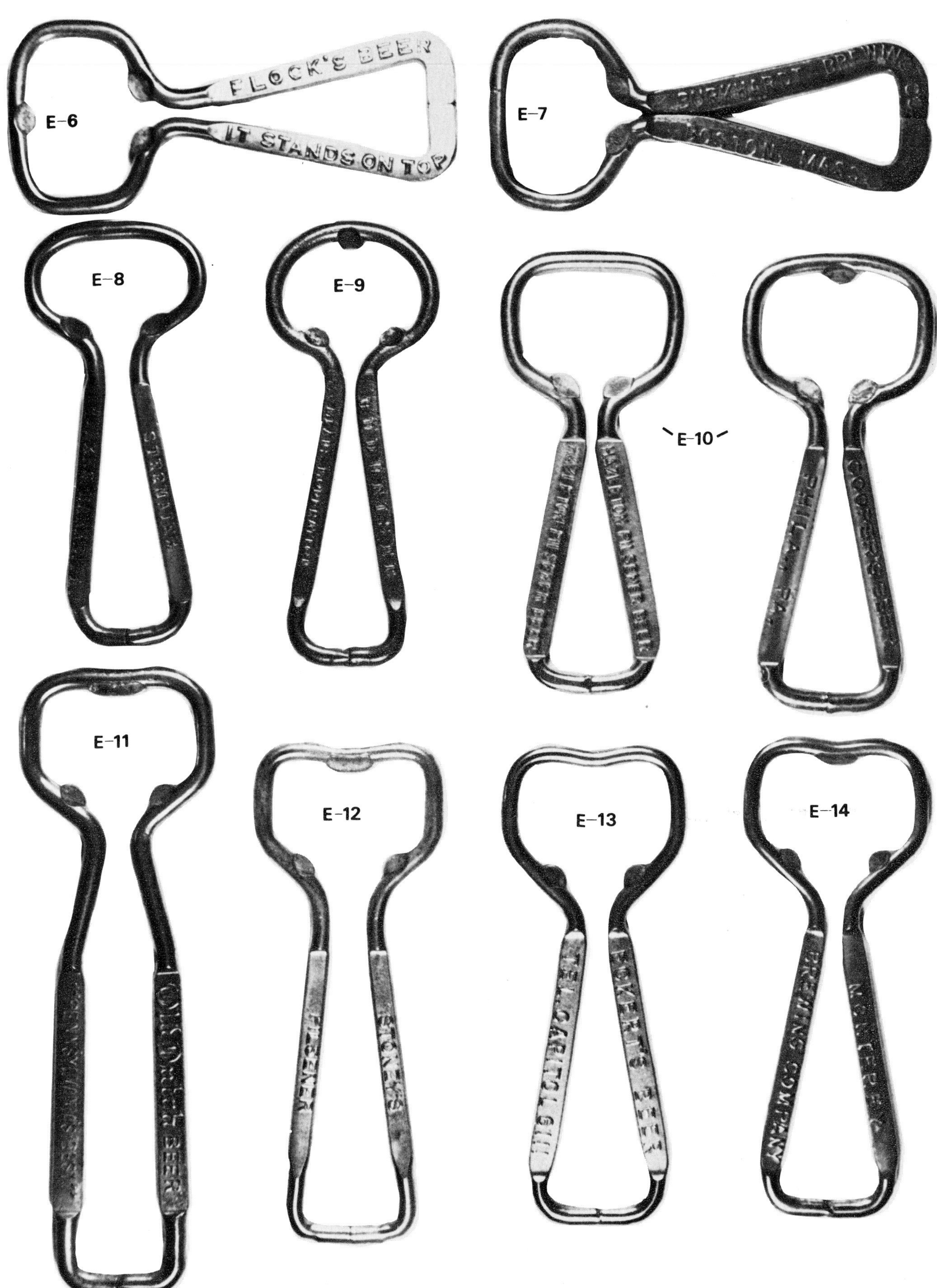
E–6
FLOCK'S BEER
IT STANDS ON TOP
E–7
E–8
E–9
E–10
E–11
E–12
E–13
E–14

TYPE F MULTI-PURPOSE OPENERS

F-1 Spoon. "Hyan Dry Ginger Ale, Lime and Lithia" / "Lang's A.A., a perfect malt brew" L.F. Dow Co.

F-2 Spoon. "Esslinger's Beer-Ale" / Design. Vaughan, Chicago

F-3 Spoon. "An Opener for friendship, Potosi Brewing Co. " B & B, St. Paul, made in U.S.A.

F-4 Spoon. "Iroquois Beverage Corp., Buffalo, N.Y." B & B, St. Paul

F-5 Cigar Cutter. "Schumann Brewing Co., Inc., Otto's Beer" / "Mantorville, Minn." (from the collection of Charles Robinson)

F-6 Pick. "Uhl's Brewery, both phones, Bethlehem, Pa." / "Celebrated beer, ale, and porter"

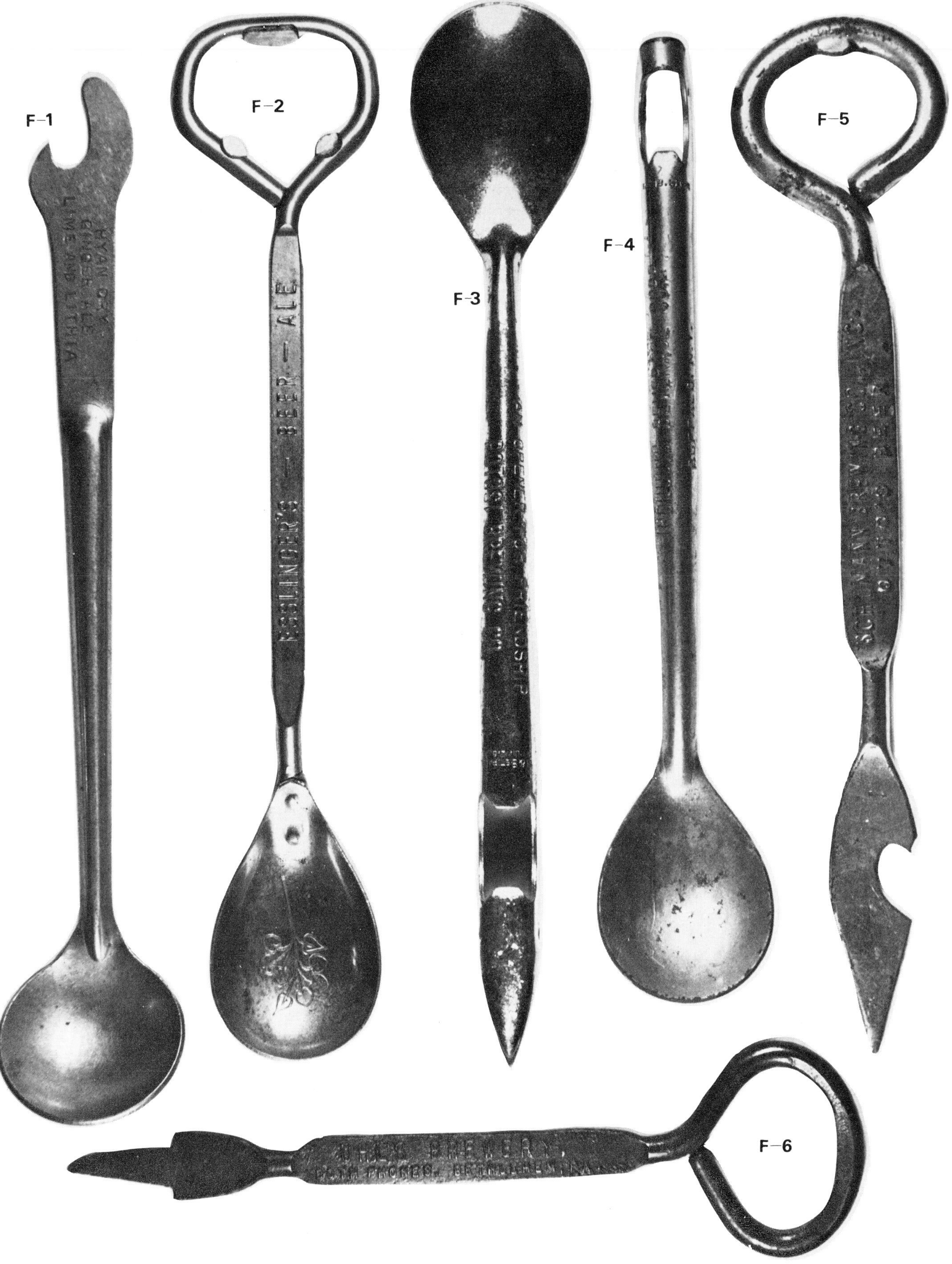
F–1
F–2
F–3
F–4
F–5
F–6
BEER — ALE

TYPE F MULTI-PURPOSE OPENERS — ICE PICKS

F-7 ''Columbia Premium Beer, the label of good taste, Columbia Brewing Co., Shenandoah, Pa.'' Plastic handle

F-8 ''Columbia Brewing Co., St. Louis, Mo., above all Alpen Brau'' (courtesy of Angelo Piccone)

F-9 ''Narragansett Brew Co., Prov., R.I., lager & ale, Brewery bottling'' Pat'd 3-24-12 (from the collection of Thomas Labeska)

F-10 ''Bullfrog Beer'' Pat'd Feb. 6, '94 (from the collection of Harry Richards)

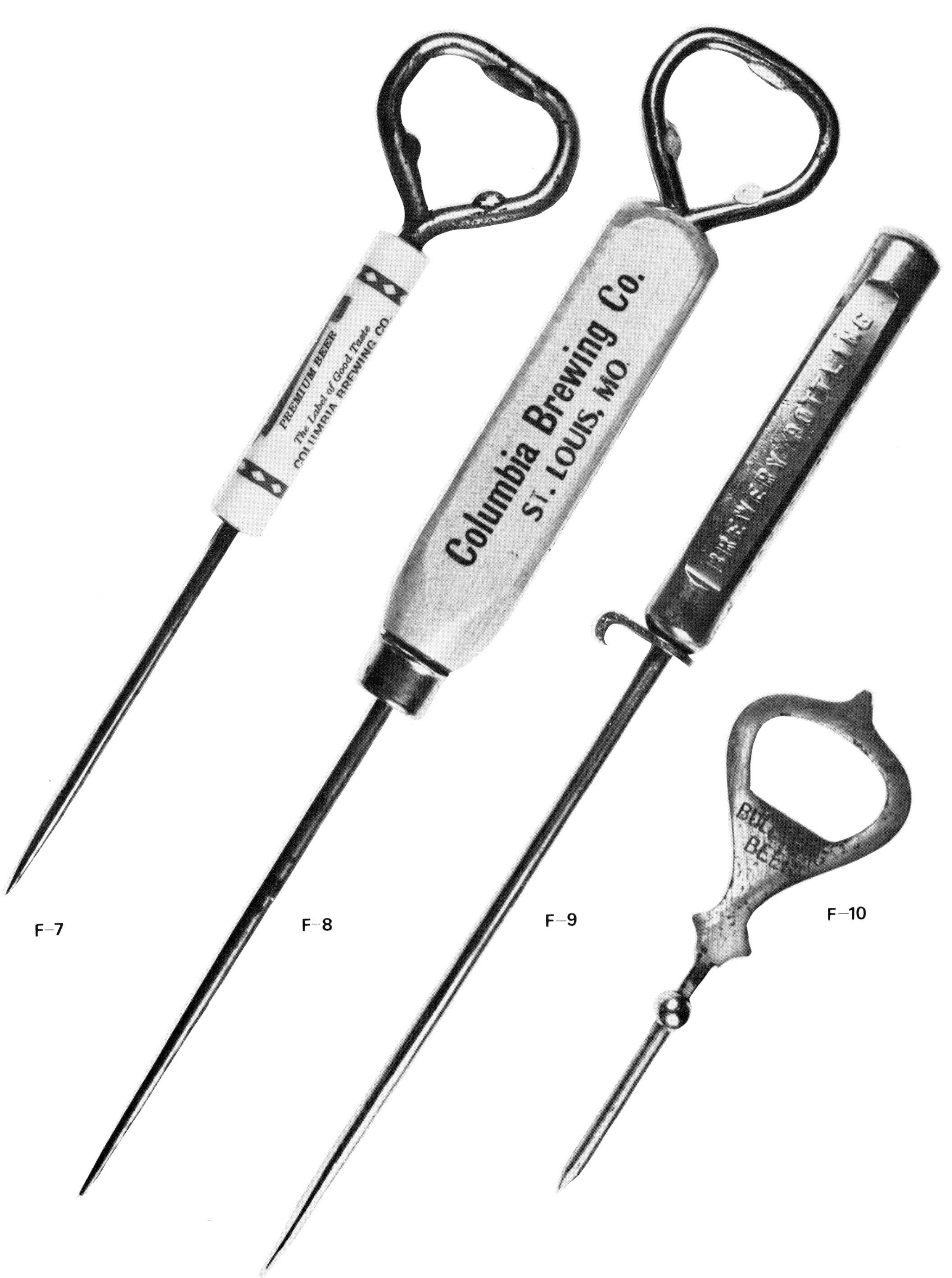

F–7 F–8 F–9 F–10

TYPE G CAP LIFTERS

G-1 ''Quandt's Ale & Lager, Troy, N.Y.'' Vaughan, Chicago

G-2 ''Hacker's Ale, Cold Spring Brewing Co., Lawrence, Mass.''

G-3 ''Hamm's Beer, leads them all''

G-4 ''Frederick's Brewery''

G-5 ''Liberty Brewing Co., Springfield, Mass.'' Mf'd by Ryede Specialty Works, patents pending

G-6 ''Bartels Beer'' Walden, Cambridge 38, Mass.

G-7 ''Pickwick Beer, light ale, ale'' Walden, Camb., Mass.

G-8 ''Beck's, Buffalo's best beer'' / same on reverse. Vaughan, made in U.S.A.

G-9 ''Ortlieb's Beer, Phone Market 4728'' Edlund Co., pat. Nov. 7, '33, made in U.S.A.

G-10 ''Moerlbach Beer'' Corkscrew. (from the collection of Bruce Clark)

Type G-9 openers were manufactured by the Edlund Co. of Burlington, Vermont. The wood handles were imprinted with a hot foil process. The purchaser paid a $10-$20 brass die charge for the imprint, and minimum order was 25,000. (Willett Foster, Edlund Co.) In the index the first color is the color of the imprint, the second is the color of the handle.

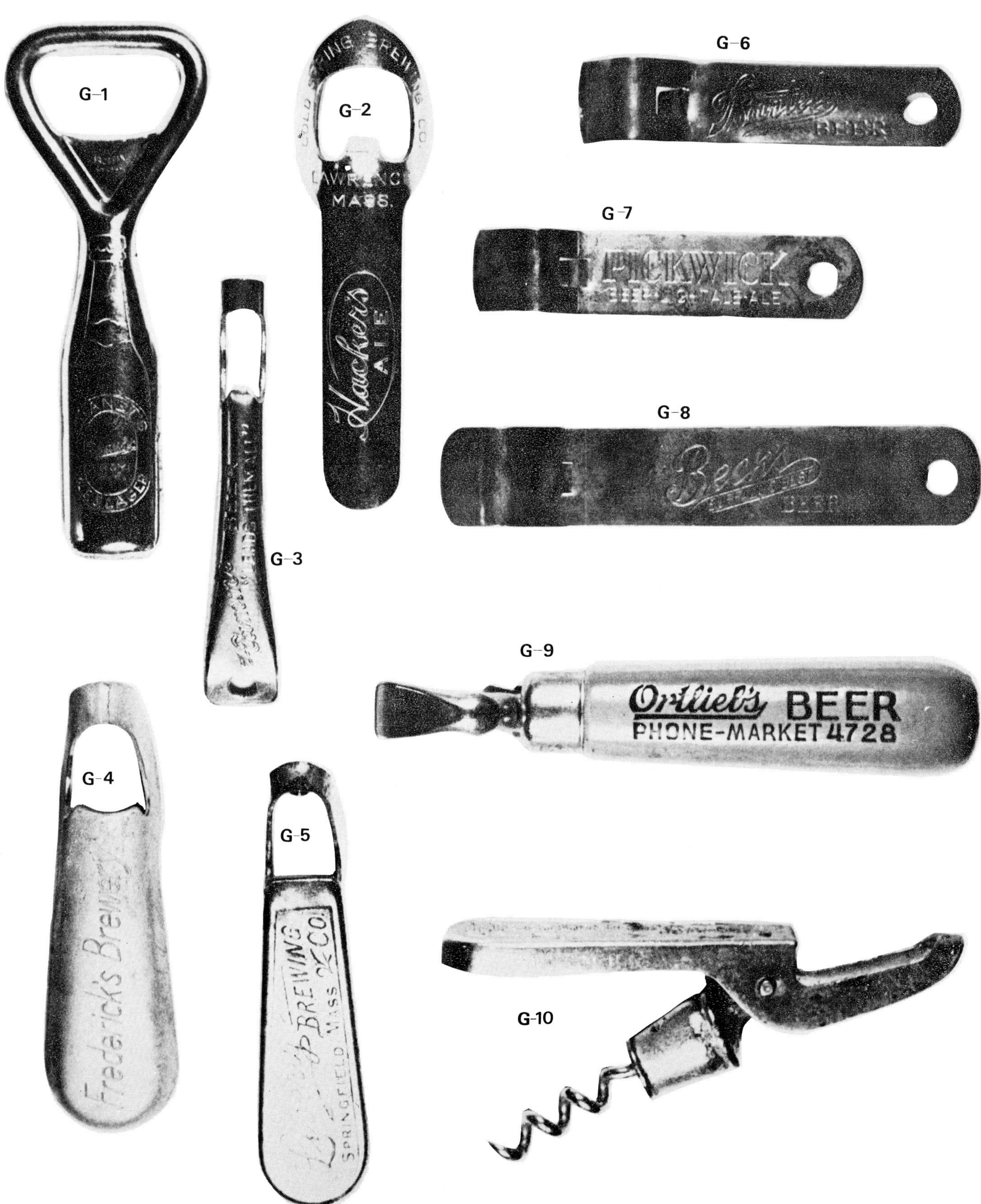
G–1
G–2
COLD SPRING BREWING CO.
LAWRENCE
MASS.
Hacker's
ALE
G–3
G–4
Frederick's Brewery
G–5
BREWING
CO.
SPRINGFIELD MASS
G–6
BEER
G–7
PICKWICK
G–8
Beck's
BEER
G–9
Ortlieb's BEER
PHONE-MARKET 4728
G–10

TYPE H OVER THE TOP STYLE CAP LIFTERS

H-1 "Sunshine Beer-Ales-Porter"

H-2 "Say Hanley's for ale, The James Hanley Co." Bulldog. Over the top trademark, made in U.S.A., Vaughan, Chicago.

H-3 "Koehler's, there is no better beer" G.G. Greene, Warren, Pa.

H-4 "Enjoy Prima Beer" Corkscrew.

H-5 "Jolly Scot Ale — Silver Stock Beer"

H-6 "What'll you have? Pabst Blue Ribbon" / "Pabst Blue Ribbon, Pabst Brewing Co., Milwaukee — Peoria Hts. — Newark — Los Angeles" No. U-263, Vaughan, Chicago. 1948 Pabst promotional opener. (Grace Ellis, Pabst Brewing Co.)

H-7 "Always serve Potosi Beer, Pilsener & Export"

H-8 "Buckeye Beer, The Buckeye Brewing Co., Toledo, Ohio" / Muth, Buffalo, N.Y., copyright 1940, Pat. Pending.

Type H-7 openers made in two varieties: one dimple or two dimples in head of opener.

All type H-8 openers noted have lifter at the top of the bottle except Pabst which has lifter at the bottom.

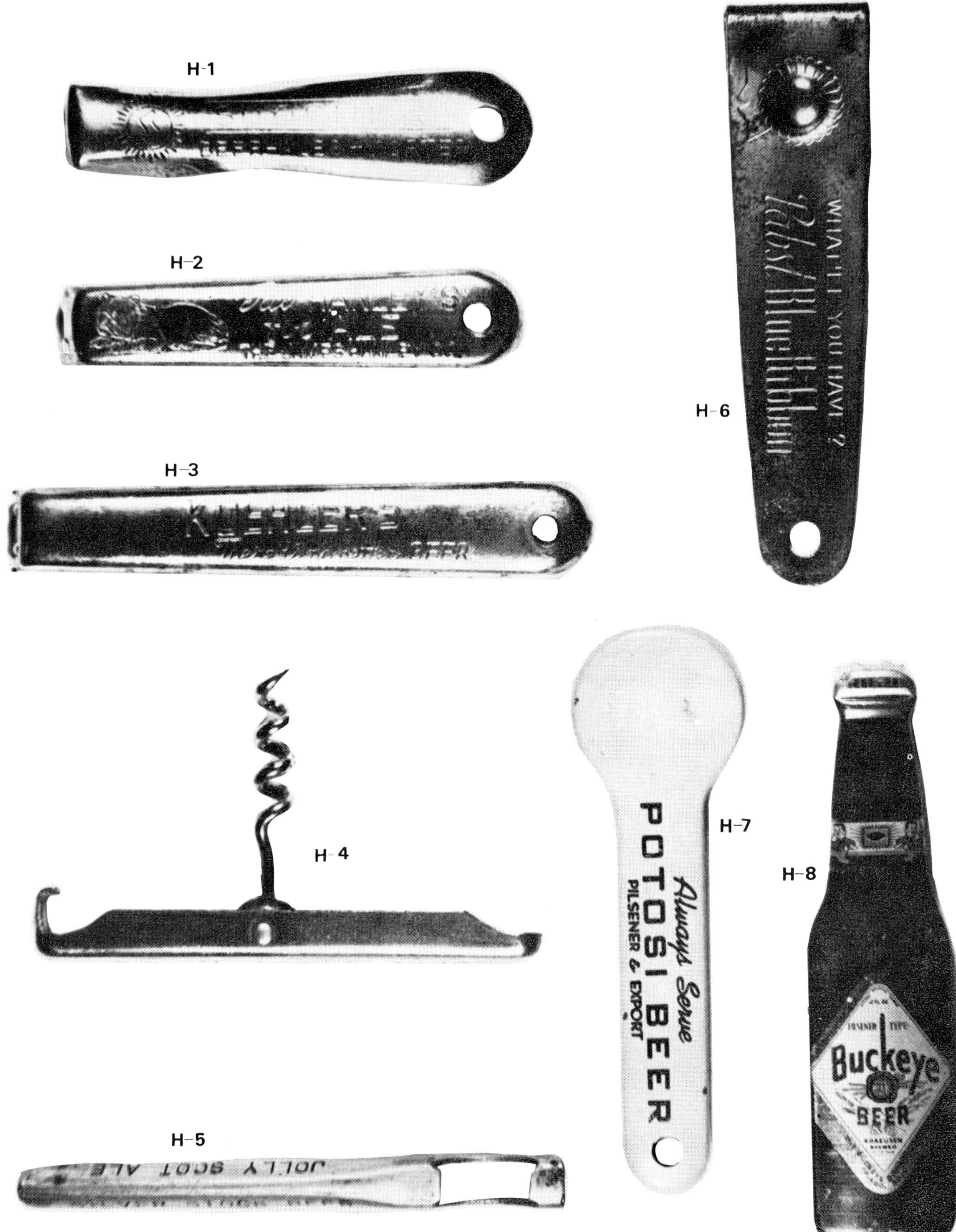
H-1
H-2
H-3
H-4
H-5
JOLLY SCOT ALE
H-6
WHAT'LL YOU HAVE ?
Pabst Blue Ribbon
H-7
POTOSI BEER
Always Serve
PILSENER & EXPORT
H-8
PILSENER TYPE
Buckeye
BEER

TYPE I COMBINATION CAP LIFTER / CAN PIERCER

I-1 "Coors, America's fine light beer" / same on reverse. Emro, St. Louis

I-2 "Hampden Mild Ale" Walden Pat. 1,996,550

I-3 "Gunther's Premium Dry Beer" Walden Pat. 1,996,550

I-4 "Genesee Beer-Ale" Pat. 143,327 & 1,996,550, made in U.S.A., Vaughan, Chicago

I-5 "Wieland's Beer" / "Wieland's Beer" Crown, U.S.A., Pat. 1,996,550

I-6 "Fox Head '400' Beer" / "Fox Head '400' Beer, brewed with Waukesha Water" Vaughan, U.S.A., Pat. 1,996,550

I-7 "Handy way to order Ballantine's Ale-Beer" / For beer in cans marked Keglined, trade mark Am. Can Co., Canco, Patent 1,996,550

I-8 "Tru-Blu Beer and Ale, Northampton Brewery Corp., Northampton, Pa." Pat. Pend. (from the collection of Stan Taylor)

I-9 "Waldorf" / "Ale & Lager"

I-10 "Tru-Blu Beer-Ale, Northampton Brewery Corporation, Northampton, Pa." Pats. Pend., Soss Mfg. Co., Roselle, N.J.

The widths of Types I-2 through I-6 vary.

I–1
I–2
Hampden Mild Ale
I–3
Gunther's Premium Dry Beer
I–4
GENESEE BEER-ALE
I–5
I–6
FOX HEAD 400 BEER
I–7
I–8
I–9
ALE & LAGER
I–10

TYPE I COMBINATION CAP LIFTER / CAN PIERCER

I-11 "Rolling Rock Premium Beer" / "Rolling Rock Premium Beer" Ekco-Chicago

I-12 "Bosch Beer — Bright bold flavor" / "Bosch Brewing Co." Not for resale. Ekco-Chicago.

I-13 "Olympia Beer — 'It's the water' " / same on reverse. Vaughan U.S.A. 61

I-14 "Leisy's Fine Beer" / same on reverse. Ekco-Chicago

I-15 "Little Man, Esslinger's Beer-Ale" / same on reverse. Vaughan, U.S.A., Pat. 1,996,550

I-16 "Lancer's Beer" / same on reverse. Ekco, Chicago. U.S.A. Pat. Pending.

I-17 Brewster the Goebel Rooster only / same on reverse. cm/App. Mod., Vaughan U.S.A. 55

I-18 "Meister Brau" / "Meister Brau" Western Newell, Freeport, Ill., Pat. 1,996,550 (from the collection of Al Kroeger)

I-19 "Drink Pearl Beer" / "Drink Pearl Beer" Vaughan, U.S.A.

I-20 "Leinenkugel Beer" / "Chippewa Falls, Wis." Vaughan, U.S.A. Pat'd

I-21 "Stegmaier Gold Medal Beer" / "Stegmaier Brewing Co., Wilkes Barre, Pa."

I-22 "A-1 Pilsner Beer, Arizona Brewing Co., Phoenix, Arix." / H.R. Ransom & Co., Detroit, Mich., Easi-Ope, Pat. No. 2,517,442 — other patents pending

The Type I-11 3¼" opener predated the Type I-12 3½" opener. The 3½" opener was added to manufacturers' lines at the request of a brewery executive who could not get his four fingers along the "handle" of the 3¼" opener.

Variations (not distinguished in the catalog of openers):
Types I-11 & I-12. Ears on sides designed to prevent dropping opener into bottle and ultimately raising havoc with bottle washing machinery.

Types I-11 — I-14. Bottle and can ends reversed.

Types I-11 — I-18. With and without hanger hole.

Types I-11 — I-18. Made of hardened tool steel and plated in nickel, copper, or non-tarnish chromate. A few brass plated Miller High Life openers were made in 1959 by the Handy Walden Co. as samples.

Types I-11 — I-18. Piercers with rounded, medium, and sharp points in keeping with types of cans on market to be punched. Angle of ends also varies.

Types I-11 — I-18. Varying widths.

Types I-16 — I-18. Openers with ribs around ends manufactured by Vaughan Co.; straight ribs manufactured by Handy Walden.

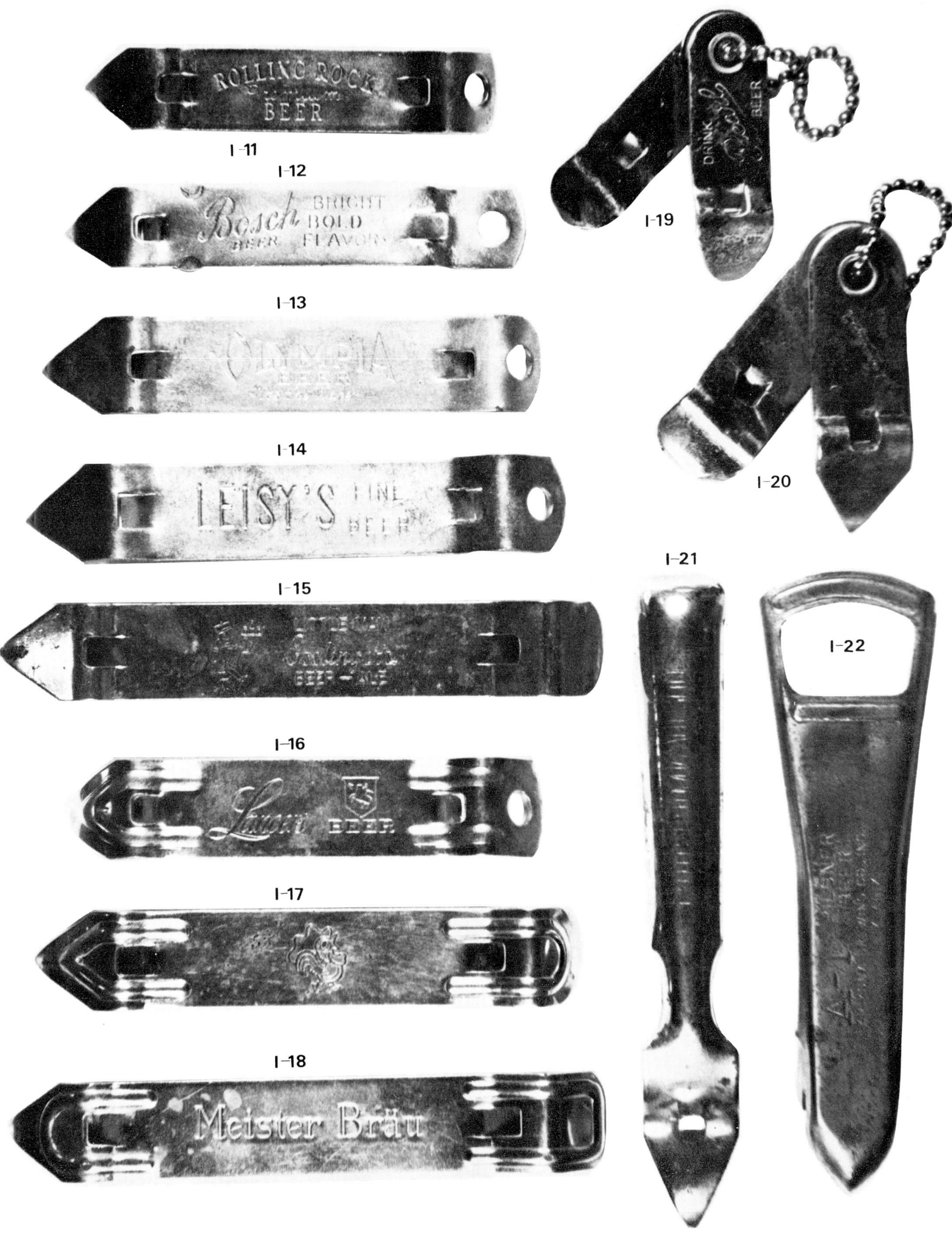

I-11 I-12 I-13 I-14 I-15 I-16 I-17 I-18 I-19 I-20 I-21 I-22

TYPE J CAN PIERCERS

J-1 "Haffenreffer Malt Liquor" / Walden, Cambridge, Mass., Pat. 1,996,550

J-2 "Hanley Beer Ale"

J-3 "Sterling" / Walden, Inc., Cambridge 38, Mass., Pat. 1,996,550

J-4 "Embassy Club Beer, Best Brewing Co., Chicago" / same on reverse. Vaughan, U.S.A., Pat. 1,996,550 (from the collection of Al Kroeger)

J-4 "Pabst Blue Ribbon" / same on reverse. Vaughan, U.S.A., Pat. 1,996,550

J-5 "Walter's Beer tastes better" / same on reverse. Vaughan, U.S.A., Pat. 1,996,550

J-6 "Acme Beer" / Pat. 143,327, 1,996,550, others pending, Vaughan, Chicago, made in U.S.A.

J-7 For beer in cans marked Keglined, trade mark Am. Can Co., Canco, Patent 1,996,550

J-8 "Good Old Reading Beer, traditionally Pennsylvania Dutch" Use on cans or bottles. Pat. Pend.

J-9 "Coors America's fine light beer, Adolph Coors Company, Golden, Colo., U.S.A." Pat. No. 1,996,550, other pat's pend.

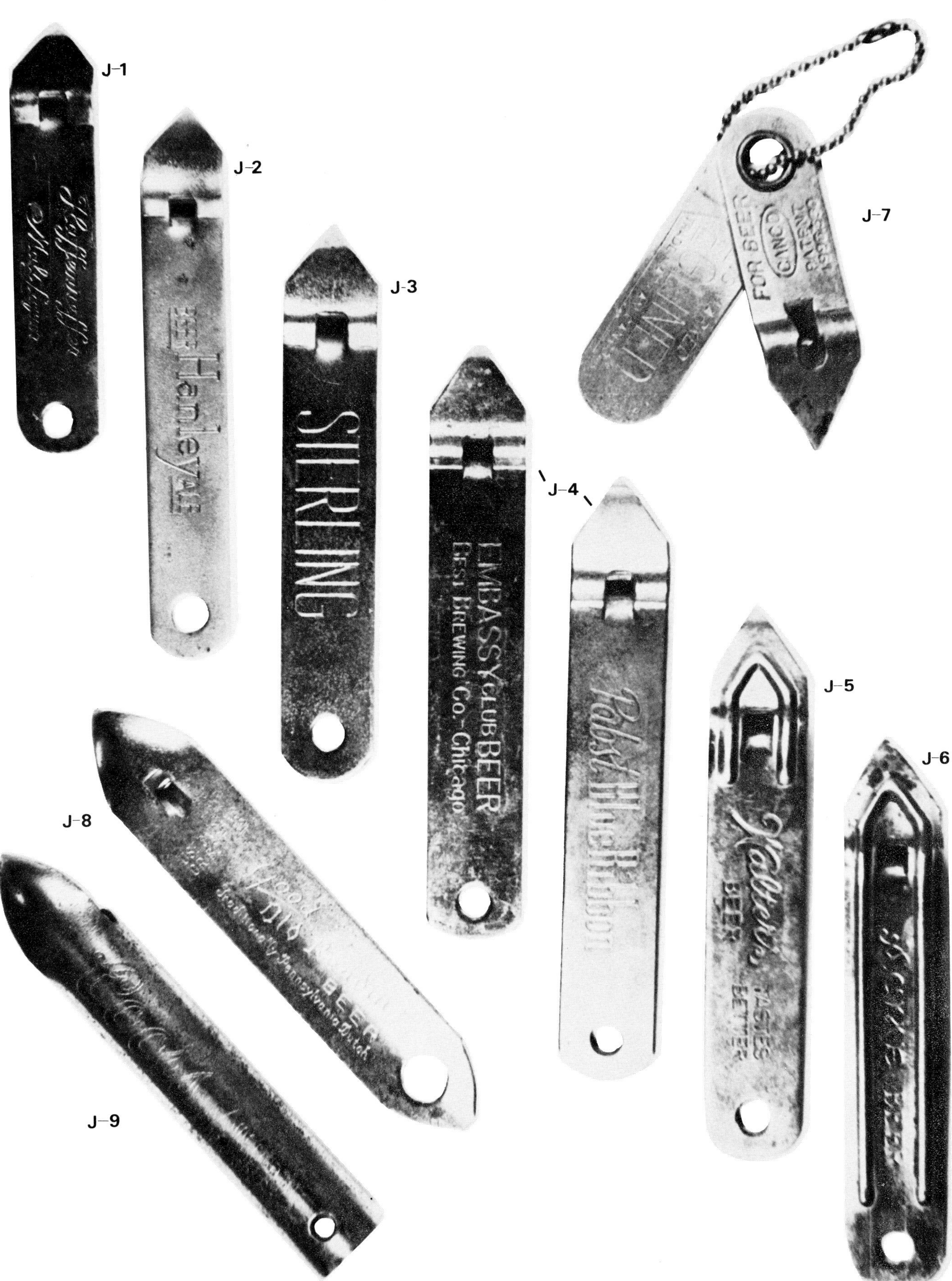
J-1
J-2
Hanley
J-3
STERLING
J-4
EMBASSY CLUB BEER
BEST BREWING Co. Chicago
J-5
BEER
J-6
J-7
FOR BEER
PATENT
J-8
BEER
J-9

TYPE K SPECIAL CAN PIERCERS (Photographs not actual size)

K-1 ''Old Milwaukee, America's light beer'' Heavy cast iron opener, insert 7,11,12, or 16 oz. can, lower handle, can is pierced.

K-2 ''Falstaff'' Pot metal opener. Pierces 12 oz cans.

K-3 ''Rheingold Extra Dry Lager Beer'' Combination opener and handle by Handy Walden Co. Fits 12 oz. can.

K-4 The Tapster by The Revere Copper Co. of Rome, N.Y. Open lid, insert can, close lid, pour. No beer advertising.

The K-3 ''Can handle'' was manufactured in 1960 for the Rheingold Brewing Co. by the Handy Walden Co. The order called for one half million at a cost of 8 cents each. The production run was made and samples were distributed. In a very short time the police department realized the danger of the can handle as a weapon and asked the Handy Walden Co. to discontinue its manufacture. According to Elliot Baritz of Handy Walden almost one half million of the openers were poured into the foundation of one of Rheingold's construction projects.

K–1

FALSTAFF

K–2

CONTENTS 12 FL.

K–3

CONTENTS 12 FL. OZ.
Rheingold
EXTRA DRY
Lager Beer
Brewed with: water,
barley malt, corn,
imported and domestic hops.

K–4

TYPE L CAN AND BOTTLE SHAPED OPENERS

L-1 "Miller High Life" made in West Germany. Push button on bottom to release retractable can piercer.

L-2 "Anheuser Busch" Williamson Co., Newark, N.J., Patented June 1, '97. Corkscrew inside. Distributed by Anheuser-Busch in the 1890's and early 1900's. (Mrs. Joan Hanselman, Archives Department, Anheuser-Busch)

L-3 "Milchelob Beer" Anheuser-Busch promotional item during the 1960's. Sold for 84 cents each. (Mrs. Joan Hanselman)

L-4 "Fehr's X/L" Miniature bottle with opener at top on cap.

L-4 "Canandaigua Extra Dry Lager Beer" Miniature bottle with opener at top on cap.

Heights and diameters of Type L-4 openers vary.

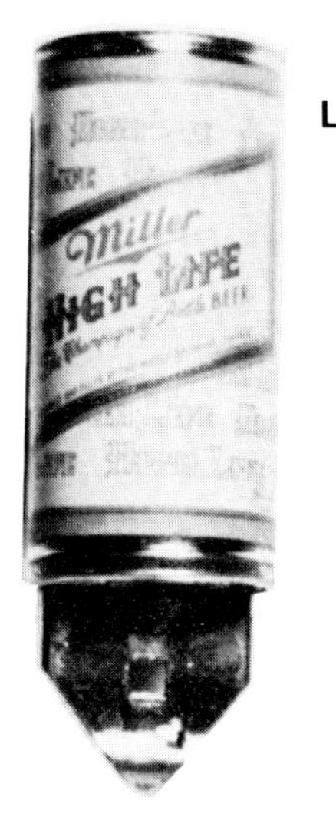

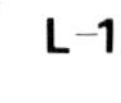

L–1

L–2

L–3

L–4

TYPE M MISCELLANEOUS OPENERS

M-1 Lithographed opener by H.D. Beach Co., Coshocton, O. "Old Colony Brews, compliments of Old Colony Brewing Co., Boston, Mass" / same on reverse.

M-2 Lithographed opener by H.D. Beach Co., Coshocton, O. "Harvard Beer" / Pat. Sept. 11, 1911

M-3 Retractable opener. "Gunther's, the word for quality beer, Brewers since 1881, Baltimore, Md."

M-3 Retractable opener. "The Original Gold Medal Beer, Stegmaier's Beer, The Stegmaier Brewing Co., Wilkes-Barre, Pa."

M-3 Retractable opener. "S-K Lager Beer, Schorr-Kolkschneider Brewing Co., Healthful and refreshing."

M-4 "Blatz Milwaukee"

M-5 "Tivoli Beer, Tivoli Brewing Company, Denver, Colorado" Plastic handle, (from the collection of William Frederick)

M-6 Bell. "Gibbons Beer, ring for it" Pat. Pending.

Most Type M-3 retractable openers have a regular lifter type action, a few were made in the over the top style.

M–1
OLD COLONY
BREWS
Compliments
of
OLD COLONY BREWING CO.
BOSTON, MASS.
OC
HARVARD
M–2
BEER
M–3
GUNTHER'S
THE WORD FOR QUALITY BEER
S-K
LAGER
BEER
THE ORIGINAL GOLD MEDAL BEER
Stegmaier's Beer
M–4
M–6
GIBBONS
BEER
RING FOR IT
M–5

TYPE M MISCELLANEOUS OPENERS

M-7 ''Silver Top Beer, Old Nut Brown Ale, Duquesne Pilsener, The finest beers in town, Duquesne Brewing Co., Pittsburgh, Pa.'' / same on reverse (from the collection of Don Reed)

M-8 ''Stoney's Beer'' (from the collection of Don Reed)

M-9 ''Ballantine Beer'' (courtesy of Midge Melchior)

M-10 ''Handy Way to Order Ballantine's'' Vaughan, Chicago

M-11 ''P. Ballantine & Sons, Newark, N.J., Drink Ballantine Ale-Beer — Purity, Body, Flavor''

M-12 ''P. Ballantine & Sons, Newark, N.J., Drink Ballantine Ale-Beer — Purity, Body, Flavor''

M-13 ''Ballantine's — Purity, Body, Flavor''

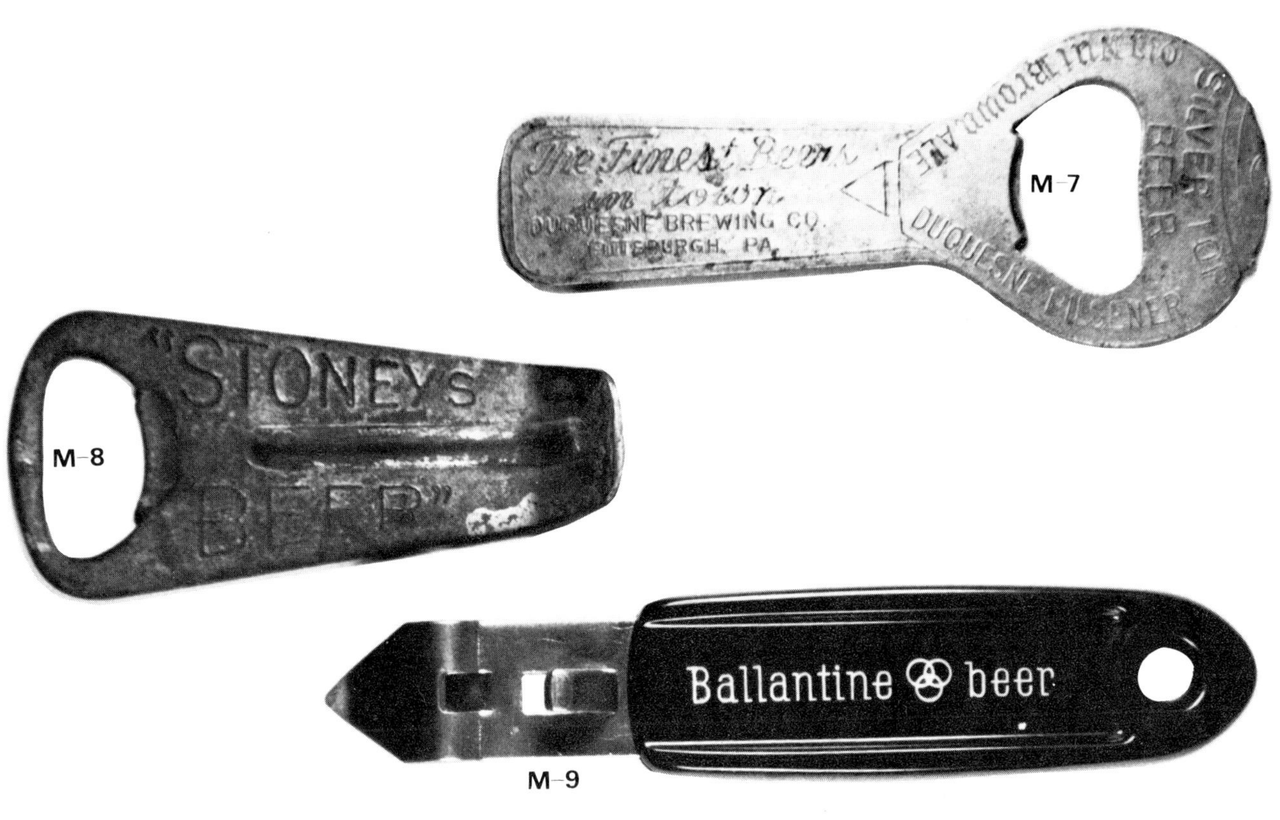
M-7
The Finest Beers in Town
DUQUESNE BREWING CO.
PITTSBURGH, PA.
SILVER TOP BEER
DUQUESNE PILSENER
M-8
"STONEY'S BEER"
Ballantine beer
M-9

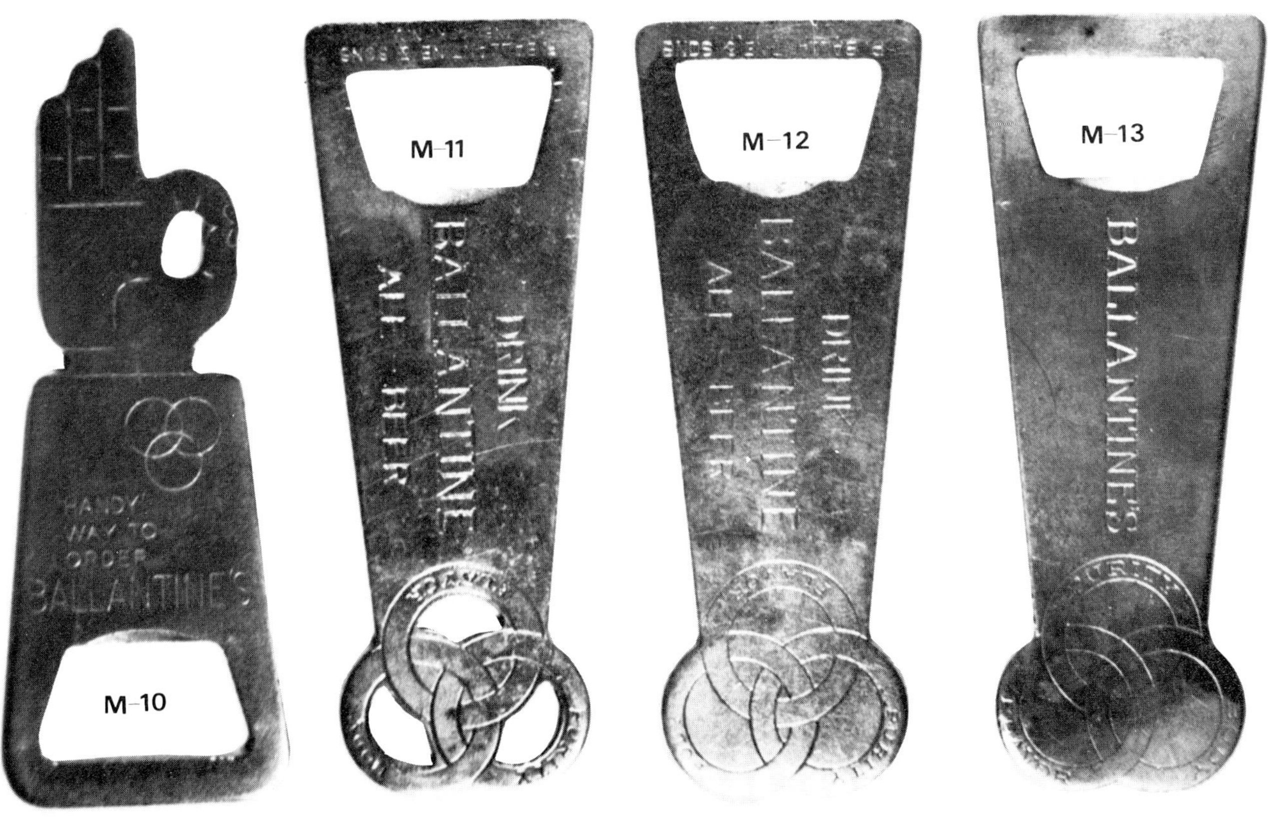
HANDY WAY TO ORDER BALLANTINE'S
M-10
M-11
DRINK BALLANTINE ALE BEER
M-12
DRINK BALLANTINE ALE BEER
M-13
BALLANTINE'S

TYPE M MISCELLANEOUS OPENERS

M-14 ''Schmidt's of Philadelphila'' Opener produced in Germany and purchased in 1963 as a gift for persons on tour through the Schmidt's Philadelphia plant. (John G. Strommer, Director of Merchandising and Sales Promotion, Schmidt's of Philadelphia)

M-15 ''Miller — 100 years in America, 1855-1955, Miller High Life'' / ''High Life'' Anniversary opener.

M-16 ''Budweiser'' / ''Beechwood'' Opener courtesy of Hamp & Sue Miller who advise that the opener is partially made from Budweiser's aging tanks. The openers were given to Anheuser-Busch executives at a special company meeting.

M-17 ''Budweiser King of Beers'' (from the collection of Jerry Schele)

M-18 ''Honorary Budweiser Brewmaster, 7 Golden Keys'' / ''This calls for Bud — 7 Golden Keys' The Golden Key was an advertising-promotional item during the 1950's. The seven keys referred to various aspects of Budweiser. (Mrs. Joan Hanselman, Archives Department, Anheuser-Busch, St. Louis.)

M–14
Miller
100 YEARS IN AMERICA
M–15
M–16
BUDWEISER®
M–17
Budweiser®
KING OF BEERS®
HONORARY
BUDWEISER® BREWMASTER
GOLDEN KEYS
M–18

TYPE M MISCELLANEOUS OPENERS

M-19 ‘‘Narragansett Lager-Ale’’ / ‘‘Narragansett Brewing Co., Cranston, R.I.’’ (from the collection of Duane Dummer)

M-20 ‘‘The Gutsch Brewing Co.’’ (from the collection of Harry Richards)

M-21 ‘‘Rainier’’ Bone Handle. (from the collection of Andy Growe)

M-22 ‘‘Edelweiss’’ D.R.G.M., Germany / ‘‘Green River’’ Supplied in box marked ‘‘Compliments of Schoenhofen Co., Chicago. (from the collection of Bob Brockmann, information courtesy of Dick Wilkey)

M-23 ‘‘Coors, America’s fine light beer’’ Ekco, U.S.A.

M-19
M-20
M-21
M-22
Coors
M-23

TYPE M MISCELLANEOUS OPENERS

M-24 ''Coors'' for opening new push tab cans.

M-25 ''Lemp, St. Louis'' Bullet shaped opener with corkscrew inside. (from the collection of William Frederick)

M-26 ''Coors-Golden'' Corkscrew in sleeve. (from the collection of William Frederick)

M-27 ''Lone Star Beer — Long Live Long Necks''

M-28 ''Coors'' with case (from the collection of William Frederick)

M-24

M-25

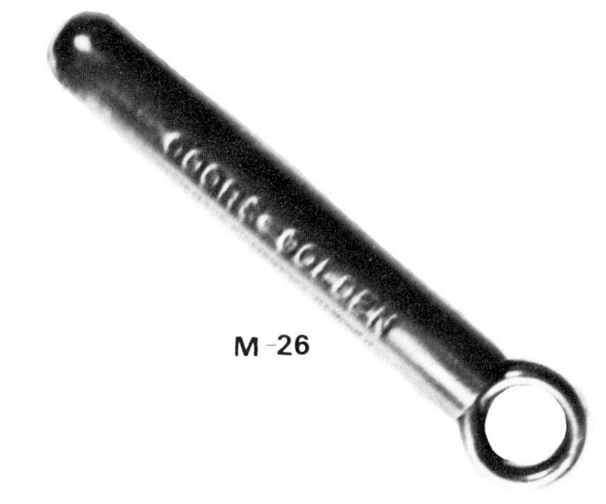

M-26

M-27

M-28

TYPE N NOVELTY OPENERS

N-1 Combination cap lifter, screw driver (inside). "Pabst Blue Ribbon" (from the collection of Don Reed). Vintage-1939. (Grace Ellis, Pabst Brewing Co.)

N-2 "Drink Dixie Beer" (from the collection of Phil Fouch)

N-3 Knife / opener. "Schmidt's Light Beer" Bassint, U.S.A. 73

N-4 Knife / opener. "Congress Beer" / "Haberle Congress Brewing Co., Inc."

N-5 Knife / opener. "Compt's West End Brg. Co." / "Utica Club, it's in the taste, Pilsener — Wuerzburger — Ginger Ale"

N-6 Knife / opener — corkscrew. "Drink American Club Beer made by" / "Lembeck & Betz, Eagle Brewing Co., Jersey City, N.J." (from the collection of Harry Richards)

N-7 Cigar Cutter / opener. "Hoster-Schlee's & Columbus, delightful beers" Pat. 10.12.09. (from the collection of Duane Dummer)

N-8 Cigar Cutter / opener. "Compliments of Schuster Brewing Co., Rochester, Minn." Pa. 10.12.09

N-9 Cap Lifter / bottle sealer. "Neuweiler's Beer-Ale 'Nix Besser' " Vaughan, Chicago, Made in U.S.A., Pat. Pend.

N-10 Cap Lifter / bottle sealer. "Drink Krueger's Beverages" Pat'd U.S.A. Dec. 9, '19. (from the collection of Don Reed)

N-11 Cap Lifter / shoehorn. "Stoney's America's Best Beer" Pat. Apl. for U.S.A.

N-12 Cap Lifter / lighter. "Beck's Buffalo's Best Beer" B & B, St. Paul, Minn.

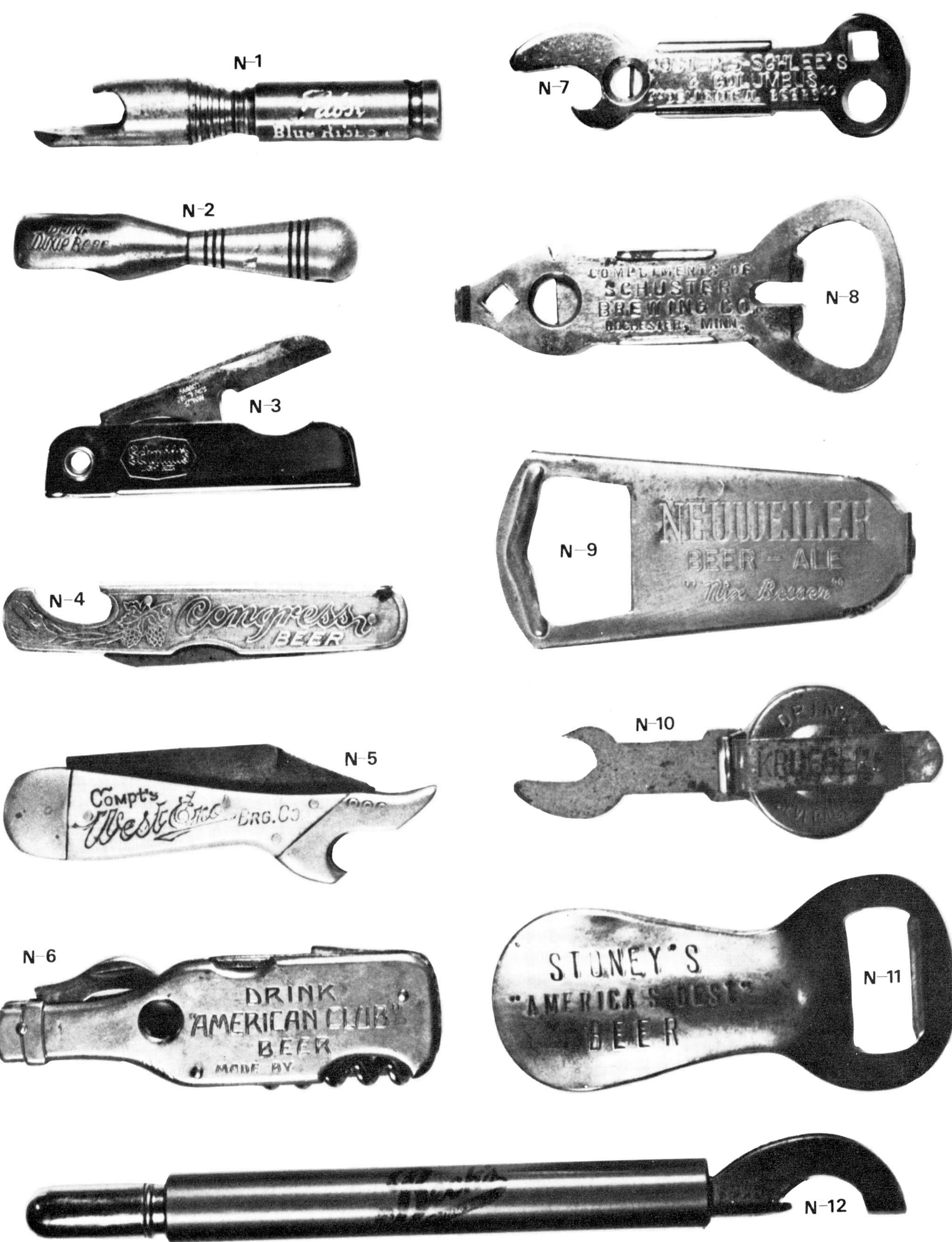
N-1
N-2
N-3
N-4
Congress
BEER
N-5
Compt's
West End
BRG. Co.
N-6
DRINK
"AMERICAN CLUB"
BEER
MADE BY
N-7
N-8
COMPLIMENTS OF
SCHUSTER
BREWING CO.
ROCHESTER, MINN.
N-9
NEUWEILER
BEER - ALE
"Nix Besser"
N-10
N-11
STONEY'S
"AMERICA'S BEST"
BEER
N-12

TYPE O WALL MOUNT STATIONARY OPENERS

O-1 "Hamm's Beer" (from the collection of Al Kroeger)

O-2 "Simon Pure Beer, Old Abbey Ale, Extra Pale Ale, William Simon Brewery, Buffalo, N.Y." Erickson, Des Moines

O-3 "Valley Forge Beer" (from the collection of Don Reed)

O-4 "Coors, America's fine light beer" Vaughan, Chicago, Never Chip, Pat'd, made in U.S.A.

O-5 "Grand Prize Lager Beer" Starr X, Pat. 2,333,088. N. News, Va.

O-6 "Drink Esslinger's Premium Beer" (from the collection of Don Reed)

O-7 "Drewrys Beer" B & B, St. Paul, Minn. (from the collection of Don Reed)

O-1
HAMM'S BEER
O-2
SIMON PURE
BEER
Old Abbey Ale
EXTRA PALE ALE
WILLIAM SIMON BREWERY
BUFFALO, N. Y.
O-3
Valley
Forge
BEER
O-4
Coors
America's Fine Light Beer
O-5
GRAND PRIZE
LAGER BEER
O-6
DRINK
Esslinger's
PREMIUM
BEER
O-7
DREWRYS
BEER

TYPE P CORKSCREWS

P-1 "Anthony & Kuhn Brewing Co." (from the collection of Jerry Schele)

P-2 "Compliments of The Greenway Brew'g Co., Syracuse, N.Y." The Davis Corkscrew, pat. June 14, 1891. (from the collection of Don Reed)

P-3 "Pabst Milwaukee" Patented Feb. 24, 1891. (from the collection of Jerry Schele)

P-4 "Sequoia Beer, Phone 3 7391" (from the collection of Stan Taylor)

P-5 "Anheuser-Busch" (from the collection of Don Reed)

P-6 "Drink F and S Beer, Shamokin, Pa." (from the collection of Don Reed)

P-7 "Burkhardt's, the Genuine, copyright 1912, beer, ale, and porter, received the Grand Prize and Gold Medal at the International Pure Food Exhibition at Paris, 1914, bottled by the Burkhardt Brewing Co., Roxbury Crossing, Mass."

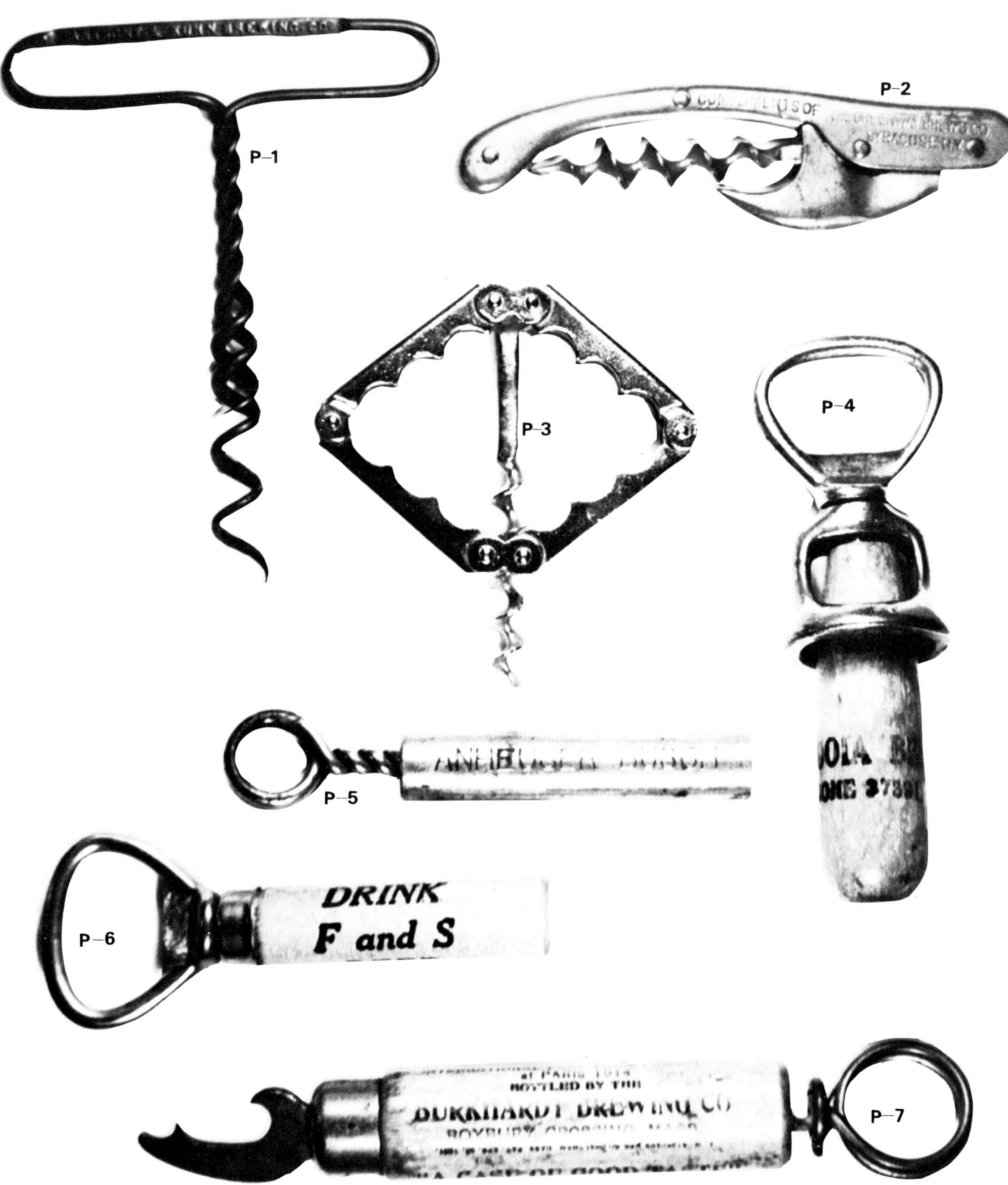
P–1
P–2
P–3
P–4
P–5
DRINK
F and S
P–6
P–7

TYPE P CORKSCREWS

P-8 "The Koppitz Melchers Brewing Co., Detroit, U.S.A." / "Pale Select"
P-9 "Heim Beer, Kansas City, Mo."
P-10 "Genesee Brew Co., Rochester, N.Y."
P-11 "Monterey Beer, Salinas Brewing Company" (from the collection of Stan Taylor)
P-12 "J.C. Helb, wholesaler and bottler, 420-422 E. Market St., East York, Pa."

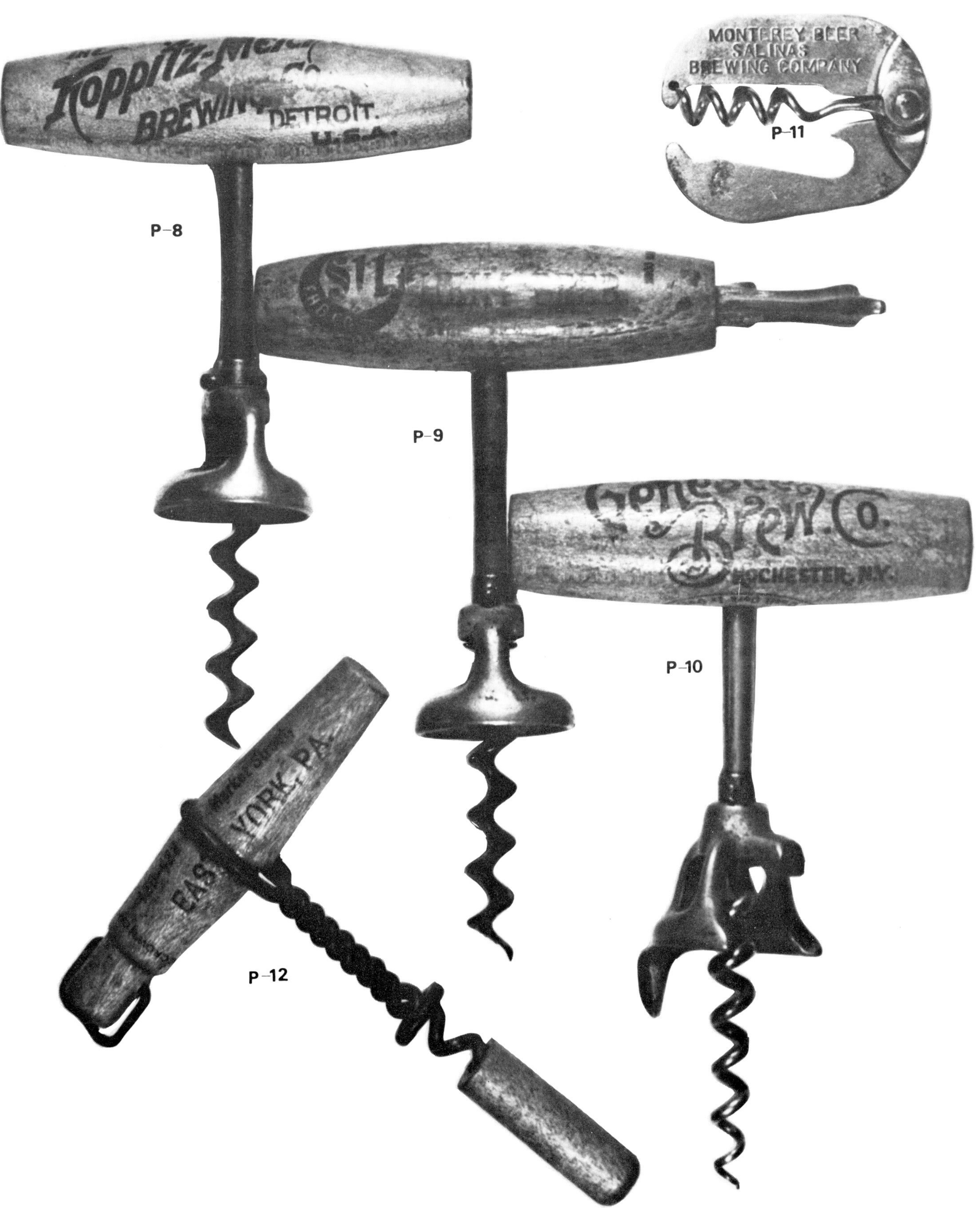
MONTEREY BEER
SALINAS
BREWING COMPANY
P–11
DETROIT.
P–8
P–9
Brew. Co.
ROCHESTER, N.Y.
P–10
EAST YORK, PA.
P–12

Compliments
of
OLD COLONY BREWING CO.
OC
BOSTON, MASS.

BREWING CO.
Hudepohl
FINE
BEER

MADE UNDER
FORMULA OF
JAMES AITKEN & COMPANY
FALKIRK, SCOTLAND
BY
LIEBMANN BREWERIES INC.
NEW YORK

"ALE that is ALE"
ASK FOR
PICKWICK
ALE
Haffenreffer

America's Finest Ale
PICKWICK
ALE
Haffenreffer
& Co

MASS.
Harvard
BEER

HARVARD
MASS.
Harvard

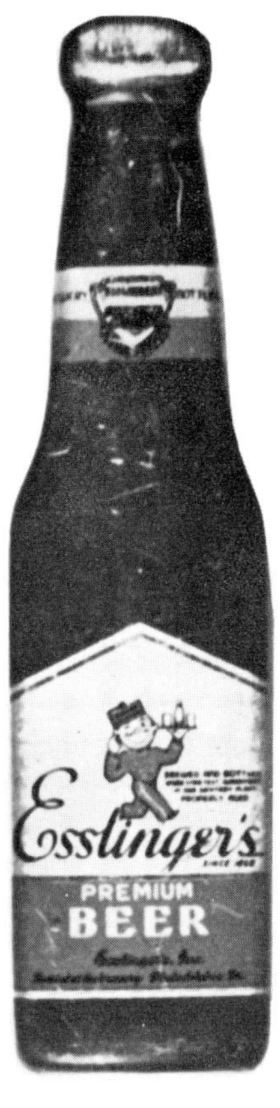

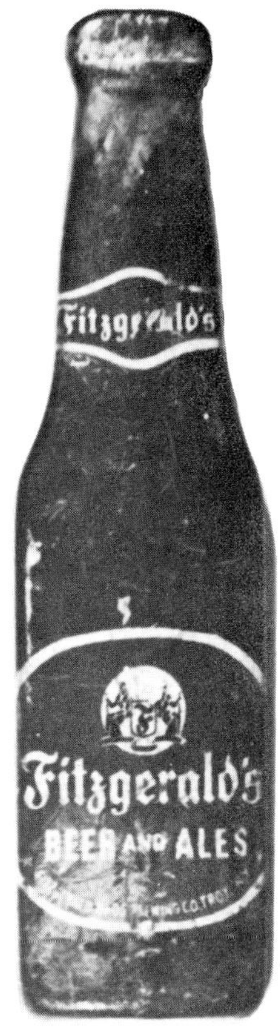

SECTION II CATALOG OF OPENERS

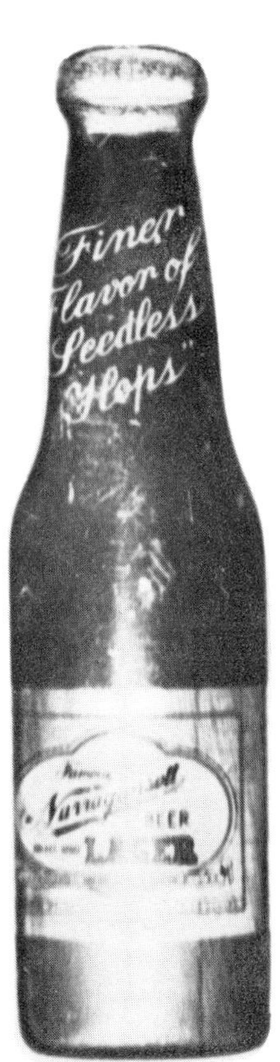

A-1

1. Argonaut Beer, San Francisco
2. That good Aurora Beer
3. Copeland's Ale — Lager
4. That good Crystal Rock Beer
5. Excelsior Beer, Manildi & Daea Agt's, San Mateo
6. Fink Brewing Co., Harrisburg, U.S.A.
7. Drink Fitgers Beer
8. Globe Brewing Co., San Francisco, Phone SU-0120
9. Golden Glow Beer and Ale
10. Grafs, Drink Lemon Lime
11. Compliments of The Gutsch Brewing Co., Sheboygan, Wis.
12. K & S Brg. Co., call for Premona
13. J.C. Kreusch, Anderson, Ind.
14. Maltop Co., Buffalo, N.Y., Use genuine "Maltop" Malt and Hops
15. Mohawk Malt Products
16. Montana Brewing Co., "My Favorite"
17. Mt. Shasta Bottling Works, It's the water
18. Old Style Beer
19. Santa Cruz Brewing Co., Golden Ribbon Beer
20. Souris Breweries Ltd., Estevan, Sask.
21. Beer El Capitan, S.F.

A-2

1. Sweet Adeline's Bar, Ashland, Wis.

A-3

1. Compliments of Indestro Mfg. Co., Chicago, Ill. (no beer advertisers noted)

A-4

1. Louis Bergdoll Brewing Co., Philadelphia
2. Chicago National Beverage Co., Drink Buck
3. Cascade Export Beer
4. Clinton Br'g Co's Pointer Beer
5. Drink Copeland's Ale & Lager
6. The Crockery City Brew. Co., E. Liverpool, Ohio
7. Crystal Rock Beer, Sandusky, O.
8. Drink Falls City Brg. Co. Beer
9. Leisy Beer, Peoria, Ill.
10. Star Brewing Co., Saginaw, Mich.
11. Warsaw Beer / Popel-Giller Co., Warsaw, Ill.
12. Widman & Co's Bohemian Beer

A-5

1. Drink Golden Ribbon Beer
2. Drink Grafs "The best what gives"
3. Dog Head Guinness
4. Highland Lager
5. Leisy Beer, Peoria, Ill.
6. Sebewaing Beverage Co., Sebewaing, Michigan
7. Ask for Utica Club Pilsener
8. Ask for Utica Club Pilsener, Ginger Ale

A-6

1. Compt's West End Brg. Co. / Utica Club, it's in the taste, Pilsener, Wuerzburger-Ginger Ale

A-7

1. Buffalo Brewing Co., Sacramento, Cal.
2. Drink Capitol Beer, Denver
3. Frontenac Export Ale
4. Frontenac Old Brew
5. Marx Malt Company, 86 S. 4th St., 643 N. 4th St., 1068 W. Broad St., Call MA 8261
6. Compliments of Star Brewing Co., Lomira, Wis.
7. The Weibel Brewing Co., New Haven, Conn.
8. White Bock Beer

A-8

1. In your home use Jacob Ruppert Knickerbocker

A-9

1. Buffalo Brewing Co., Sacramento, Cal.
2. F & S Beer, Frank F. Seiss, Harrisburg, Pa.
3. The Hoster-Columbus A.B. Co., Drink Gold Top "That's the beer"
4. Isaac Leisy Brewing Co., Cleveland, Ohio, Phones Cuyahoga-Erie 234, Bell-Harvard 780
5. Antonio Manieri Bottler of Poth & Schemm Dark Beers, wine & liquors, 1225 Tasker St.

A-10

1. Drink Muehlebach's Pilsener Beer

A-11

1. Drink Wooden Shoe Beer

A-12

1. Burgermeister, a truly fine pale beer / Shrine Victory Convention, July, 1946, San Francisco
2. Compliments of Maier Brewing Co., Inc., Los Angeles / Al Malaikan
3. O'Keefe's Beverages Ltd. / O'Keefe's Dry
4. Pointer Brewing Co., Clinton, Iowa
5. Reine Co., S.F. / Use Best Ever Hop Malt Syrup
6. White Label, East India Ale / Regal — spell it backwards

A-13

1. Drink Star Beer, brewed by Star Brewery, Lomira, Wis.
2. Key to Schell's Vacuum Tonic, New Ulm, Minn.

A-14

1. Rainier Beer

A-15

1. Aurora Brewing Co., Aurora, Ill. / Drink that good Aurora Beer
2. Birk Bros. Brew. Co., Phone Lincoln 496, Chicago / Superb Beer
3. The Cleveland & Sandusky Brewing Co. / Crystal Rock Beer
4. Cook's, Evansville, Ind.
5. Edelbrau Beer / Drink Schreiers Beer, Sheboygan, Wis.
6. Elgin National Brg. Co., Phone 28, Elgin, Ill.
7. Excelsior Beer, Santa Cruz, Cal.
8. Fortune Bros. Brewing Co., Chicago / Topaz, Good to the last drop on the lip
9. Hyde Park Bottled Beer / C.G. Pauly, wholesale dealer, Iowa
10. Liberty Brewing Corp., Pittston, Pa.
12. Leisy Beer
12. Drink Neuweiler's Purity, Allentown, Pa.
13. Terre Haute Brewing Co., Terre Haute, Ind. / Champagne Velvet that ever welcome beer

A-16

1. Blakeslee Brothers Beverages
2. Compliments of Huether Brewing Co., Ltd., Kitchener, Ontario, Pure Ice

A-17

1. Cook's, Evansville, Ind.
2. Cream City Brg. Co., Famous Milwaukee Pilsener Beer
3. Drink Fremont Beer
4. Drink Gold Label Beer

5. The Kamm & Schellinger Brg. Co., Mishawaka, Ind. / Our brands — Private Stock, Export, K & Standard
6. Kazmaier's Beer & Stout, Altoona, Pa.
7. S. Priebe for Masterbrus, Tel. Pontiac 2743J
8. Key to Rainier Beer
9. Ritter Brau "Far Better"
10. C. Schmidt & Sons, Inc., Philadelphia, Pa. / Brewers since 1860

A-18

1. Buck & Century Beer, fresh & salt sea foods — Southern Fish & Oyster Co. / Phone 3-6176
2. Buffalo Brewing Co., Sacramento, Cal.
3. Star Beer, Lancaster, Pa. / same on reverse

A-19

1. The Goebel Brewing Co., Detroit, Mich. / The Pure Food Beer

A-20

1. Enterprise Bohemian Lager / King Philip Ales
2. Goebel's at the Wharf, Santa Cruz
3. Ask for Hoffbrau today's best beer, phone Homestead 4242
4. Hoster-Columbus, Columbus, Ohio / Drink Gold Top, Old Top, that's the beer
5. P.O.N. Bar & Grill, 467 Clinton Ave., Newark, N.J.
6. Renner's, order a case, phone 44467, Youngstown
7. Seitz Brewery, Easton, Pa. / Seitz Beer
8. Wayne: Wayne Products & Brw'g Co., 3601 E. Hancock, Detroit, Mich., Plaza 0800
9. Wehle Ale-Lager / spin to see who wins

A-21

1. Beck's, Buffalo's best beer
2. Blatz Milwaukee / Blatz Old Heidelberg
3. Try Carling Red Cap Ale, Black Label Beer, Twin Dist. Co., 855 Lancaster

A-22

1. Ballantine Export Beer / Newark, N.J.

A-23

1. Blackhawk Beer
2. Pearl Beer

A-24

1. Independent Brewing, Duquesne Silver Top
2. Miller Brewing Co., Milwaukee, Wis., U.S.A., High Life Beer

A-25

1. Hamm's Famous Beers, Hamm's, St. Paul

A-26

1. Empire State Brewing Corp., Olean, N.Y., Empire State Lager Beer
2. Zett's Sparkling Ale

A-27

1. First Prize Beer — Peter Doelger First Prize Brewery, N.Y. / Peter Doelger first prize bottled beer, best beer brewed

A-28

1. Buffalo Brewing Co., Sacramento, Cal.
2. Consumers Products Co., Brooklyn, N.Y. / Use Pilser Brand Malt & Hops
3. Bottled at the Brewery by The Deppen Brewing Co., Reading, Pa. / Queen quality
4. The Dominion Brewery Co., Ltd., Toronto / White Label Ale

A-29

1. Cosgraves Ale
2. Drink Eberle's delicious beverages, Jackson, Mich.
3. K-B Beer
4. Maier Beer
5. Pabst Blue Ribbon Beer / The brew that brings back memories
6. Use Pilser Brand Malt & Hops
7. Rainier Old German Lager / Rainier Lime Rickey
8. Reine Co., S.F., try Best Ever Malt & Hop Syrup
9. Schlitz, the brew that made Milwaukee famous / the brew that made Milwaukee famous
10. Stein King Beer, Columbia, S.C.

B-1

1. Drink Ben Brew absolutely pure beer, Columbus, Ohio, U.S.A.
2. Fort Pitt Brewing Co., Sharpsburg, Pa.
3. Fuhrmann & Schmidt Brewing Co., Shamokin, Pa.
4. Gund's Peerless Beer, Gund, LaCrosse, good since 1854
5. Pittsburgh Brewing Co., Tech Beer
6. Wagner's Beer, Sidney, O., always the same
7. Welz and Zerweck, Gambrinus Brau, better than imported

B-2

1. Drink Blatz Private Stock Beer, Milwaukee
2. Drink Eagle Beer, made in Utica, Peerless Lager, Monarch Ale
3. Edelweiss Beer
4. Feigenspan P.O.N., the beer that builds
5. Compliments of Fresno Brewing Co., Fresno, Cal., patronize home industry
6. Hamm's Famous Beer, Hamm's, St. Paul
7. Fred Krug Brewing Co., Luxus, The beer you like
8. Menk's bottle beer
9. Oakland Brewing & Malting Co., Oakland, Cal. / Blue & Gold Lager
10. Old Mission Lager, traditionally good, made in San Diego
11. Old Style Beer, the beer with a snap to it
12. United States Brg. Co., Drink Savoy Special Brew

B-3

1. Peter Doelger First Prize bottled beer, expressly for The Home
2. Edelweiss Beer
3. Compliments of Reno Brewing Co., Inc., Reno, Nev.

B-4

1. Feigenspan Private Seal
2. Scheidt's Valley Forge Special Beer
3. Schoenhofen's Edelweiss Beer

B-5

1. Anchor Brewing Com'y, Brackenridge, Pa.
2. Key to Kustenbader Beer, Catasaqua, Pa.
3. Compliments of Palouse Brewing Company, Palouse, Washington
4. Compliments of Reno Brewing Co., Reno, Nev. / same on reverse
5. Spokane Brewing & Malting Co., Gilt Top Bottled Beer, the kind your neighbor drinks
6. Key to Storz Triumph Beer, the delicious artesian brew, Storz Brewing Co., Omaha, U.S.A. / Key to Storz Old Saxon Brau, the best beer in America, Storz Brewing Co., Omaha, U.S.A.

B-6

1. Bridgeport
2. Drink Canada Dry Pale Ginger Ale
3. Pacific Brewing & Malting Co.

B-7

1. Bartholomay's Beer & Ale
2. Bartholomay's Beer & Ale, Buckley's, 166 E. Main
3. Key to Hauenstein's Beer, New Ulm, Minn.

B-8

1. Drink Crystal Rock Brew
2. National Brewing Co., Steelton, Pa. / same on reverse

B-9

1. Compliments of Centennial Brewing Co., Butte, Mont. / We make a specialty of bottle beer for family trade.

B-10

1. Congress Beer / Congress Beer

B-11

1. Key to Rainier Beer

B-12

1. Fink's Beer, Harrisburg, U.S.A.

B-13

1. Ambrosia Brewing Co., Yards 7-2213-19 / Nectar Premium Beer
2. Insist on Blue Ribbon Malt
3. Daisy Beer / Golden City Brewery
4. Fink's Beer, Harrisburg, U.S.A.
5. Drink Golden West Beer
6. Griesedieck Bros., St. Louis
7. Haberle Congress Beer, Syracuse / National Derby Cream Ale, Syracuse
8. Heileman Brewing Co., LaCrosse, Wis. / Old Style Lager
9. Iron City Lager / Tech Dry Ginger Ale
10. Star Beer, Lancaster, Pa.
11. Storz Beer / Storz Beer

B-14

1. Atlas Brewing Company Special / Tonic Canal 6200
2. Drink Berghoff / Dry Ginger Ale
3. Berghoff, Fort Wayne, Drink Dortmunder Beer / Made in U.S.A.
4. Berghoff, Fort Wayne, Drink Dortmunder Beer / Vaughan, Chicago
5. Blatz Heidelberg Beer / Eat Cor-Betta Ice Cream, Denver, Colo.
6. Peter Bub Brewery, Winona, Minn.
7. Calgary Brewing & Malting Limited
8. Central Products Co., Jackson, Mich. / Blue Star Malt Extract
9. Dow Old Stock Ale
10. Drink Drewry's Dry Ginger Ale, Winnepeg, Canada / 1877 Canada Special Export
11. Drink Dutch's Beer
12. Pull for Blue Star Beer, E.B. Co.
13. Fecker's High Grade Beer
14. Frankenmuth Products Co., Frankenmuth, Mich. / Use Gold Medal Malt Extract
15. The Franklin Brewing Co., Columbus, Ohio / Ask for "Bennie"
16. Gluek, Gluek's Pilsener Pale
17. Gluek Pilsener Pale / Indian Made Ginger Ale
18. Goebel Beer — Pure Food
19. Goetz Country Club / M.K. Goetz Brewing Co., St. Joseph, Mo.
20. M.K. Goetz Brew. Co., St. Joseph, Kansas City, Mo. / Flavor blended Country Club Beer
21. M.K. Goetz Brew Co., St. Joseph, Kansas City, Mo. / Goetz Country Club Pilsener Beer
22. Drink Golden Glow / made from 5% lager brew
23. Drink Golden Glow / made from a fully fermented lager brew
24. Grand Prize Beer / GP-20 Vintage Brew
25. Grand Prize Beer / Top of the Brew
26. Drink Hamm's Beverages, St. Paul, Minn. / Windsor Club, the real beer taste
27. Drink Hamm's Special Brew / Oxford Club Pale, Dry Ginger Ale
28. Hauenstein's, New Ulm, Minn., Quality beverages
29. Hoosier Beer (lion head) / Hoosier Beer
30. K & S Co., Pull for Kamm's Beer
31. Keeley's, Chicago, Pull for Blue Bell Beer
32. Manitowoc Products Co., Manitowoc, Wisconsin, Kingsbury Pale
33. Manitowoc Products Co., Kingsbury Pale / The Aristocrat of them all, Manitowoc, Wis.
34. Marathon City Brwg. Co. / Tannenbaum Beer
35. Drink Monroe Ale, Rochester, N.Y.
36. Oakland / The Wests best bet
37. Pittsburgh Brewing Co., Drink Iron City Beer / same on reverse
38. Pittsburgh Brewing Co., Drink Tech Beer
39. Drink Mathie Ruder Red Ribbon Beer, Wausau
40. Salinas Brewing Co., Salinas, Cal., Schloss Brau
41. Jacob Schmidt Brewing Co., St. Paul, Minn. / Schmidt's City Club
42. Silver Spring Beer, Victoria, B.C.
43. South Fork Brewing Co., South Fork, Pa.
44. Walter Brewing Co., Pueblo, Colo. / Walter's Triple Brewed Beer & Ale
45. Washington Pilsner
46. Drink Yuengling's Fine Beer

B-15

1. Demand the Brown Label, Old German Lager
2. Drink Zang's Beverages, Denver / same on reverse

B-16

1. Gold Label Beer, Menasha, Wis.

B-17

1. Compliments of Buffalo Brewing Co., Sacramento, Cal.
2. Strohs Bohemian Beer / America's Favorite

B-18

1. American Beer, Rochester
2. American Beer, Rochester, N.Y.
3. American Brewing Co., Rochester, N.Y. / Tam O'Shanter Ale, Liberty Beer
4. Bartholomay, Rochester, Beer in bottles / same on reverse
5. Bartholomay, Rochester, N.Y., in bottles only, Tam O'Shanter Ale / Bartholomay, Rochester, N.Y., in bottles only, Rienzi Beer
6. Berkshire Brewing Ass'n, Pittsfield, Mass., key to Lenox Half Stock Ale
7. Berlin Brewing Co., Berlin, Wis.
8. Key to Brownsville Beer
9. Buffalo Co-Op Brewing Co's Extra 6 Lager
10. Bushkill Lager / Easton, Pa.

11. Drink Old Bohemian Brew, California Bottling Assn.
12. Canandaigua Ale
13. Carling's Red Cap / Black Lager Rice Beer
14. Compliments of Carrington Bottling Works
15. Chattanooga Brew Co's Home Bottling / Drink Imperial Pilsener
16. Cold Spring Lager, Sunbury, Pa.
17. Key to Cook's Beer, Evansville, Ind.
18. Crescent Brewing Co. of Irwin, Pa.
19. Drink Daeufers Beer / Brewed & Bottled by Daeufer Lieberman Brewery, Allentown, Pa.
20. Dawson's Ale-Lager (on bottle)
21. Drink Dick's Beer
22. Dubuque Brewing & Malting Co., Dubuque, Iowa / Banquet the beer for you
23. Dubuque Brewing & Malting Co., Dubuque, Iowa / Vimalt the Health Tonic
24. Key to the famous Dubuque Star Beer
25. Duquesne Silver Top Beer / Duquesne, American, Lutz, 1st National, Char. Valley, Hilltop, Home, Homestead, Charleroi, Globe, Monessen, Anderton, Butler, New Kensington, Loyalhanna
26. Enterprise Brewing Co., Ale & Lager, Fall River, Mass.
27. Eulberg Brewing Co., Crown Select Beer, Portage, Wis.
28. Key to Franz Bros. Brewing Co., Freeport, Ill. / same on reverse
29. Drink Fresno Beer
30. Key to German Brew'g Co's Beer, Cumberland, Md.
31. Bottle opener for Gipps Beer, Peoria, Ill.
32. Key to Goetz Beer, St. Joseph, Mo.
33. Key to Gold Medal Wilkes Barre Beer
34. Golden Grain Belt Beer is good
35. Compliments of Grand Rapids Brewing Co. / Silver Foam & Export
36. J. Gund Brg. Co., LaCrosse, Wis., Key to Peerless Bottle Beer, Awarded Gold Medal St. Louis 1904, Established 1854
37. J. Gund Brg. Co., LaCrosse, Wis., Key to Peerless Bottle Beer, Medal for Purity, Paris Exposition 1900, Established 1854
38. Drink Horlachers 7 months old Perfection Beer
39. Inter-State Brg. Co., Sioux City, Iowa, Drink Nu Life Beer
40. Kamm & Schellinger Co., Mishawaka, Ind. / Drink Arrow Beer
41. Karmaiers Beer
42. Kingsbury Pale
43. Use Koch's Beer
44. Lembeck & Betz, Eagle Brewing Co., Jersey City, N.J.
45. Manitowoc Products Company, Manitowoc, Wisconsin / Kingsbury Pale
46. Key to Metz Bros. Br'g Co., Omaha's favorite beer
47. Key to Michels Perfection Beer, LaCrosse, Wis.
48. Minneapolis Brewing Co., Gold Grain Belt Beers
49. Drink Moerlein's Barbarosa, the finest bottled beer brewed
50. Drink Moerlein's Cincinnati Beers
51. Drink Old Monarch Beer
52. Key to North Yakima Brewing & M. Co's Bottle Beer
53. Key to Northampton Brewing Co., Valhalla Beer
54. Old Lockport Lager "The Better Beer" / same on reverse
55. Return these keys to Olympia Brewing Co., Olympia, Washington and receive reward / (a different number on each 1 through 10,000)
56. Drink Overland Beer
57. Oxford Club Ale
58. Use with satisfaction only on Pacific Club Beer
59. Key to Park Brewing Co's Sunshine Beer, Winona, Minn.
60. Drink Phoenix Beer, Buffalo's famous brew
61. Piel's Beer
62. Drink Pierson's Bottle Beer, Phone Home 113-7
63. Pointer Brewing Co., Clinton, Iowa
64. Drink Primo Beer
65. Key to Rainier's Beer
66. E. Robinson's Sons, Scranton, Pa., bottlers of Pilsener Beer
67. Key to Jacob Ruppert's Beer
68. Drink Schlitz Beer, bottled by A.W. Schrader
69. Schlitz in brown bottles / The beer that made Milwaukee famous
70. R.J. Serwasi, Manayunk Bottler / Drink Betz's Phila. Porter pasturized
71. Shamokin Brewing Co's Beer, Key to Rising Sun
72. Key to Simon Pure Beer, Buffalo, N.Y.
73. Key to Silver Top Beer
74. Standard Bottling Works, Silverton, Colo. / Key to Anheuser Busch or Budweiser
75. Standard Brewing Co., Manka, Minn. / Drink Standard 1776
76. Drink Stegmaier's Wilkes Barre Beer
77. Compliments of Sunset Brewing Co., Wallace, Idaho
78. Tacoma Beer, Anti-Katzenjammer
79. The Thieme & Wagner Brewing Co., Lockweiler Special Brew / T & W Special
80. Tivoli Brewing Co's Altes Lager
81. Valley Brew Lager, Stockton, Cal.
82. West End Brewing "The Famous Utica Beer" / same on reverse

B-19

1. Drink Acme Beer for health
2. Ask for Bartels Beer
3. Drink Bartl's Beers, LaCrosse, Wis.
4. Berghoff, a real German beer
5. Buffalo Brewing Co., Sacramento, Cal.
6. Drink Centlivre's Nickel Plate, Ft. Wayne Beer
7. Drink Dick Bros' Pilsener Beer, Quincy, Ill.
8. Duluth Brewing & Malting Co., Duluth, Minn.
9. Edmonton Beer, Oscar Heyman & Co., H3 Park Place
10. Flower City Brewing Co., Maltop Acme Ale
11. Fresno Brewing Co., Fresno, Cal.
12. Drink Gunds Keg & Bottle Beers, LaCrosse, Wisc., Gold Medal 1904
13. Gund's Peerless Bottled Beer, LaCrosse, Wis.
14. Gund's Peerless Beer, good since 1854, LaCrosse, Wis.
15. Haberle Congress Beer, Syracuse / same on reverse
16. Key to Hamm's Famous Beers
17. Key to Hamm's Famous Beers / Digesto Malt Tonic
18. Heidel Brau Bottled Beer / Western Brew Bottled Beer
19. King's Bohemian Beer
20. Lemp, St. Louis / J.S. Wahl, Caruthersville, Mo.
21. The Lima Brewing Co., Lima, Ohio / Drink Lima Beer
22. Compliments of Maier Brewing Co., Incorporated, Los Angeles, U.S.A. / Drink Old Fashion German Brew
23. Compliments of Maier Brewing Co., Incorporated, Los Angeles, U.S.A. / Drink Select Beer
24. Minneapolis Brewing Co., Golden Grain Belt Beers
25. Moerlbach
26. Order Neef's Gold Belt, Tel 1105 Main
27. Drink Oertel Brew Cream Beer, Louisville, Ky.
28. Ohio Brewing Co., Columbus, Ohio "Try a case"

29. Key to Pittsburgh Brewing Co's Select Beer / same on reverse
30. Key to Pittsburgh Brewing Co's Tech Beer / Pittsburgh Brewing Co., P.B. Co. Special
31. Key to Rainier Beer
32. Drink E. Robinson's Sons Pilsener Beer / same on reverse
33. Ruhstallers Lager, best beer brewed / Sacramento, Cal.
34. Drink Saskatoon Beer
35. Seattle Brewing & Malting Co., Seattle, Wash., U.S.A. / Key to Rainier Beer
36. Star Brewing Co., Minster, Ohio
37. The Washington Brewing Co., "Pilsener for Me"
38. Call for Wieland's Beer
39. Wilhelm, Moschim & Ramsey, drink Sunshine
40. Willow Springs Beverage Co., Omaha

B-20

1. King's Bohemian Beer

B-21

1. Drink Acme Beer for health
2. Drink Akron Brewing Company's White Rock Export
3. Drink Aurora Brew'g. Co's Bottled Beer
4. Ask for Bartels Crown Beer, Syracuse
5. Batholomay Rochester Beer and Ale in Bottles
6. Becker Products Co., Ogden, Utah / Drink becco nourishing as beer
7. Blue and Gold Beer
8. The Cleveland & Sandusky Brewing Co., Sandusky, Ohio / Drink Crystal Rock Beer
9. Cold Spring Lager, Sunbury, Pa.
10. Coors Golden Beer
11. The Christ Diehl Brewing Co., Defiance, Ohio / Diehls Beer, try it, you always buy it
12. Call for Ehrenpreis, the beer extraordinary
13. Enterprise Brewing / Yosemite Beer
14. Evans Ale
15. Evans Ale has trade mark on Crown Corks
16. Call for Evansville Brewing Ass'n Beer, Sterling, Rheingold, Pale Export
17. Drink Flocks, it stands on top
18. Fredericksburg Beer
19. Call for Fredericksburg Beer
20. Garden City Brewing Co., Missoula, Mont.
21. The Goebel Brewing Co., Detroit / Key to Goebel Beer
22. Drink Gold Bond Cream of Table Beer
23. Key to Gold Medal Wilkes Barre Beer
24. Compliments of Grands Rapids Brewing Co. / Silver Foam & Export
25. Drink Gund's Keg and Bottle Beer, LaCrosse, Wis., Gold Medal 1904 (mug)
26. Haberle Congress Beer, Syracuse
27. Hamm's St. Paul
28. Key to Hennepin Brg. Co., Minneapolis, Minn., Use It.
29. Hopsburger Beer
30. Drink Horlachers 9 months old Perfection Beer
31. Key to J.B. Hronecz Bottling Works, Shenandoah, Pa.
32. Drink Huehners Toledo Beer
33. Drink Humboldt Beer / Good? Yes
34. Hyde Park / same
35. Hyde Park Bottled Beer, Seldom equaled, never excelled / Brewed only at the Hyde Park Bottled Beer Plant, St. Louis, Mo.
36. Hyde Park Brewing Co., Hyde Park, Pa. / Drink Purity Beer
37. Independent Brg. Co. of Pittsburgh / American Pale Export Beer
38. Independent Brg. Co. of Pittsburgh
39. Independent Brg. Co. of Pittsburgh / Duquesne, Silver Top Beer
40. Independent Brg. Co. of Pittsburgh / Silver Top
41. Indianapolis Brewing Co., Duesseldorfer, The World's standard of perfection
42. Jamestown Brewing Co., Jamestown, N.Y., Drink Chautauqua Brew
43. Call for Frank Jones Portsmouth Ale
44. Call for the brew from Kalamazoo, Kalamazoo Brewing Co., Kalamazoo, Mich.
45. Compliments of John Kazmaier, Altoona, Pa.
46. Kings Bohemian Beer
47. Try a case of Zang's Beer bottled by the C.A. Lammers Bottling Co., Denver, Colo.
48. Drink Majestic Beer Best of all / Bottled at the Brewery, 3036 N. 6th St., Phila., Pa.
49. Maltosia
50. C & J Michel Brewing Co., LaCrosse, Wis.
51. C & J Michel Brewing Co., LaCrosse, Wis., Felsenbrau
52. Drink Moerlein's Barbarossa / The finest bottled beer brewed
53. The Muessel Brewing Co., South Bend, Ind.
54. Compliments of Muskegon Brewing Co., Muskegon, Mich. / Drink Muskegon Old Time Lager Beer
55. Call for Mutual Beer in Golden Bottles
56. Mutual Union Brewing Co., 279 Main, Phone 3143 Grant / Ask for Pilsener Style and Pennsy Select
57. The Famous Narragansett Lager / The Famous Narragansett Ale
58. National Beer
59. National Beer / Best in the West
60. Order Neef's Gold Belt, Tel. 1105 Main
61. The Old Brewing Co., Dayton, Ohio
62. Old Standard Beer
63. Call for Quandt's Famous Lager Beer, Tel. 587, Troy, N.Y.
64. Key to Peru Beer, Fine Beer
65. Pfaff's Beer
66. Watch P.O.C. Extra Pilsener Bottled Beer
67. Drink Potosi Brewing Co's Beer
68. Drink Radeke's Beer
69. Key to Rettig Brewing Co., Pottsville, Pa. / same
70. Ritter Brau, good as gold
71. E. Robinsons Sons, Scranton, Pa., Bottlers of Pilsner Beer
72. Ruhstaller's Lager, best beer brewed, Sacramento, Cal.
73. Ryans Pure Beers, Syracuse, N.Y. / same
74. San Antonio Brg. Assn. City Brewery / A key to the city
75. Adam Scheidt Brewing Co., Norristown, Pa., Philadelphia, 963 N. Ninth St. / Drink Lotos finest pale beer brewed
76. Schlitz in brown bottles / The beer that made Milwaukee famous
77. Key to Schlitz Beer, John A. Sheenan, Williamsport, Pa.
78. Key to Schreiber Beer, Buffalo, N.Y.
79. Seitz Brewing Co., Easton, Pa.
80. Silver Spring Brewery Limited, Sherbrooke, Que.
81. So. Bethlehem Brewing Co., the home favorite — Supreme
82. Tacoma Beer, Anti-Katzenjammer
83. Tacoma Beer "Get it"
84. Tacoma Extra Pale — Get it!

85. The Thieme & Wagner Brewing Co., Lockweiler Special Brew / T & Special
86. Tivoli Brewing Co., Detroit, Mich. / Call for "Altes Lager" The beer in the green bottle
87. U.S. Standard Beer, the Reading Beer
88. The Victor Brewing Co., Jeanette, Pa., Gilt Edge
89. Walter's Gold Label, Menasha, Wis.
90. White Eagle Brewing Co., 3755 S. Racine Ave., Chicago, Ill.
91. Wielands Beer
92. Compliments of York Brewing Co.

B-22

1. American Liberty Brew. Co.
2. Berghoff, a real German beer
3. Centlivre Beer, Ft. Wayne
4. Falstaff Bottled Beer / same
5. Drink Foss-Schneider Bottle Beer
6. Key to Gluek Root Beer, Glix Beverage, Gluek Brg. Co., Minneapolis
7. Gold Medal Wilkes Barre Beer
8. Key to Hamm's Famous Beers
9. Jetters "Old Age"
10. Jung Beer, Milwaukee, serves you right
11. Kessler, the beer for you
12. Drink Leisen & Henes' "Old Craft Brew"
13. Lexington Brewing Co.
14. Minneapolis Brewing Co., Golden Grain Belt Beers
15. Mutual Union Brewing Co., Phone Grant 3143 / Ask for Pennsy Select
16. Ottawa Brg. Ass'n Beer
17. Drink Radeke's Beer
18. Key to Schell's Deer Brand Beer, New Ulm, Minn.
19. Schlitz in brown bottles / The beer that made Milwaukee famous
20. West Louisville Brewing Co., Inc.

B-23

1. Adanac Beer, A bottle of good taste
2. Bartholomay Apollo Beer, Rochester, N.Y. Bartholomay Chic Ale, Rochester, N.Y.
3. Blumers Special Brew Beverage
4. Burgermeister Beer / same
5. Centlivre Beer, Ft. Wayne, Ind. (spinner)
6. Dub-Lin-Stout Malt
7. Duquesne Brewing Co. of Pittsburgh, the finest beers in town / Duquesne, Silver Top, Old Carnegie, 3 Star
8. Try Ehret's Extra / (trademark)
9. Genesee Liebotschaner
10. Golden Glow Beer / Golden Glow (spinner)
11. Peter Hand Brewery Co., Chicago / Meister Brau
12. Drink Harding's Special Brew / Enjoy Harding's just wonderful food, Chgo.
13. Wm. G. Jung Beverage Co. / Random Lake, Wis.
14. Lethbridge Breweries Ltd., The beer without peer
15. Kessler Brwg. Co., Lorelei
16. Drink King of Clubs
17. Mausner's Lager Beer "Like the old days"
18. Miller High Life Beer
19. Drink Miller High Life Beer
20. Miller High Life Beverages
21. Famous Narragansett Beers
22. Drink Old Style Lager
23. Oshkosh Brewing Co., 1631 Doty St., Oshkosh, Wis. / Chief Oshkosh Special Old Lager, B'Gosh it's good
24. Overland Beverage Company, Nampa, Idaho
25. Piel's Beer
26. Renner, Youngstown, Ohio / Lager Beer, Oxford Ale
27. Key to Schreiber Beer, Buffalo, N.Y.
28. Key to Schreiber's Manru Beer, Buffalo, N.Y.
29. Manufactured by Terre Haute Brewing Co. / Drink C-V non intoxicating
30. The Wehle Brewing Co., Quality beer and ale, West Haven, Conn.

B-24

1. Acme Beer
2. Auto City Beer
3. Berlin Brewing Co.
4. Buffalo Brewing Co., Sacramento, Calif.
5. Burgermeister Beer / same
6. Burkhardt's Beer / Mug Ale
7. Canada Bud Breweries, Toronto / Drink Canada Bud Beer, Stout, WA 1885
8. Carnegie Pils'ner / Frontenac Ale
9. Dawson's Ale & Lager / Two Royal Brews
10. Drink Dutch Club Beer / same
11. Drink Edelweiss Beer / A case of good judgement
12. Effinger Beer, Baraboo, Wis.
13. GB Lager
14. Gipps Amberlin Peoria
15. Gluek's
16. Golden Glow Beer
17. Griesedieck Bros., St. Louis
18. Homestead Brewery, HO-4242, Heigh-Ho Premium Beer / Hofbrau Beer HO-4242, by case-barrel-or-truckload
19. Howell & King Brewery, Pittston, Pa., Joyce's Perfection Beer
20. Drink Iron City Beer "The talk of the town" / same
21. Kingsbury Breweries Co., Kingsbury Pale Beer
22. Enjoy Lucky Lager Beer
23. Mathie-Ruder Brew. Co., Wausau, Wis., Enjoy Red Ribbon & Gold Star Beer
24. Drink Mineral Spring Beer, Mineral Spring Brewing Co.
25. Monterey Beer
26. Famous Narragansett Ale
27. Old Tap Ale
28. Light Pickwick / Pickwick Ale
29. Pointer Brewing Co., Clinton, Iowa / Pointer Beer
30. Rainier Beer / Rainier Ale
31. Schmidt, St. Paul, Minn. / City Club
32. Jacob Schmidt Brewing Co., St. Paul, Minn. / City Club
33. K.G. Schmidt's Beer, Logansport, Ind.
34. Walters Pilsener Beer
35. Walter Brewing Co., Colorado & Wisconsin / Walters Pilsener Beer
36. D.G. Yuengling & Son, Inc., Pottsville, Pa. / Drink Yuengling Fine Beer

B-25

1. C & J Michel Brewing Co., LaCrosse, Wis. / Elfenbrau

C-1

1. The Central Brewing Co. (Horse)
2. Peter Doelger First Prize Quality Beer
3. Edelweiss Beer, A case of good judgement

C-2

1. Phoenix Beer, Buffalo's Famous Brew, taste the difference (Eagle)
2. Pittsburgh Brewing Co., Tech Beer (bottle)

C-3

1. Don't say beer, say Schlitz

C-4

1. Pabst Blue Ribbon / The Beer of quality

C-5

1. Pablo made by Pabst Milwaukee / Pablo the happy hoppy drink
2. Pabst Blue Ribbon / The Beer of quality

C-6

1. Black Bass Ale / Congress Lager, Derby Pale Ale
2. Falls City Lager Beer
3. Iroquois Ale-Beer-Porter, Buffalo, N.Y.
4. Pabst Blue Ribbon, the beer of quality

C-7

1. Utica Club Pilsener-Wuerzburger, it's in the taste — pale dry Ginger Ale / same

C-8

1. Congress Beer
2. Grain Belt

C-9

1. Acme Beer
2. Famous Beverwyck Beer, Albany, N.Y.
3. Blatz, Milwaukee
4. The Bruckmann Co., Cincinnati
5. Chelmsford
6. Edelweiss Beer / A case of good judgement
7. Storz Beer, Omaha
8. Regal, Detroit, Mich., King of Beers (lion head)
9. Schmidt, St. Paul
10. Sebewaing Old Style Lager
11. Tivoli Brewing Co.
12. Drink Valley Forge Special / Philadelphia Branch 2815 Ridge Ave.

C-10

1. Famous A-B-C Beer
2. American Brewing Co., Rochester, N.Y. / Tam O'Shanter Ale, Apollo Beer
3. American Brewing Co., Rochester, N.Y. / Tam O'Shanter Ale, Liberty Beer
4. Famous Beverwyck Beers & Ale, Albany, N.Y.
5. Blatz Milwaukee / Blatz Old Heidelberg
6. Drink Dotterwyck Beers & Ale
7. Eagle Ales & Lager, Utica, N.Y.
8. General Brewing Corporation, Lucky Lager Bonded Beer
9. General Brewing Corporation, Lucky Lager — plainly age-dated
10. Iron City Beer
11. Kamm & Schellinger Co., Mishawaka, Ind., Drink A-R-R-O-W
12. Koerber's Beer, Age-Strength-Purity
13. Manz Beer
14. Drink Neuweiler's Beverages, Purity Porter, Frontenac Ale
15. Newark "Olde Towne" Beer and Ale / same
16. Phoenix Beer-Ale / same
17. Phoenix Beer-Ale / Conserve steel for defense, don't lose this opener
18. Piel's Beer
19. Regal, King of Beers, Detroit, Mich., Good beer for the good times (lion head)
20. Rochester Brewing Co., Inc., Old Topper Ale (man in top hat)
21. Stein's Beer and Ale
22. Tivoli Beer
23. Yough Brewing Co., Connellsville, Pa.

C-11

1. Conn. Valley Brew Co., Meriden, Conn., Beers - Ales
2. Independent Milwaukee Brewery, Phone Mitchell 0880 / Bill's Braumeister, the brew with that old time flavor

C-12

1. Famous A-B-C Beer / same
2. Peter Breidt Brewing Co., Elizabeth, N.J., Breidt's Beer - Ale
3. Camden Beer
4. Cremo Brewing Co., Inc., New Britain, Ct., Cremo Ale and Lager
5. Cremo Sparkling Ale and Beer
6. Fidelio Beer, quality since 1852
7. Drink Fort Pitt the good beer
8. Fort Pitt Special Beer
9. The Franklin Brewing Co., Ben Brew Beer, 100% grain product
10. Genesee Old Fashioned Goodness Beer & Ale
11. From the Cypress casks of Goebel
12. Hamm's smooth mellow beer
13. Hawaii Brewing Corporation Ltd., Primo Beer, Honolulu, T.H. (bottle)
14. Drink Jax Beer
15. Lebanon Valley Beer / same
16. Monarch Beer
17. Neuweiler's Ale & Beer
18. The National Brewing Co., Baltimore, Md., National Premium Beer / same
19. National Brewing Co., Above Ale Eagle Beer Special (bottle)
20. Old Stock Beer
21. Piels Light Beer (man)
22. R & H Beer
23. Regal Lager Beer
24. Riekers Beer (bottle)
25. Jacob Schmidt Brewing Co. / City Club Beer
26. South Bethlehem Brewing Co., Supreme Beer
27. So. Bethlehem Brewing Co., Bethlehem, Pa. / Supreme Bottles & Cans
28. Tacoma Beer best East or West (bottle)
29. Ask for Tivoli Beer
30. The Victor Brewing Co., Jeanette, Pa., Victor Beer (bottle)
31. Weibel's Ales-Lager / New Haven, Conn.
32. White Eagle Beer

C-13

1. Alpen Brau Beer (bottle) / same
2. Bartels Beer — Ales
3. Bethlehem Brewing Co., Bethlehem, Pa. / Supreme Bottles & Cans
4. Biere Champlain Porter
5. Birk Bros. Brewing Co., Lincoln 7600, Birk's Superb Beer
6. Drink Black Forest Beer
7. Breidt's Beer — Ale, Since 1867
8. Brockerts Brewing Co., Inc., Worcester, Mass., Brockert's Ale
9. Brucks distinctive beers, Cincinnati, over 80 years
10. Cadillac Brewing Co., Detroit, Mich.
11. Camden Beer, full quart (bottle)
12. Canandaigua Beer — Ale

13. Carnegie Pils'ner or Lager, the beer everyone likes, Chartier Valley Brewery, Carnegie, Pa. / Frontenac Ale, the perfect pale ale
14. The Cleveland Home Brewing Co., Black Forest Beer
15. Columbus Brewing Co. — All American
16. Cook's Beer / F.W. Cook Co., Evansville, Ind.
17. Corona Extra / La Cerveza Mas Fina
18. Cream City Brg. Co., Famous Milwaukee Pilsener Beer (bottle)
19. Detroit Brew. Co., Old Bru Beer (bottle)
20. Diamond Spring Ale — Porter
21. Dobler P.O.N.
22. Dobler since 1865
23. DuBois Brewing Co., DuBois, Pa., "Let's meet and be friends" / DuBois Budweiser
24. DuBois Brewing Co., DuBois, Pa. / "Let's meet and be friends"
25. Duquesne Brewing Co., Pittsburgh, Duquesne Old Nut Brown Ale (squirrel) / Duquesne Brewing Co., Pittsburgh, The Prince of Pilseners, Duquesne Pilsener (prince)
26. Dutch Maid Beer, Gold Mule Ale
27. The Ebling Brewing Co., Inc., New York, N.Y., Ebling's that grand old beer (bottle)
28. Carl Ebner Brg. Co., Atkinson, Wis.
29. Eldredge Portsmouth Ale (bottle)
30. F & S Beer — Ale
31. Fuhrmann & Schmidt Brewing Co., Shamokin, Pa. / F & S Beer (bottle)
32. Falls City Beer
33. Falls City Brewing Co., Louisville, Ky., Falls City Beer (bottle)
34. Fecker's Beer
35. Fehr's since 1872
36. Feigenspan P.O.N.
37. Fitzgerald Bros. Brewing Co., Troy, N.Y., Burgomaster Beer (bottle)
38. Fitzgerald's Beer — Ale
39. Flocks, Williamsport, Pa.
40. Fort Pitt Beer
41. Fort Pitt Double Lagered Beer
42. Fort Pitt Special Premium Beer
43. Drink Fort Pitt the good beer
44. Fox's DeLuxe Beer (bottle)
45. The Franklin Brewing Co., Ben Brew 100% Grain
46. Genesee Old Fashioned Goodness Beer — Ale
47. Genesee Premium Quality Beer
48. Made only by The German Brewing Co., Cumberland, Md. / The Original Old German Beer
49. Geyers, Drink Frankenmuth Lager Beer
50. Good Old Glennon's Beer
51. Globe Brewery, Arrow Beer — it hits the spot
52. Gold Glow Beer
53. Goenner & Co., Johnstown, Pa., Old Monarch Beer
54. Graupner's Beer — Ale, Harrisburg, Pa.
55. Gunthers Lager Beer (bottle)
56. Hamm's smooth mellow beer
57. Hanley's for ale
58. Highland Beer (bottle)
59. Hohenadel
60. Iron City Beer / same
61. Frank Jones Ale
62. Ask for K-B Beer
63. Kings Beer (bottle & crown)
64. Knapstein Brg. Co., Phone 100, New London, Wis.
65. Koerber's Beer Age-Strength-Purity
66. G. Krueger Brg. Co., Newark, N.J., Krueger Beer-Ale (waiter)
67. Lake of the Woods Brewing Co., Ltd., Kenora, Ontario, Beer-Ale-Stout / Bentz Beer
68. Lebanon Valley Beer
69. Magnolia Beer / same
70. Manz Beer
71. Miller High Life Beer (bottle)
72. Moore & Quinn Ale
73. Muessel Silver Edge Beer
74. National Premium Beer
75. Neuweiler's Ale & Beer
76. North American Brewing Co., Brooklyn, N.Y. / Doerschuck Beer
77. North American Brewing Co., Brooklyn, N.Y. / Paramount Beer
78. Old Style Lager, Chicago, Phone Spaulding 6800 / Drink Old Style Lager the beer with a snap to it (man with glass & bottle)
79. Ortlieb's Beer (bottle)
80. Pabst Blue Ribbon Beer (bottle)
81. Pabst Blue Ribbon Beer (bottle) / The brew that brings back memories (bottle)
82. Peerless Beer, LaCrosse, Wis.
83. Peerless Beer, LaCrosse, Wisconsin, spin — you pay (spinner)
84. Pelissier's
85. Penn Brewing Co., Diplomat Beer, Steelton, Penna.
86. Pfeiffer Beer, Detroit, Est. 1889
87. Piels Real Lager Beer
88. Pilser's Original N.Y. Extra Dry
89. R & H Beer
90. Rainier Brewing Co., Inc., San Francisco, Cal. / Rainier Beer old original (bottle)
91. Ruppert Beer Ale
92. Ruppert Beer — Old Knickerbocker Beer
93. Ruppert Knickerbocker Beer
94. Schaefer Beer at it's best
95. Schaefer Fine Beer
96. Schlitz (bottle) / Schlitz the beer that made Milwaukee famous
97. Jacob Schmidt Brewing Co. / City Club Beer
98. Schmidt's Beer, no sugar, no glucose / same
99. Schmidt's Famous, America's finest beer, Est. 1873 (bottle)
100. Schmidt's Famous Beer / same
101. Schmidt's Wurzburger Beer / Schmidt's Famous Beer
102. Schultz Brewing Co., Inc., Union City, N.J.
103. Silver Top — Duquesne — Old Carnegie
104. Simon Pure Ale and Beer
105. Standard Brewing Co., Rochester, N.Y. / Old Ox Cart Sturdy Ale
106. Standard Brewing Co., Inc., Rochester, N.Y., Phone Glen 363, Standard Always (bottle) / Standard Brewing Co., Inc., Rochester, N.Y.
107. Standard Brewing Co., Inc., Rochester, N.Y., Phone Glen 363, Standard Always (bottle) / 420-46 Lake Ave, Rochester
108. Standard Brewing Co., Inc., Rochester, N.Y., Phone Glen 363, Standard Always (bottle) / Ox Head Sturdy Ale
109. The Stanton Brewery, Inc., Troy, N.Y.
110. Sterling Brewing, Inc., Evansville, Ind., Sterling Beer (bottle)
111. South Bethlehem Brewing Co., Supreme Beer
112. Terre Haute Brewing Co., Inc., Champagne Velvet Beer / Champagne Velvet Beer (bottle)
113. Ask for Tivoli Beer
114. Two Rivers Bobbie Ale / Two Rivers Golden Drops Beer

115. Von Brewing Co., 1800 East Forest Ave., Detroit, Mich. / Von the beer of distinction
116. Wehle Mule Head Ale, Ox Head Beer
117. Weibels Ales-Lager / New Haven, Conn.
118. White Eagle Brewing Co., 3755 So. Racine Ave., Tel Yards 7460 / Allweiser Beer
119. Yoerg's Cave Aged Beer, St. Paul
120. Ziegler's Beer

C-14

1. Buckeye Beer (B in circle)
2. Burkhardt's since 1880, Beer, Mug Ale
3. Fort Pitt Beer & Ale
4. Hauenstein's New Ulm Beer
5. Horlacher's
6. Jones Brewing Co., Smithton, Pa., Satisfying Stoney's (man with glass of beer)
7. Manz Beer
8. Old Dutch Beer — Ale, Brooklyn, N.Y.
9. Pfeiffers Beer, Detroit, Est. 1889
10. Regal Lager Beer (lion head)
11. Rheingold
12. Rheingold Extra Dry
13. Rochester Brewing Co., Old Topper Ale (man in top hat)
14. Rochester Brewing Co., Inc., Old Topper Ale
15. Ruppert Ale
16. Ruppert Beer — Old Knickerbocker Beer
17. Scotch Thistle Brand Ale
18. Simon Pure Beer — Ale
19. Storz Gold Crest Beer

C-15

1. Camden Beer, tastes as good as it looks!
2. Fort Pitt Special Beer
3. Genesee Old Fashioned Goodness Beer & Ale
4. Be happy with Harvard Ale or Export
5. Pour on the Iron, Rally round returnables / Rally round the Pirates
6. Iroquois Beverage Corp., Buffalo, N.Y., Iroquois Ale — Beer (Indian head)
7. Piel's Light Beer
8. Rheingold Extra Dry
9. Ruppert Knickerbocker Beer / same
10. Schaefer America's oldest lager beer / same
11. Utica Club for Natural beer — one punch / same
12. Valley Forge Beer / same

C-16

1. Iroquois, the bold beer (Indian head), International Breweries, Inc., Buffalo, N.Y., Covington, Ky., Findlay, Ohio
2. Iroquois Indian Head Beer
3. G. Krueger Brg. Co., Newark, N.J., Krueger Beer — Ale (K-man)
4. Monarch Brg. Co., Chgo. / Monarch Beer
5. Moose Brewing Co., Pennsy Beer
6. Rheingold Extra Dry
7. Rolling Rock Premium Beer
8. Rubsam & Horrmann Brewing Co., New York City, N.Y. / Crown Premium Beer
9. Schaefer America's Oldest lager beer / same
10. Schaefer Fine Beer / same
11. Schoenling Beer, Cincinnati's finest, Phone Cherry 4344

C-17

1. Arrow Beer — it hits the spot
2. Atlas Prager Beer, Got it? Get it!!
3. Time out for Dawson's Ale & Beer, Dawson's Brewery, Inc., New Bedford, Mass. / Time out for Dawson's Ale & Beer
4. Ehret's Extra Beer
5. Fox DeLuxe Beer
6. Gretz Beer, Phila. (cone top can)
7. Haberle Beer — Ale / same
8. Hanley's for ale
9. Hazleton Pilsener Beer
10. Hudepohl Beer, Cincinnati, O.
11. Iroquois Indian Head Beer
12. Lebanon Valley Beer (bottle)
13. Lebanon Valley Beer (shield)
14. London Dry the Topper of all drinks (man in top hat)
15. The Milwaukee road
16. Monarch Beer
17. Moore & Quinn Ale
18. Moose Beer
19. Ortlieb's Beer
20. Pabst Blue Ribbon (short bottle)
21. Pabst Blue Ribbon (tall bottle)
22. Phoenix Beer — Ale
23. Pioneer
24. Prior Beer
25. Rochester Brewing Co., Golden Old Topper Ale — Beer, Rochester Brewing Co. (man in top hat)
26. Schaefer Beer at its best / same
27. Schaefer Fine Beer / same
28. Schoenling Beer, Cincinnati's finest, Phone Cherry 4344
29. The Stanton Brewery, Inc., Troy, N.Y.
30. Valley Forge Beer
31. Wayne Beer Ale
32. Wayne Beer Ale / Lager Pilsner Ale
33. White Eagle Brewing Co. 3755 So. Racine Ave., Tel Yards 7460 / Drink Chevalier Beer

C-18

1. Blatz, Milwaukee's finest beer
2. Drink Esslinger's Beer — Ale (little man)
3. Fort Schuyler, Don't say beer, say Fort Schuyler
4. Independent Milwaukee Brewery, Drink Braumeister, "Milwaukee's choicest beer"
5. Iroquois Beverage Corp., Buffalo, N.Y., Iroquois Indian Head Beer and Ale (Indian head)
6. Knickerbocker Beer
7. Metz Quality beer since 1864
8. R & H Beer — Ale
9. Rolling Rock Premium Beer
10. Simon Pure Ale and Beer, The William Simon Brewery, Buffalo, N.Y.
11. Trommer's Beer
12. Trommer's White Label, the all malt beer, Trommer Brewing Co., Bklyn, N.Y.

C-19

1. Cremo Ale and Beer
2. Fort Pitt Special Beer — something special / Old Shay DeLuxe Beer — for particular people (2 varieties — red on nickel, blue on nickel)
3. Gretz Beer (man on bicycle)
4. Harvard (red)
5. Hudepohl Pure Lager Beer
6. Independent Milwaukee Brewery, Braumeister Special Pilsener Beer

7. Rochester Brewing Co., Inc., Old Topper Ale-Beer, the flavor that's in flavor (two varieties — red and nickel)
8. Rolling Rock the premium beer

C-20

1. Betz Ales-Beer-Porter
2. Famous Beverwyck Beers and Ales
3. Burkhardt's Beer and Ale, Akron, Ohio
4. Kaier's Special Beer, union made / Kaier's Old Dominion Ale & Port, union made
5. Lebanon Valley Export Beer-Ale-Porter / same
6. Lion, New York City, Beer — Ale (lion & keg)
7. Drink Neuweiler's Famous Beers, Allentown, Pa. / same
8. Drink Neuweiler's Purity Beer, Allentown, Pa.
9. North American Brewing Co., Brooklyn, N.Y. / Paramount Beers — Ales
10. The Wm. Peter Brewing Corp. / Peter Brau
11. Wehle Mule Head Ale

C-21

1. Crystal Rock Beer
2. Kaier's Special Beer, famous as anthracite / Kaier's Old Diamond Ale & Porter, famous as anthracite
3. Old Timers Ale
4. The Wm. Peter Brewing Corp.
5. R & H Beer — Ale

C-22

1. Molson's / Molson's
2. Jacob Ruppert, Brewer — New York / Save this opener, order by the case, Knickerbocker the brew that satisfies

C-23

1. Drink Jax, best beer in town, Jackson Brewing Co., N.O., La. / same

C-24

1. Hoffman
2. Compliments of United States Brewing Co.

D-1

1. Budweiser / A.B.B. Ass'n, St. L.
2. Chief Oshkosh
3. Delta Beer
4. Denmark Brewing Co.
5. Mellow Brew
6. Newman / Pittsburg
7. Jac. Ruppert / Knickerbocker
8. Storz
9. Stroh's Beer / same
10. Zoller's Beer

D-2

1. Chief Oshkosh
2. Dinkelacker
3. Kupper / Beer
4. Maier Beer / Select
5. Rahr Beer
6. Schlitz / same
7. Zoller's Beer

D-3

1. K B Lager / T B Ale
2. Lion Ale / Pilsener Lager
3. Miller High Life
4. Ushers / is better beer
5. Velvet / Terre Haute

D-4

1. Leisys
2. Marchants Ltd.

D-5

1. Berlin Beer
2. Blatz
3. Chief Oshkosh
4. Cook's Beer
5. Delta Beer
6. Kato Beer
7. Kingsbury Beer
8. Mellow Brew
9. Miller High Life
10. People's / Wurtzl
11. Point Beer / same
12. Pointer Beer
13. Rahr Beer / Oshkosh
14. Schoenhofen / Edelweiss
15. Zoller's Beer / same

D-6

1. Bruck's
2. Fehr's / Louisvlle

E-1

1. Compliments of Auto City Brg. Co.
2. Bankers Ale, Bankers Ale / Lucky Lager, Lucky Lager
3. Daeufer's Beer, Allentown's Favorite / Thirsty just call Daeufer's 4733
4. Derby Brewing Co. / Moerlein Beer, Old Coach Ale
5. Fisher Beer, since 1884 / same
6. Fox Head Beers and Ale / same
7. Haffenreffer & Co., Boylston Lager Beer
8. Hull Brewing Co., New Haven, Conn. / Hull's Cream Ale & Lager
9. Drink Kamm's Quality Beer / same
10. Kuebler Brewing Co., Phone 4225, Easton, Pa. / Beer-Ale-Porter, Quarts-Pints-Steinie --- (?!)
11. Mount Carbon Ale — Porter / Mount Carbon Lager Beer
12. Stegmaier Brewing Co., Wilkes Barre, Pa. / Wilkes Barre Tel 28171, Scranton 41167
13. The Tivoli Union Co., Denver, Colo. / Tivoli Beer first for thirst
14. Trommer's Genuine Ale, Taste and compare / Trommer's Malt Beer, taste & compare
15. John F. Trommer, Inc., Brooklyn, N.Y. / Trommers Malt Beer, taste & compare

E-2

1. Drink Bushkill Lager Beer / same
2. Croft Ale, Croft Ale / same
3. The Cumberland Brewing Co. / Old Export Beer
4. Diamond Spring Ale, Diamond Spring Ale / same
5. Griesedieck Bros., St. Louis Beer / same
6. Holihan's Ale-Beer, Lawrence, Mass.
7. Hornung's, Phila., White Bock Beer / Hornung's, Phila., Londonderry Ale
8. Drink Kamm's Quality Beer
9. Koppitz Select Beer / same
10. Adam Scheidt Brewing Co. / Valley Forge Beer
11. Star Beverages, Philadelphia / Maxwell Pale Dry
12. Suffolk Brewing Co.

E-3

1. Belmont Beer, John L. Ale
2. Boyertown Brewing Co., Boyertown, Pa. / Drink Boyertown Beer

3. Delmarva Beer, Wilmington, Del. / same
4. Effinger, Baraboo
5. Fisher Beer since 1884 / same
6. Ernst Fleckenstein Brewing Co. / Faribault, Minn.
7. Fox Head Beers and Ale / same
8. Griesedieck Bros., St. Louis Light Lager / same
9. Holihan's Ale, Holihan's Beer / same
10. Holihan's Ale-Beer, Lawrence, Mass. / same
11. Drink Good Old Hoosier Beer / same
12. Joliet Citizens Brewing Co.
13. Drink Kamm's Quality Beer / same
14. The Lion, Inc., Brewery, Wilkes Barre, Pa.
15. Mt. Carbon Ale — Porter / same
16. C. Schmidt & Sons, Inc., Philadelphia, Pa. / Beer-Ale, brewers since 1860
17. Sioux City Brewing Co., Heidel Brau / Western brew, best in the West
18. Standard Brewing Co., Inc., Rochester, N.Y.
19. Standard Brewing Co., Inc. Rochester, N.Y. / Old Ox Head Ale, properly aged always
20. Standard Brewing Co., Inc., Rochester, N.Y. / Standard Ale, Porter-Half & Half
21. Standard Brewing Co., Inc., Rochester, N.Y., Tel. Glen 0373 / Standard Dry Ale, Old Ox Cart Beer
22. Standard Brewing Co., Scranton, Pa. / Scranton Tel. 41143, Kingston Tel. 72300
23. Standard Dry Ale, Old Ox Cart Beer / same
24. Trommer's Malt Beer, taste and compare / Trommer's Genuine Ale, taste and compare
25. Wacker Brewing Co., Lancaster, Pa.

E-4

1. Acme Beer / Old Bohemian Beer
2. American Bev. Co., Detroit / Cream Top Beer
3. American Brewing Co. of Mich. / Cream Top Beer
4. American Brewing Co., Rochester, N.Y. / Rochester Special Brews
5. Drink Arrow Beer / It hits the spot
6. Atlantic Brewing Co. / Tavern Pale Beer
7. Atlas Br'g. Co., Canal 6200, Chicago / Atlas Prager Beer
8. Atlas Br'g. Co., Canal 6200, Chicago / For lovers of beer Atlas Certificate Brew
9. Atlas Br'g. Co., Canal 6200, Chicago / Imported quality — regular price Prager Beer
10. Atlas Br'g. Co., Canal 6200, Chicago / Reach for a treat drink Atlas Special Brew
11. Berghoff Fort Wayne / Drink Dortmunder Beer
12. Black Eagle Beer / Class Ale & Beer
13. Blatz Milwaukee / Old Heidelberg Brew
14. Blatz Milwaukee / Drink Old Heidelberg Brew
15. Buckeye Beer picks you up / Krauesen brewed as of old
16. Buffalo Brewing Co. / Buffalo & Gilt Edge
17. Burgermeister Beer / Golden State Beer
18. Bushkill Beer / same
19. Cataract Brewing Co., Inc., Cataract Cream Ale / Canandaigua High Hopped Ale, Cataract Brewing Co., Inc.
20. Centlivre Beer, Fort Wayne
21. Centlivre Brewing Corp., Fort Wayne / Nickel Plate Beer
22. Clevelander / Meister Brau
23. Cold Spring Brewing Co. / Ales — Beer
24. Commercial Brewing Co. / Old India Pale
25. Drink Coors Golden Beer / same
26. Derby Cream Ale / same
27. Dick Brother's / Drink Dick's Beer
28. Dick Brothers Brewing Co. / Drink Dick's Beer
29. Christ. Diehl Brewing Co., Defiance, Ohio / Drink Centennial Beer
30. Peter Doelger First Prize Beer / same
31. Doelger's Malt Brews / same
32. The John Eichler Brewing Co., Inc., New York City, N.Y. / Eichler's Beer
33. Falls City Brewing Co., Louisville, Ky. / Falls City Beer
34. Falls City Extra Pale Lager / Falls City Special Lager
35. Falstaff / The choicest product of the brewer's art
36. Fidelio Brewery, Inc., New York, N.Y. / Fidelio Beer quality since 1852
37. General Brewing Corporation, San Francisco / Here's luck with Lucky Lager
38. The Globe Brewing Co., Balt., Md. / Drink Arrow Beer
39. Golden West Brewing Co., Oakland, Calif. / Order Golden Glow by the case
40. Golden West Brewing Co., Oakland-San Francisco-Los Angeles / Golden Glow Beer
41. Grace Bros. Beer / same
42. Grace Bros. Brewing Co., Santa Rosa-San Francisco-Oakland / Grace Bros. Beer
43. Drink Heurich's Beer / Famous for quality since 1873
44. Hollencamps Golden Glow Beer / same
45. Hornung's White Bock / "Es Schmeckt"
46. Horton / same
47. Hudepohl Brewing Co. / Cincinnati, Ohio
48. Humboldt Beer / same
49. Independent Milwaukee Brewery / Braumeister Beer
50. Manitowoc Products Co., Manitowoc, Wis. / Kingsbury Pale
51. Koehler's Beer / same
52. G. Krueger Brg. Co., Newark, N.J. / Krueger's Finest Beer — Lord Essex Stout — Old Surry Porter — Boar's Head Ale — Kent Ale
53. Lang's Extra Fine Ale / Lang's Extra Fine Beer
54. Liebmann Breweries, Inc. / same
55. Lion Brewery of N.Y.C. / same
56. Lucky Lager / One of America's really fine beers
57. Manhattan Brg. Co., Chicago, Ill. / Old Manhattan Lager Beer
58. Original Manitou / Natural gas carbonation makes it better naturally
59. McDermott for taste / McDermott, Yards 7200, Chicago
60. The Miami Valley Brewing Co., Phone East 737, Dayton, Ohio / Old Reliable — Raun's Pilsner — Nick Thomas — Red Crown Malt Tonic
61. Miller High Life Brew / Miller High Life Syrup
62. Miller's High Life Beer / University Club
63. Monarch Beer / same
64. Neustadt Brewing Corp., Stroudsburg, Pa. / Drink Gesundheit Beer
65. Louis F. Neuweiler's Sons, Allentown, Pa. / Neuweiler's Beer
66. Old Bru Beer, Detroit, Mich. / same
67. Potosi / Potosi Beer always good
68. Prima Beer / Chicago, Phone Mohawk 2300
69. Rubsam & Horrmann, Stapleton, S.I., N.Y. / R & H Pilsener Wurzburger
70. Rainier Brewing Co., Inc., San Francisco, Cal. / Beer-Rainier-Ale
71. Rainier Brewing Co., Inc., San Francisco, Cal. / Drink Rainier Beer
72. Regal Amber Brewing Co. / Regal Amber Lager Beer
73. Regal India Ale / Regal Pale Beer

74. Regal Pale Beer / same
75. Rochester Brewing Co. / Old Topper Ale
76. Jacob Ruppert, Brewer, New York / Order Knickerbocker by the case
77. St. Claire Brewing Co., San Jose, Cal. / St. Claire Beer
78. San Francisco Brewing Corp. / Golden State Beer
79. San Francisco Brewing Co., San Francisco, Cal. / Golden State Beer
80. Schmidt's City Club
81. Schmidt's City Club / same
82. Schneider's Grand Prize and Ginger Ale / Brooklyn, N.Y.
83. Schoen's Wausau Brewing Co. / Adel Brau, Wausau Brewing Co.
84. Schultz Brewing Co., Inc. / Union City, N.J.
85. Seitz Brewery, Easton, Pa. / Drink Seitz Beer
86. Southeastern Brewing Co., Chattanooga, Tenn. / Old South Beer and Ale
87. The Star Beverage Co., Minster, Ohio / Drink Wooden Shoe Beer
88. Geo. F. Stein Brewery, Inc., Buffalo, N.Y. / Steins Dry Hop Ale and Pilsener Beer
89. Stroh's Bohemian Lager / Old Gold Pale Dry Ginger Ale
90. Stroh's Bohemian Beer / same
91. The Tacoma Brewing Co., San Francisco, Cal. / Drink Tacoma Beer
92. Trommer's Malt Beers / Trommer's Malt Brews
93. Wagner Beer / same
94. Walker's Brewing Co., Center Line (Detroit), Mich. / Walker's Famous Beer
95. Wehle Ox Head Beer / Wehle Mule Head Ale
96. Drink Wieland's Extra Pale / Fredericksburg Extra Lager
97. White Crown Beer—Ale
98. Yuengling's Winner Beer / same

E-5

1. Dubuque Star Brewing Co., Reach for a star, Iowa's only beer
2. Esslinger's since 1868, beer and ale, Philadelphia, Pa. (waiter)
3. Fort Pitt Beer and Fort Pitt Pilsner Beer (bottle)
4. Fort Pitt Beer, Old Shay DeLuxe Beer and Ale
5. Fort Pitt Old Shay Ale (horse drawn carriage)
6. Hochgreve Brewing Co., Green Bay, Wis., Phone Adams 653 "Hochgreve's Please"
7. Heigh-Ho, the premium beer, phone Homestead 4242 (bottle)
8. Hofbrau, Homestead 4242, Bohemian Style Hofbrau Beer, Homestead Brewery (bottle)
9. Hyde Park the Diamond Jubilee Beer
10. Rolling Rock the Premium Beer brewed with pure mountain spring water, try a nip of Rolling Rock Extra Pale Beer, Latrobe Brewing Co. (bottle)
11. Compliments of Marathon City Brewing Co.
12. Compliments of Matz Brewing Co., Bellaire, Ohio, Merry Xmas, Happy New Year Favorites — Golden Rite Beer, 1884 Golden Ale
13. Ortlieb's Premium Lager Beer since 1864
14. Rheingold
15. Storz Beer, year after year the same fine beer
16. G. Weber Brewing Co., Theresa, Wisconsin, Pioneer Brew for quality since 1849
17. The Wehle Brewing Co., West Haven, Conn., Indian Pale Ale, Ox Head Beer, Mule Head Ale

E-6

1. Acme Beer / same
2. Banker's Ale, Lucky Lager
3. Banker's Ale, Lucky Lager / same
4. Banner Beer, Balanced blend / same
5. Val. Blatz Brg. Co., Milwaukee, Wis. / Blatz Private Stock leads them all
6. Blitz Weinhard, Blitz Weinhard / same
7. Bohemian Club / same
8. Burkhardt's, Akron, O. Select Beer / Key to Burkhardt's Beer
9. Chartiers Valley Bry., Carnegie, Pa. / Old Carnegie Beer, Salbo Ale
10. Chester Brewery, Inc., Chester, Pa. / Chester Pilsner, Silver Dime Premium
11. Chester Pilsner, Silver Dime Premium
12. Cold Spring Brewing Co., Hacker's Ale / same
13. Drink Coors Golden Beer / same
14. Dallas Fort Worth Brewing Co. / Ask for Bluebonnet Beer
15. The Deppen Brewing Co., Reading, Pa.
16. Drewrys, South Bend, Ind. / Drink Drewrys Ale — Lager Beer
17. Original DuBois Beer / Let's meet and be friends
18. DuBois Brewing Co., DuBois, Pa. / Key to DuBois Beers
19. Eagle Brewing Co., Catasaqua, Pa. / same
20. Put Eastside Inside / same
21. Put Eastside Inside / Perfectly brewed beer
22. Felsenbrau Beer, Cincinnati, Ohio / same
23. Fesenmeier Brewing Co., Huntington, W. Va. / W. Va. Special Beer & Ale
24. Flock's Beer, it stands on top
25. Don't say beer, say Fort Schuyler
26. Frontenac Breweries Limited
27. Genesee Liebotschaner / same
28. Genesee Liebotschaner / Genesee 12 Horse Ale
29. Graham's Vita Brew / Graham's XXX Ale
30. Hanley's Extra Pale / Quality guarded since 1876
31. Hoffman Beer and Ale / Hoffman Beverages
32. Drink Horton's Beer / same
33. The Hudepohl Brewing Co. / Cincinnati, Ohio
34. G. Krueger Brg. Co., Newark, N.J. / Ambassador Beer, Krueger's finest beer
35. G. Krueger Brg. Co., Newark, N.J. / Krueger's Finest Beer Lord Essex Stout, Old Surrey Porter, Boar's Head Ale, Kent Ale
36. McHenry Lager Beer / Famous since 1861
37. Harry Mitchell's Good Honest Beer / same
38. Drink Northern Blue Label Beer
39. Old Dutch Brewers, Inc., Brooklyn, N.Y. / Old Dutch Lager, Tudor Beer
40. Pilsen Brewing Co., Chicago, Ill. / Yusay Beer, Yusay Beer
41. Pittsburgh Brewing Co. / Iron City Pilsener, Lager — Fox Hunt Ale
42. Rainier Brewing Co., San Francisco / Beer-Rainier-Ale, Beer-Rainier-Ale
43. Red Ribbon Beer, Tonic Stout / Finest Ale, Nut Brown Ale
44. Red Top Brewing Co., Red Top Ale / Barbarosa Beer, Cincinnati, Ohio
45. Rochester Brewing Co., Old Topper Ale / same
46. Schmidt Brewing Co., Drink City Club / same
47. Schoenhofen Edelweiss Co., Chicago, Illinois / Edelweiss Beer, a case of good judgement

48. Southern Select Beer / same
49. Sterling Brewing Co., E. Mauch Chunk, Pa.
50. Sunbury Brewing Co., Sunbury, Pa. / same
51. Sunshine Beer-Ales-Porter / Keep "Sunshine" in your home
52. Sunshine Extra Light / Sunshine Premium
53. Tip a "Topper" Topper Beer / same
54. Utica Club, "U.C. for me" / same
55. The Victor Brewing Co., Jeanette, Pa. / same
56. The August Wagner & Sons Brewing Co., Columbus, O. / Augustiner Gambrinus
57. Drink Wieland's Extra Pale / same

E-7

1. Atlas Brg. Co., Chicago / same
2. Burkhardt Brewing Co., Boston, Mass.
3. Burton Brewing Co., Paterson, N.J. / same
4. Drink Coors Golden Beer / same
5. Eichler Brewing Co. / same
6. Drink the favorite Gilt Top Beer
7. M.K. Goetz Brewing Co., St. Joseph, Mo. / Drink Country Club, Country Club Special
8. Hazleton Pilsener, Hazleton Pilsener / same
9. Milwaukee Brg. of S.F., Golden State Beer
10. Prima Company Beverages, Chicago, Phone Lincoln 4302
11. Tru Blu Beer, Northampton
12. Wiedenmayer's Pure Beer

E-8

1. Consumers Brewing Company of New York Limited
2. Goebel Brewing Co., Detroit, Mich. / Goebel Pure Food Beer, Goebel Extract
3. Frank Jones Brewing Co. / Homestead Ale, Portsmouth, N.H.
4. Lion Brewery Pilsener / same
5. Red Ball Brewery, XXX Old Stock Ale / same
6. Rice Bros. "New Life Ale" / Pittsfield, Mass.
7. Stegmaier, Wilkes Barre, Pa. / same
8. West Side Brg. Co., Detroit / Mundus, Waldbrau
9. H. Weinhard Brewery, Portland, Ore. / Drink Weinhard's Columbia Beer

E-9

1. Anheuser-Busch, St. Louis, Missouri / same
2. Anheuser-Busch, St. Louis, Mo. / Budweiser means moderation
3. Val. Blatz Brg. Co., Milwaukee, Wis. / same
4. Val. Blatz Brg. Co., Milwaukee, Wis. / Blatz Private Stock leads them all
5. Burton Brewing Co., Paterson, N.J. / same
6. Put Eastside Inside, its frankerized
7. Feigenspan Private Seal Beer / same
8. Free State Brewery, Baltimore, Md. / The thirst choice of a nation
9. Graupner's Por-Der / Graupner's Select
10. Gutsch Brg. Co., Sheboygan, Wis. / same
11. Haberle Brewing Co., Congress Beer / same
12. Horlacher's Beer
13. E.G. Irvin, Graupner Beer/same
14. Krueger's High Grade Beer / same
15. Krueger's Special Brews / same
16. Mass. Brew. Co., Boston
17. Neef Gold Belt / same
18. Old Towne Ale / same
19. Jacob Ruppert's Knickerbocker / same
20. Drink Seitz Pale Beer
21. C.F. Wagner, S.F., Alpenweiss
22. Welz & Zerweck, Brooklyn, N.Y. / Gambrinus Brau, Pilsener Beer

E-10

1. Enjoy Acme Beer / same
2. American Ale, Baltimore, Md. / American Beer, Baltimore, Md.
3. American Brewery, Inc., Baltimore, Md. / American Beer, American Ale
4. Bleser, Better Beer / Manitowoc, Wis.
5. Bowler Beer, Tadcaster Ale / Heidelbrau Lager, Matchless Porter
6. Boyertown Brewing Co., Boyertown, Pa. / Drink Boyertown Beer
7. Good Old Brucks Beer / Cincinnati's oldest brewery
8. Burger Beer, Burger Ale / Burger Brewery, Cincinnati
9. Central Brewing Co., New York, N.Y. / High grade beers, brewery bottling
10. Cold Spring Brewing Co., Hacker's Ale / same
11. Columbia Brewing Co., Alpen Brau / same
12. Cooper's Beer, Phila., Pa. / Namar Premium Beer
13. Cooper's Beer, York, Pa. / same
14. Drink Coors Golden Beer / same
15. Peter Doelger First prize brews / same
16. Eagle Brewing Co., Catasauqua, Pa. / same
17. Eastside Beer, Eastside Beer / same
18. Enterprise Brewing Co., Fall River, Mass. / Old Tap Ale, Old Tap Beer
19. Felsenbrau Beer, Cincinnati, Ohio / same
20. German Brewing Co., Cumberland, Md. / The original Old German Beer
21. Graupner's Por-Der / Graupners Select
22. Greenway's Ale, Greenway's Lager / same
23. Griesedieck Bros., St. Louis Beer / same
24. Gunther's Beer, Baltimore, Md. / A good head on a fine boy
25. Haberle Brg. Co., Congress Beer / same
26. Haberle, Syracus / same
27. Hazleton Pilsner Beer / same
28. Holihan's Ale-Beer / same
29. Kuebler Brewing Co., Easton, Pa. / Mellow light Kuebler
30. Loewer's Beer / Loewer's Ale
31. Lucky Lager / same
32. Moerschbacher's Phillipsburg Beer / same
33. Mount Carbon Ale-Porter / Mount Carbon Lager Beer
34. Old Stock Lager, Old Stock Pilsener
35. Henry F. Ortlieb Brewy. Co., Philadelphia, Pa. / Ortlieb's Beer, Ortlieb's Ale
36. Pickwick Beer, Pickwick Ale / same
37. Pickwick Ale, Light Pickwick / same
38. Queen City Brg. Co., Cumberland, Maryland / The original Old German Beer
39. Rochester Brewing Co., Inc., Rochester, New York / Golden Old Topper Beer
40. Schmidt Brewing Co., Drink City Club / same
41. Stag Beer / same
42. Sunshine Extra Light / Premium Sunshine
43. Walter Brewery, Triple Brew Beer / same
44. Drink Wausau Brg. Co. Beer / same
45. Wehle Mule Head Ale / Wehle Colonial Ale

E-11

1. Atlas Brewing Company, Chicago, Illinois / Atlas Prager, best beer in town
2. Brewers Association of America / 1957 Convention, Emro Mfg. Co., Chicago, Ill.
3. Budweiser, Anheuser-Busch / same
4. Budweiser, King of beers / same

5. Budweiser, trademark of Anheuser-Busch / same
6. Kaier's Outstanding Beer / same
7. Kaier's Special Beer Ale and Porter / same
8. Kaier's Special Beers, famous as anthracite / Kaier's Old Diamond Ale & Porter
9. Lone Star Beer, it's certified / same
10. Old Dutch Beer "Pennsylvania's Best"
11. Regal Beer, American Brewing Co. / same
12. Schoenhofen-Edelweiss Co., Chicago, Illinois / Edelweiss Beer a case of good judgement
13. Stegmaier Brewing Co., Wilkes Barre, Pa. / Brewers and bottlers of Gold Medal Beer
14. Straub Brewery, Inc., St. Marys, Pa. / Brewers since 1872

E-12

1. A-1 Premium Beer / Western way to say welcome
2. Chester Brewing Co., Inc., Chester, Pa. / Chester Pilsener, Silver Dime Pilsener
3. Dixie Beer, it speaks for itself / same
4. Duquesne Pilsener / Silver Top Beer
5. Free State, Baltimore, Md. / Supreme Beer, Hackney Ale
6. A. Gettleman Brewing Co., Milwaukee, Wis. / $1,000 Natural Process Rathskeller Brew
7. Golden Grain Belt / Friendly beer, friendly flavor
8. R.H. Graupner, Inc., Harrisburg, Pa. / same
9. People's Brewing Co., Oshkosh, Wis. / Peoples Beer, 7 and 12 ounce
10. Piel Bros., New York, Piel's Fine Beer / same
11. Rochester Brewing Co., Old Topper Ale / same
12. Aug. Schell Brg. Co., Pleasure pack / same
13. Schmidt Brewing Co., St. Paul, Minn. / Drink Schmidt's City Club Beer
14. Schmidt Brewing Co., St. Paul, Minn. / Real draft beer flavor
15. Spencer Brewing Co., Lancaster, Pa.
16. Stag Beer / same
17. Standard Brewing Co., Rochester, N.Y., Tel. Glen 392 / Standard Dry Ale, Old Ox Cart Beer
18. Stoney's Pilsener
19. Trommer's Beer, taste & compare / Trommer's Beer, it's all malt & hops

E-13

1. Anheuser-Busch, Budweiser / same
2. Blatz, Milwaukee Beer / same
3. Drewrys, South Bend, Ind. / Drink Drewrys Ale-Lager Beer
4. Eckert's Beer, Tel. Capitol 6111 / Wins any test of taste
5. Enterprise Brewing, Fall River, Mass. / The best — Old Tap Ale
6. Genesee Beer, 12 Horse Ale / same
7. R.H. Graupner, Inc., Harrisburg, Pa. / same
8. Theo. Hamm Brg. Co., St. Paul, Minn. / America's most refreshing beer
9. Theo. Hamm Brg. Co., St. Paul, Minn. / Hamm's smooth mellow beer
10. Hazleton Pilsener Beer / same
11. Krueger's Special Brews / same
12. Mankato Brg. Co., Mankato, Minn. / Kato Beer, Jordan Beer
13. Minneapolis Brg. Co., Minneapolis, Minn. / Grain Belt Beer, Canterbury Ale
14. Oertels Brewing Co., Louisville, Ky. / same
15. Pabst Brewing Co., not for resale / same
16. What'll you have? Pabst Blue Ribbon / same
17. Primo Beer / same
18. Royal "58" Beer, make a date with "58" / same
19. Schmidt Beer of St. Paul / Enjoy Schmidt Beer
20. Utica Club Beer & Ale / The famous Utica Beer
21. Warsaw Brewing Corp. / Burgermeister Beer
22. Warwick Club Beverages / same

E-14

1. Famous A-B-C Lager Beer / same
2. A-1 Pilsner Beer, Phoenix, Ariz. / same
3. Acme Beer / Bohemian Distributing Co.
4. Acme Beer / Acme Breweries, San Francisco
5. Acme Brewing Co., Los Angeles / Acme Beer
6. Enjoy Acme Beer / same
7. Altes Lager / The only Eastern beer made in the West
8. American Ale, Baltimore, Md. / same
9. American Brewery, Inc., Baltimore, Md. / American Beer, American Ale
10. Anderson Beverages, famous for quality
11. Atlas Prager Beer, tops for taste / Atlas Brewing Co., Chicago, Ill.
12. Good Old Balboa Beer / same
13. Banner Beer, balanced blend / same
14. Bavarian Beer-Ale-Porter
15. Bavarian Brewing Co., Covington, Ky. / Bavarian's Old Style Beer
16. Magnus Beck Brg. Co., Buffalo, N.Y. / Beck's Beer
17. Becker Brewing & Malting Co., Becker's Beer
18. Becker's Beer, Ogden, Utah
19. Becker's Best Beer
20. Best Brewing Co. of Chicago / Drink Hapsburg Beer
21. Beverwyck Breweries, Inc., Albany, New York / same
22. Billings Brewing Co., Billings, Montana
23. Black Eagle Beer / Class Ale & Beer
24. Blackhawk Beer
25. Blatz Beer / same
26. Blatz Milwaukee Beer / same
27. Blitz Weinhard / same
28. Bobbie Ale, White Cap Beer / same
29. Don't say ale, say Boston Light / same
30. Brackenridge Brew. Co., Inc., Highland 2929 / Old Anchor Beer
31. Bridgeport Brewing Co., Bridgeport, Conn. / Pioneer Beer, Dugans Ale
32. Good Old Brucks Beer / Cincinnati's oldest brewery
33. Peter Bub Brewery, Inc., Winona, Minn.
34. Buffalo Brewery, Inc., Sacramento, Cal. / Quality brews, Buffalo & Bohemian
35. Burger Beer, Zinzinnati / Burger Beer, Burger Ale
36. Burgermeister a truly fine pale beer / same
37. Burgermeister Beer / Golden State Beer
38. Burkhardt's Beer, Mug Ale / same
39. Butte Beer is "Better" Beer / same
40. Butte Special Beer is better beer / same
41. Butte Special Beer, it's better beer / same
42. Canandaigua, it's desugarized / Canadian Cream Ale
43. Casper Brewing Co., Casper, Wyoming / Hilcrest Pilsener Pale Dry
44. Cataract Lager, the pride of Rochester
45. Cold Spring Brewing Co., Hacker's Ale / same
46. Columbia Brewing Co., Alpen Brau / same
47. F.W. Cook Company, Inc., Evansville, Indiana/ / Cook's Beer bottles — cans
48. Cook's Goldblume Beer
49. Cooper's Beer-Ale-Porter / Namar Nips Beer-Ale
50. Coors America's Fine Light Beer / same
51. Coors Fine Light Beer / same
52. Drink Coors Golden Beer / same

53. Croft Cream Ale / same
54. Crown Cork & Seal Co., Inc. / same
55. Crown Cork Specialty Corp. / 5622 Natural Bridge, St. Louis, Mo.
56. Dallas-Fort Worth Brewing Co. / Ask first for Bluebonnet Beer
57. Dawson's Ale & Beer / same
58. Delmarva Beer, Wilmington, Del. / same
59. Dick Bros., Brg. Co., Quincy, Illinois / same
60. DuBois Budweiser / DuBois Export
61. DuBois Budweiser / Let's meet and be friends
62. Dubuque Star Beer, Product of Iowa / same
63. Duquesne Pilsener / Silver Top Beer
64. Eagle Brewing Co., Catasauqua, Pa. / same
65. Eastern Beverage Corp., Brewers / Holland Beer and Ale
66. Eastside Beer / same
67. Now taste Eastside / same
68. Now taste Eastside Beer / same
69. Put Eastside Inside / same
70. Put Eastside Inside / Perfectly brewed beer
71. Edelweiss Beer / A case of good judgement
72. Effinger, Baraboo
73. El Dorado Brewing Co. / Valley Brew Beer, Stockton, Calif.
74. Engesser Brewing Co., St. Peter, Minnesota
75. Enterprise Brewing Co., Fall River, Mass. / The Best — Old Tap Ale
76. Enterprise Brewing Co., Fall River, Mass. / Old Tap Beer, Old Tap Ale
77. Erlanger DeLuxe / Erlanger DeLuxe Half & Half
78. Erlenger's Beer Ale Porter / same
79. Esquire Premium / Stoney's Pilsener
80. F & S Beer, Shamokin, Pa. / same
81. Falstaff Brewing Corp., St. Louis, Omaha, New Orleans / The choicest product of the brewer's art
82. Fauerbach CB Beer / Fauerbach, ask for CB
83. Fehr's X/L Beer / same
84. Fehr's X/L Beer, Louisville, Ky. / Drink Fehr's, it's good
85. Feigenspan Private Seal Beer / same
86. Fesenmeier Brg. Co., Huntington, W. Va. / West Virginia Beer and Ale
87. Fisher Beer, since 1884
88. Fitger's Beer, Duluth, Minn. / Naturally brewed, naturally better
89. Drink Fitger's Nordlager / Brewed in Duluth, Minn.
90. Drink Fitger's Rex Beer / Brewed in Duluth, Minn.
91. Ernst Fleckenstein Brewing Co. / Faribault, Minn.
92. Fort Pitt Special Beer / Old Shay DeLuxe Beer and Ale
93. Don't say beer, say Fort Schuyler / same
94. Fox DeLuxe Beer / same
95. Fox Head Lager Beer, made with Waukesha Water
96. Free State Brewery Corp., Balt., Md. / Hackney, the prince of ales
97. Free State Brewery, Baltimore, Md. / The thirst choice of a nation
98. Fresno Brewing Co., Fresno, Calif. / Drink Mt. Whitney Beer
99. Fresno Brewing Co., Fresno, Calif. / Quality brews Fresno & Bohemian
100. GB Beer, GB Ale / same
101. Genesee Beer, 12 Horse Ale / same
102. A. Gettelman Brewing Co., Milwaukee, Wis. / Get... Get...Gettelman
103. A. Gettelman Brewing Co., Milwaukee, Wis. / $1,000 Natural Process Rathskeller
104. Gibbons Beer — Ale
105. If it's ... Gibbons ... it's Good / same
106. Gipps Amberlin / same
107. Gluek Brg. Co., Minneapolis, Minn. / The beer for the man who knows
108. Gluek Brg. Co., Minneapolis / Enjoy Gluek's Beer
109. M.K. Goetz Brewing Co., St. Joseph, Mo. / Country Club Beer, Goetz Lager Beer
110. M.K. Goetz Brewing Co., St. Joseph, Mo. / Country Club Beer, Pilsener Beer
111. M.K. Goetz Brewing Co., St. Joseph, Mo. / Drink Country Club, Country Club Special
112. M.K. Goetz Brewing Co., St. Joseph, Mo. / Country Club Pilsener, Country Club Special
113. Golden Glow Beer and Ale / same
114. Golden West Brewing Co., Oakland, Calif. / Golden Glow Beer and Ale
115. Grace Bros. Beer and Ale / same
116. Graham's Vita Brew / Graham's XXX Ale
117. Friendly Grain Belt / same
118. Grain Belt Beer ... from perfect brewing water / same
119. Grand Prize Lager Beer / same
120. Grand tasting Grand Prize Beer / same
121. Grand Prize Beer, top of the brew / same
122. R.H. Graupner, Inc., Harrisburg, Pa. / same
123. Graupner's Beer, Harrisburg, Pa. / Graupner Beer, first by far
124. Great Falls Beer, Great Falls, Mont.
125. Great Falls Lager Beer
126. Greenway's Ale / Sparkling Grenay
127. Griesedieck Bros. St. Louis — Beer / same
128. Griesedieck Bros. St. Louis Light Lager / same
129. Gunther's Beer, Balt., Md. / It's dry and Beer-y
130. Haberle, Syracuse / same
131. Haberle Brg. Co., Congress Beer / same
132. Hamm's Beer, born in the land of sky blue waters
133. Hamm's Beer, it's the refreshingest / From the land of sky blue waters
134. Theo. Hamm Brg. Co., St. Paul, Minn. / America's most refreshing beer
135. Theo. Hamm Brg. Co., St. Paul, Minn. / The beer refreshing
136. Theo. Hamm Brg. Co., St. Paul, Minn. / Hamm's Smooth Mellow Beer
137. Hamden Brewing Co., Hampden Mild Ale / same
138. Peter Hand Brewery Co., Meister Brau
139. Hanley's Extra Pale / Quality guarded since 1876
140. Harvard Brewing Co., Lowell, Mass. / Harvard has what it takes
141. Hauenstein's, New Ulm, Minn. / same
142. Hauenstein's Brg. Co., New Ulm, Minn. / Hauenstein's Beer
143. Heileman's Old Style Lager / same
144. Helb's Beer, York, Pa. / same
145. Hensler a swell beer / same
146. Hensler Beer, you'll like it / same
147. Highlander Pale Beer / same
148. Hofbrau Royal Export / Hofbrau today's best beer
149. Hoffman Beverages / Hoffman Beer & Ale
150. Enjoy Holihan's Ale / same
151. Horlacher's Beer, Made in U.S.A. / same
152. Hornell Brewing Co., Inc., Hornell Beer / Hornell Brewing Co., Inc., K.D.K. Cream Ale
153. Hornell Brewing Co., Inc., K.D.K. Cream Ale / Old Ranger Beer and Ale
154. Drink Horton's Beer / same
155. Drink Hudepohl Beer / same
156. Hyde Park Beer / same

157. Hyde Park Bottle Beer / seldom equaled, never excelled
158. Frank Jones Portsmouth Ale / same
159. Jung Beer, Random Lake, Wis. / same
160. Kaier Brewing Co., / Mahanoy City, Penna.
161. Drink Kamm's Quality Beer
162. Keeley Half & Half, blend of beer & ale / same
163. Kessler Brewing Co., Kessler Beer / same
164. Kessler Brewing Co., Lorelei
165. King Cole Beer, Chicago Heights, Ill.
166. Kingsbury Pale Beer, Manitowoc and Sheboygan, Wis.
167. Fred Koch Brewery, Dunkirk, N.Y. / same
168. G. Krueger Brg. Co., Newark, N.J. / Old Surrey Porter, Cream Ale & Kent Ale
169. G. Krueger Brg. Co., Newark, N.J. / Krueger's Finest Beer Cream Ale
170. Krueger Cream Ale, Finest Beer / same
171. Krueger's Finest Beer Ambassador Beer / same
172. Kuebler Brewing Co., Phone 4225, Easton, Pa. / Beer Ale Porter, Quarts Pints Steinie
173. Chippewa's Pride, Leinenkugel
174. Chippewa's Pride Beer, Leinenkugel
175. Liebmann's XXX Cream Ale / Liebmann's Export Lager Beer
176. Lone Star Beer, San Antonio, Texas / same
177. Lucky Lager age dated beer / same
178. Lucky Lager, Lucky Ale / same
179. Maier since 1875 / Maier Select Beer
180. Mankato Brg. Co., Mankato, Minn. / Jordan Beer, Kato Beer
181. Mankato Brewing Co., Kato Lager Beer / same
182. Mankato Brewing Co., Mankato and Jordan / same
183. Marathon Superfine Beer / same
184. Metz Beer since 1864, Metz Jubilee Beer / Metz Beer since 1864, Golden Spike Beer
185. Bottle of Metz Please, Metz Jubilee Beer / same
186. Drink Metz Jubilee, Extra Dry Beer / same
187. Miller Brewing Company, Milwaukee, Wisconsin / Miller High Life Beer
188. Miller High Life Beer / same
189. Minneapolis Brewing Co., The Minneapolis Beer / Golden Grain Belt Beer, Canterbury Ale
190. Mishicott Brewing Co., Mishicott, Wis. / Our special quality beer
191. Monarch Beer / same
192. Monterey Brewing Co. / Monterey Beer
193. Muehlebach Beer quality since 1868 / same
194. Narragansett Brewing Company / same
195. National Beer / same
196. National Premium / same
197. Northern Brewing Co., Superior, Wis. / Drink Northern it's superior
198. Oertel Brewing Co., Louisville, Ky.
199. Oertel Brewing Co., Louisville, Ky. / Cheer up with Oertel's '92 Beer
200. Old Bru Beer, Detroit, Mich.
201. Old Dutch Beer, Pennsylvania's Best
202. Old Faithful, Bozeman / same
203. Old Hill-Top Ale, Old Hill-Top Beer / same
204. Old Hill-Top Brew / same
205. Old Imperial, Green Bay, Wis.
206. Old Reading Beer and Ale / Pale Reserve, Berkshire Ale
207. Old Tap Ale, Bohemian Beer / same
208. Olympia, it's the water / same
209. Oshkosh Brewing Co., Oshkosh, Wis. / same
210. Always ask for Overland
211. What'll you have? Pabst Blue Ribbon / same
212. Pearl Beer / same
213. Pearl Brewing Co. / Pearl Beer
214. Peerless, LaCrosse, Wis. / same
215. Peoples Brewing Co., Oshkosh, Wis. / Peoples Beer, Old Derby Ale
216. Peoples Brewing Co., Oshkosh, Wis. / Peoples Beer, 7 and 12 ounce
217. Pfeiffer Brewing Co., Drink Pfeiffer's Beer / same
218. Philadelphia Brg. Co., Old Stock Beer-Ale / same
219. Phoenix Brewery, Buffalo, N.Y. / Light Lager, Cream Ale
220. Pickwick Beer, Light Pickwick / same
221. Piel Bros. New York, Piel's Fine Beer / same
222. Piel's Premium Beer, always rings the bell / same
223. Pilsen Brewing Co., Chicago, Ill. / Yusay Beer, Yusay Beer
224. Pittsburgh Brewing Co., Dutch Club Beer / A fine old beer in bottles
225. Potosi Brewing Co., Potosi, Wis. / Gains by comparison
226. Queen City Brg. Co., Cumberland, Maryland / The original Old German Beer
227. R & H Light Beer since 1868 / same
228. Rainier Beer-Ale / same
229. Rainier Brewing Co., San Francisco / Beer-Rainier-Ale
230. Rams Head Ale, the Aristocrat of ales / Make friends with Valley Forge Beer
231. Red Ribbon Beer, Wausau, Wis.
232. Red Top Brewing Co., Cincinnati, Oh. / Red Top Beer, Extra Dry
233. Red Top Brewing Co., Cincinnati, Oh. / Twenty Grand Ale, a man's brand
234. Regal India Ale / same
235. Regal Pale Beer / Regal India Ale
236. Regal Pale, it tastes so good / same
237. Regal Pale Beer, light and mellow / same
238. Regal Supreme Beer / same
239. Renner Golden Amber Beer / Old Oxford Ale Phone RI-44457
240. Renners, Youngstown, O. / Bohemian Beer, Premium Ale
241. Rhinelander Beer, Rhinelander, Wis.
242. Rochester Brg. Co., Old Topper / The flavor that's in favor
243. Rochester Brewing Co., Old Topper Ale / same
244. Rochester Brewing Co., Inc., Rochester, N.Y. / Golden Old Topper Ale-Beer
245. Royal "58" Beer / Make a date with "58"
246. Ruppert Beer and Ale / Ruppert for that smile of pleasure
247. St. Claire Beer, America's finest
248. Salinas Brewing and Ice Co. / Monterey Beer
249. San Antonio Brewing Ass'n / Pearl Beer, Pearl Beer
250. San Antonio Brewing Ass'n / Pearl Beer, Texas Own
251. San Antonio Brewing Ass'n / Pearl Beer, Texas Pride Beer
252. Peter Sayers Old Reading Beer / same
253. Adam Scheidt Brewing Co. / Valley Forge Beer
254. Aug. Schell Brg. Co., New Ulm, Minn. / Schell's Deer Brand Beer
255. Aug. Schell Brg. Co., Pleasure pack
256. Schlitz Beer, Milwaukee, Wis. / same
257. Schlitz Lager in cap sealed cans / same
258. Jos. Schlitz Brg. Co., Milwaukee, Wis. / Schlitz Beer bottles — cans

259. Schmidt Beer of St. Paul / Enjoy Schmidt Beer
260. Schmidt Brewing Co., St. Paul, Minn. / Drink Schmidt's City Club Beer
261. Schmidt Brewing Co., St. Paul, Minn. / Schmidt Brewing Co., Drink City Club
262. Schmidt Brewing Co., Drink City Club / same
263. The Schmidt Brewing Co., Schmidt's Famous Beer / same
264. Schmidts of Philadelphia / Beer-Ale Brewers since 1860
265. Schutz & Hilgers, Jordan Brewery, Inc., Jordan, Minn. / Old Style Beer, Jordan Beer
266. Sheridan, Wyoming / Sheridan Export Beer
267. Southern Select Beer / same
268. Shiner Beer, Spoetzl Brewery
269. Sick's Select / same
270. Sioux City Brg. Co. / Heidel Brau Beer
271. Stag Beer / same
272. Standard Brewing Co., Inc., Rochester, N.Y., Tel. Glen 0373 / Old Ox Cart Beer, Standard Dry Ale
273. Standard Brewing Co., Tru-Age Beer / same
274. Star-Peerless Brg. Co., Oltimer Beer / same
275. Stegmaier Brewing Co., Wilkes Barre, Pa. / Brewers and bottlers of Gold Medal Beer
276. Stegmaier Brewing Co., Wilkes Barre, Pa. / Stegmaier Gold Medal Beer
277. Sterling Brewers, Inc., Evansville, Indiana / same
278. Storck Products, Slinger, Wis. / Storck's Slinger Beer
279. Straub Brewery, St. Marys, Pa. / Brewers since 1872
280. Sunshine Beer Ales Porter / Keep "Sunshine" in your home
281. Sunshine Extra Light / Premium Sunshine
282. Superior Brewing Co., Fort Worth, Texas / same
283. Syracuse Brewery, Inc., Dickens Ale / same
284. Tivoli Beer, Denver, Colo. / same
285. Tip a "Topper" Topper Beer / same
286. Trommer's Beer, it's all malt & hops / Trommer's Beer, taste & compare
287. Tube City Premium Beer
288. Union Brewing Co., New Castle, Pa. / Royal Bru "Fit for a king"
289. United States Brewing Co., Good Old Rheingold Beer / United States Brewing Co., Call for Gold Crown Beer
290. Utica Club Beer & Ale / The Famous Utica Beer
291. Utica Club "U.C. for me"/ same
292. Vernon Brewing Co., Los Angeles, Calif. / Golden Creme Beer, Golden Creme Ale
293. Wagner Beer / same
294. August Wagner Breweries, Inc., Gimmie a "Gam" / same
295. Walter Brewing Co., Eau Claire, Wis.
296. Drink Wausau Brewing Co. Beer / Adelbrau, Schoen's Old Lager
297. Drink Wehle Ale & Beer / same
298. West Bend Lithia Co., West Bend, Wisconsin / same
299. The. Geo. Wiedemann Brewing Co., Newport, Ky. / Bohemian, Royal Amber
300. Wiedemann's Fine Beer / same
301. Drink Wieland's Extra Pale / same
302. Wieland's has the flavor / same
303. Wiessner's Regal Beer / same
304. Drink Roger William's the ale of quality
305. Drink Wooden Shoe Beer / same
306. Yoerg's Beer / Cave aged best by test
307. D.G. Yuengling & Son, Inc., Pottsville, Pa. / Drink Yuengling's Beer — Ale
308. Ziegler's Beer

F-1

1. Hyan Dry Ginger Ale, Lime and Lithia / Lang's A.A., a perfect malt brew

F-2

1. Ambrosia Brg. Co., Nectar Premium Beer
2. Blatz Pilsener Beer
3. Esslinger's Beer — Ale
4. Frederick's Brewing Co., Thornton, Ill. / Van Nestor Beer
5. A. Mirabile Beer — Ale
6. North Star Lager / Red Ribbon Beer
7. Potosi Beer / Pure Malt & Export
8. Rainier Old German Lager / Rainier Lime Rickey
9. South Bethlehem Brewing Co., Bethlehem, Pa. / Supreme Beer
10. Wacker Beer
11. Wacker Brewing Co., Lancaster, Pa., all malt brew

F-3

1. Potosi Brewing Co., an opener for friendship

F-4

1. Cataract Products Corp., Rochester, N.Y., insist on quality, Cataract Liquid Malt for baking and cooking
2. Iroquois Beverage Corp., Buffalo, N.Y.
3. Kaier's Beer
4. Thomas V. O'Connor, distributor of Beer & Ale, Corning, N.Y.
5. Oshkosh Brewing Co., Chief Oshkosh
6. The William Simon Brewery, Buffalo, N.Y., Simon Pure Beer-Ale, the best taste in town
7. Lefty Wiese Dist. Co., Blatz Pilsener Beer, Burkhardt Beverages

F-5

1. Schumann Brewing Co., Inc., Otto's Beer / Mantorville, Minn.

F-6

1. Bartel's Brewing Co. / Crown Beer the best for home use
2. Call Bartel's, Phone James 2345 / Drink Crown Beer
3. Peter Doelger First Prize Bottled Beer / Best beer brewed expressly for the home
4. Flower City Brewing Co. / Maltop Beer "Acme Ale"
5. Hauenstein's / New Ulm, Minn.
6. Hinchcliffe, Paterson, New Jersey / Bottled lagers & ales
7. Huebner Toledo Beer / Better than the imported
8. Jamaica Malt Products Co., 150-32 Jamaica Ave. / Use Muenchener Brand, Tel. Jamaica 4554
9. E. Porter Brg. Co., Joliet
10. Schemm Brewing Co. / The beer of quality
11. Drink the Schreihart Brew Co's Beer / The beer of quality
12. Uhl's Brewery, both phones Bethlehem, Pa. / Celebrated beer, ale, and porter
13. Wieland's Extra Pale
14. Wieland's Extra Pale / Wieland's Beverages

F-7

1. Columbia Premium Beer, the label of good taste, Columbia Brewing Co., Shenandoah, Pa.

F-8

1. Columbia Brewing Co., St. Louis, Mo., above all Alpen Brau

F-9

1. Cleveland & Sandusky Brewing Co., Gold Bond Beer, Cleveland, Ohio, Sixth City
2. Narragansett Brew Co., Prov., R.I., lager & ale, brewery bottling

F-10

1. Bullfrog Beer

G-1

1. A B C Pale Dry
2. Berghoff Beer 1887 (bottle)
3. Biere Black Horse Ale (bottle)
4. Buckeye Beer — picks you up (waiter)
5. Camden Beer (bottle)
6. Dr. Miller's Golden Harvest Beer, made in Crete, Nebraska, Never fails to satisfy (bottle)
7. Ebling's
8. Ebling's extra, that grand old beer (bottle)
9. Esslingers Beer, Philadelphia, Pa. (little man)
10. Foxhead, Waukesha, Wis. (bottle)
11. Goldenrod Beer tastes better
12. Drink Grand Prize Lager Beer
13. Grand Prize, South's famous beer
14. Grand Prize, Texas largest seller
15. Hazelton Pilsener Beer
16. Latrobe Brewing Co., Latrobe, Pa., Latrobe Beer (bottle)
17. Lithia Beer
18. Old Reading Beer (bottle)
19. Old Shay Ale (bottle)
20. Old Stock Lager (bottle)
21. Pabst Blue Ribbon Beer (bottle)
22. Piel's Beer (bottle)
23. Quandt, Troy, N.Y., Standard Ale & Lager (bottle)
24. Schaefer Fine Beer (bottle)
25. Tru Blu Beer and Ale
26. Yoerg's Cave Aged Beer

G-2

1. Boston Ale-Beer, the best for over 100 years / Boston Beer Co., America's oldest brewery
2. Hackers Ale, Cold Spring Brewing Co., Lawrence, Mass.
3. Hampden Light Beer, Mild Ale
4. Hampden Mild Ale
5. Harvard Beer, Ale, Porter
6. Pennsylvania Dutch, Old German Beer
7. Drink Point Beer

G-3

1. Blatz Milwaukee
2. Denmark Brewing Co., Denmark, Wis., Beer of good cheer
3. Hamm's Beer "leads them all"
4. Geo. Walter's Adler Brau, Appleton Beer

G-4

1. Bay City Beverage Co.
2. Blatz Beer for good taste
3. Frederick's Brewery
4. Drink Holland Premium Beer
5. Johnson's Premium Beer, Lomira, Wis.
6. Lithia Beer
7. Miller High Life Beer, Miller Brewing Co., Milwaukee, Wis.
8. Peter Schemms Beer and Robert Smiths Ale & Beer, Lawrence Bros., Rdg., Pa.

G-5

1. Drink Blatz Private Stock Beer, Milwaukee
2. Buck Beverages "First for thirst"
3. Johnson's Premium Beer, Lomira, Wis.
4. Jung Beer
5. Liberty Brewing Co., Springfield, Mass.
6. Lion Export Beer, Cincinnati, O.
7. Tavern Pale
8. Wetterer's Beers are the best

G-6

1. Bartels Beer
2. Enterprise Brewing Co., F.R., Mass., Old Tap for Ale, Boh for Beer
3. Fleck's, Faribault, Minn.
4. Fuhrmann & Schmidt Brewing Co., F & S Beer, Porter, and Ale
5. Fort Pitt Special Beer
6. Gluek's First Prize Beer
7. Gretz Extra Premium Beer
8. Gunther Brewing Co., Inc., Balt., Md., Gunther Premium Dry Beer
9. Holihan's Ale
10. National Brewing Co., Balt. 10, Md., National Bohemian
11. Pickwick — Light Ale — Ale
12. Schell's Beer, New Ulm, Minn.
13. Sunshine Beer, it's extra light, it's extra good
14. Walter's, Eau Claire, Wis.

G-7

1. Bartels Beer
2. Dresden Beer
3. Fort Pitt Special Beer
4. Gretz Extra Premium Beer
5. Gunther Brewing Co., Inc., Balt., Md., Gunther Premium Dry Beer
6. Harvard Ale or Export Beer
7. Holihan's Ale
8. National Brewing Co., Balt., Md., National Bohemian (Mr. Boh)
9. Pickwick Beer — Light Ale — Ale
10. Schmidt City Club Beer
11. Sunshine Beer — it's extra light, it's extra good

G-8

1. Beck's, Buffalo's best beer / same
2. Columbia / same
3. Columbia Preferred Beer / same
4. Dawson's Brewery, Inc., New Bedford, Mass. / Time out for Dawson's Ale & Beer
5. Gibbons Brewery, Wilkes Barre, Pa. / If it's Gibbons, it's good
6. Independent Milwaukee Brewery, Milwaukee, Wis., Braumeister Special
7. Marathon City Brg. Co., Marathon, Wis. / Wee Willie
8. Monarch the great beer
9. Ruppert for that smile of pleasure / same
10. Standard Tru-Age Beer / same
11. Sunshine Beer, it's extra light, it's extra good

G-9

1. Beck's Buffalo's Best Beer (white on red)
2. Carling's Red Cap Ale (white on red)
3. Daeufer's Beer "Allentown's favorite" (red on yellow)
4. Downs Beer — Ale (gold on red)
5. Globe Brewery, Balt., Md., Arrow Beer (white on red)
6. Drink Heineken Beer (brown on natural)
7. Hornung homogenized beer (black on red)
8. Murphy's Ale (white on green)
9. O'Keefe's Old Vienna Beer (black on blue)
10. Old Reading Beer, it's smoother (black on green)
11. Ortlieb's Beer, phone Market 4728 (black on green)
12. Ortlieb's Premium Lager Beer (black on green)
13. Ortlieb's Premium Lager Beer (black on blue)
14. Peoples Brewing Co., Oshkosh, Wis., Phone 334 (black on green)
15. Phoenix Beer — Cream Ale (black on yellow)
16. Pickwick Ale (white on green)
17. Scheidt's Valley Forge Beer (black on red)
18. Schmidt's City Club Beer (black on red)
19. Schreiber Brewing Co., Inc., Buffalo, New York, Manru Beer — Light & Dark, Schreiber's Beer (black on natural)
20. Simon Pure Beer — Ale (black on red)
21. Star Ale & Lager (white on red)
22. Stegmaier Brewing Co., Wilkes Barre, Pa., Stegmaier's Gold Medal Beer (black on yellow)
23. same as above (black on red)
24. same as above (white on blue)
25. same as above (gold on red)
26. Stoney's America's Best Beer (black on red)
27. same as above (black on blue)
28. Tube City Beer (black on red)
29. Wausau Brewing Co., Wausau, Wis., Adel Brau, Schoen's Old Lager (black on natural)
30. D.G. Yuengling & Sons, Inc., Pilsener Beer, brewers since 1829 (white on red)

G-10

1. Moerlbach Beer

H-1

1. Beverwyck Beers and Ales
2. Consumer's Brewing Co. of Rhode Island, Consumer's Ale
3. Erin Brew
4. Drink Falls City
5. Hof-Brau Ale and Beer, powerfully good
6. Neuweiler's Famous Brews
7. Norton's, Anderson, Ind.
8. Ortliebs Beer — Ale
9. Philipsburg Beer
10. Henry Rahr Brewing Co., Telephone 9, Chilton, Wis.
11. Sprenger's Red Rose Beer, Lancaster, Pa.
12. Stegmaier Brewing Co., Wilkes Barre, Pa.
13. Sunshine Beer-Ales-Porter
14. Yough Brewing Co., Connellsville, Pa.

H-2

1. American Brewing Co., Rochester, N.Y., Liberty Beer
2. American Brewing Co., Rochester, N.Y., Tam O'Shanter Ale and Liberty Beer
3. Atlantic Ale and Beer
4. Berghoff Fort Wayne
5. John Betz & Son, Inc., Philadelphia, Betz Beer
6. Brownsville Beer, it's pure — that's sure
7. Enjoy Burger Beer
8. Carling's Red Cap Ale
9. Carnegie Beer "The best of all"
10. Chartiers Valley Brewery, Duquesne Brewing Co., Carnegie Pilsner and Frontenac Ale
11. Cold Spring Lager Beer "It's the water"
12. Columbia Brewing Co., Columbia, Pa., Columbia Beer
13. Duquesne Can-O-Beer in crown sealed cans "Match it if you can"
14. Duquesne Kego-Beer in crown sealed cans "The keg beer flavor merits your favor"
15. Duquesne of Pittsburgh, Pa., "The finest beer in town"
16. Duquesne Pilsener "The finest beer in town"
17. Esslinger Beer, Philadelphia, Pa. (little man)
18. Fink Brewing Co., Harrisburg, Pa.
19. Fort Pitt Brewing Co.
20. Don't say beer, say Fort Schuyler
21. M.K. Goetz Brewing Co., St. Joseph & Kansas City, Mo., Country Club the bright beer
22. The James Hanley Co., say Hanley's for ale (bulldog)
23. Hochgreve Beer
24. Hornung Beer Ale
25. Kato Lager Beer
26. Koehler's there is no better beer!
27. Monarch Brg. Co., Chicago, Monarch Beer
28. Philadelphia Brewing Co., Old Stock Lager
29. Ortlieb's Beer — Ale
30. Pabst Milwaukee
31. Phoenix Beers, Moffats Ale
32. Piel's Beer
33. Queen-O
34. Rahr Green Bay Brewing Corp., Green Bay, Wis., Old Imperial and Van Dyck Beer
35. C. Schmidt & Sons, Inc., Philadelphia, Pa.
36. C. Schmidt & Sons, Inc., brewers in Philadelphia since 1860
37. Schmidt's of Philadelphia, brewers since 1860
38. Stegmaier Brewing Co., Wilkes Barre, Pa.
39. Drink Tech Beer
40. Terre Haute Brewing Co., Terre Haute, Ind., CV the beer with the million dollar flavor
41. Trommers Malt Brew
42. Tru-Blue Beer and Ale
43. Tube City Brewing Co., McKeesport, Pa.
44. Utica Club, the famous Utica Beer
45. Drink Valley Forge Special
46. Wacker Brewing Co.
47. Weber Waukesha Beer
48. Weber Waukesha Beer, Waukesha Brewing Co., Waukesha, Wis., you will enjoy Weber
49. West Bend Lithia Beer, Kilb 0606
50. West Virginia Pilsner Beer & Ale
51. D.G. Yuengling & Son, Inc., Pottsville, Pa.

H-3

1. Drink Barq's, it's good and wholesome
2. Famous Beverwyck Beers & Ale
3. Dick Brothers Brewing Co., Quincy, Illinois, Dick's Beer
4. Duquesne of Pittsburgh, Pa., "The finest beer in town"
5. Dutch Club Beer
6. Edelweiss, a case of good judgement
7. Esslinger's Premium Beer
8. Fitzgerald's Pale Beer, Burgomaster Beer, Garrytowen Ale

9. Flock Brewing Co., Williamsport, Pa., Drink Flocks Beer
10. Frederick Bros., Inc., Boulevard 2537, Four 4 Crown, Queensville, Ambrosia
11. Grand Prize Famous Beer
12. G. Heileman Brewing Co., LaCrosse, Wis., Old Style Lager
13. Hohenadel Beer Ale
14. Hornung Beer Ale
15. Drink Iron City Beer
16. Iroquois Indian Head Beer-Ale-Porter (indian head)
17. Koehler's there is no better beer!
18. Drink Monarch, the great beer
19. Ortlieb's Premium Beer, Henry F. Ortlieb Brewing Co., Phila., Pa.
20. Rolling Rock Premium Beer "Brewed with pure mountain spring water"
21. Adam Scheidt Brewing Co., Norristown, Pa., Valley Forge Beer
22. Schlitz the beer that made Milwaukee famous
23. The William Simon Brewery, Buffalo, N.Y., Simon Pure Beer Ale (?)
24. Stegmaier Brewing Co., Wilkes Barre, Pa.
25. Stegmaier Brewing Co., Wilkes Barre, Pa., Stegmaier's Gold Medal Beer
26. Tally-Ho Ale Porter Beer, New York City
27. Drink Tech Beer
28. Drink Weber Waukesha Beer
29. Yuengling's Pilsner Beer

H-4

1. Enjoy Prima Beer

H-5

1. Alberta Breweries
2. Bartels Beer
3. Columbia Beer, Shenandoah, Pa.
4. Drink Gretz Beer
5. Hazelton Pilsener
6. Kaier's Beer, Mahanoy City, Pa.
7. Jolly Scot Ale, Silver Stock Beer
8. Lucky Jewel
9. Neuweiler's Famous Brews

H-6

1. Blatz Milwaukee's famous beer / Blatz Milwaukee's finest beer, brewed at Milwaukee, Newark, Los Angeles, Peoria Heights, Blatz Brewing Co.
2. Carling's Black Label Beer
3. Olympia Beer "It's the water"
4. Original Pabst Blue Ribbon / Original Pabst Blue Ribbon, Pabst Brewing Co., Milwaukee, Peoria Heights, Newark, Los Angeles
5. What'll you have? Pabst Blue Ribbon / Pabst Blue Ribbon, Pabst Brewing Co., Milwaukee, Peoria Hts., Newark, Los Angeles
6. Schlitz the beer that made Milwaukee famous / Jos. Schlitz Brg. Co., Milwaukee, Wis., U.S.A., breweries at Milwaukee, Wis., Brooklyn, N.Y., Los Angeles, Calif., and Kansas City, Mo.

H-7

1. Adler Brau
2. Blatz Milwaukee's most exquisite beer
3. Calumet Beer
4. Fox Head Beers and Ales
5. Kingsbury
6. Knapp's Bohemian Style
7. Marathon Beer
8. Peerlesss Beer, LaCrosse, Wisconsin
9. Always serve Potosi Beer, Pilsener & Export

H-8

1. Arrow Beer
2. Buckeye Beer
3. Duquesne Pilsener Beer
4. Esslinger's Beer (little man walking)
5. Esslinger's Beer (little man standing)
6. Fitzgerald Beers & Ale
7. Griesedieck Bros., Light Lager Beer
8. Iroquois Indian Head Beer
9. Narragansett Ale
10. Narragansett Lager Beer
11. Pabst Blue Ribbon
12. Schlitz
13. Tavern Pale

I-1

1. Coors America's Fine Light Beer / same
2. Grain Belt Beer is Diamond Clear / same
3. Griesedieck Bros. Beer, St. Louis / same
4. Krantz Brewing Co., Findlay, Ohio / Old Dutch Beer

I-2

1. Atlas Prager Extra Dry Beer / Got it? Get it!
2. Quick! Quick! My Beverwyck
3. Drewrys Extra Dry Beer / same
4. Hampden Mild Ale
5. Trommer's Beer, it's all malt and hops

I-3

1. Quick! Quick! My Beverwyck
2. Budweiser King of Beers / same
3. Coors America's Fine Light Beer
4. Coors America's Fine Light Beer / same
5. Croft Cream Ale
6. Grand Prize Beer / same
7. Gunther's Premium Dry Beer
8. Hampden Mild Ale
9. Harvard Ale or Export Beer
10. Be happy with Harvard Ale or Export
11. Mitchell Premium Beer
12. Famous Narragansett Ale & Beer
13. Pabst Blue Ribbon
14. Premium Quality Pearl
15. Piel's Light Beer, Piel Bros., Brooklyn, N.Y.
16. Pilser's Original Extra Dry Beer., N.Y.
17. Adam Scheidt Brewing Co., Norristown, Pa.
18. Trommer's Beer, it's all malt and hops

I-4

1. Arrow Beer, it hits the spot
2. Atlas Prager Beer
3. Ballantine Ale Beer
4. Blatz Beer
5. Burgermeister
6. Canadian Ace Brand Beer and Ale
7. Coors
8. Buy Drewrys — for the best
9. Embassy Club Beer, Chicago
10. Esslinger's Premium Beer
11. Falls City Beer
12. Fox DeLuxe Beer
13. Genesee Beer-Ale
14. Golden Glow Beer-Ale
15. Harvard has what it takes
16. Senate, Chr. Heurich Brewing Co., Wash., D.C.
17. Hornung Beer-Ale
18. Hyde Park Beer

19. Miller High Life
20. Old Crown Ale-Beer
21. Pabst Blue Ribbon
22. R & H Beer-Ale
23. Rainier Beer Ale
24. Rheingold Extra Dry
25. Ruppert Beer Ale
26. Adam Scheidt Brewing Co., Norristown, Pa.
27. Sterling — the beer drinker's beer
28. Tavern Pale
29. Trommer's Beer

I-5

1. Coors America's Fine Light Beer
2. Lucky Lager Beer
3. Regal Pale Beer / same
4. Ruppert Beer for that smile of pleasure
5. Silver Top the most luxurious light beer in the world
6. Terre Haute Brewing Co., Terre Haute, Ind., CV the beer with that million dollar flavor
7. Wieland's Beer / same

I-6

1. Acme Beer Ale / same
2. Ambrosia Brewing Co., Nectar Beer / same
3. A-1 Pilsner Beer, Arizona Brewing Co., Phoenix, Ariz. / same
4. Blatz Beer / same
5. Enjoy Burger Beer, opens cans and bottles
6. Burger Beer a miracle of fine brewing
7. Burgermeister Beer / Burgermeister a truly fine pale beer
8. Burgermeister Pilsener Beer / same
9. Canadian Ace Brand Beer & Ale / same
10. Carling's Red Cap Ale / same
11. Croft Cream Ale / same
12. Eastside Beer / same
13. Fox DeLuxe / same
14. Fox Head "400" Beer (fox head) / Fox Head "400" Beer brewed with Waukesha Water
15. GB Lager / same
16. Genesee Beer Ale
17. Genesee Beer Ale / same
18. Globe Brewing Co., Baltimore, Md., Mighty good Arrow Beer, it hits you right
19. Goebel Brewing Co. of California, Oakland, Calif. / Goebel Beer
20. Grand Prize Beer / same
21. Grand Prize Pale Dry Beer / The top of the brew
22. Gunther Premium Dry Beer
23. Hamm's Beer / same
24. Hampden Mild Ale
25. Harvard Ale or Export Beer
26. Hensler Beer "You'll like it"
27. For opening Hull's Ale and Lager, New Haven, Conn.
28. Drink Jax Beer / same
29. Lucky Lager Beer / No finer beer made East or West
30. Miller Select Beer
31. Famous Narragansett Lager & Ale
32. Pabst Blue Ribbon / same
33. Prior Beer
34. R & H Beer, taste the difference
35. Drink Rainier Beer / Drink Rainier Ale
36. Regal Beer / same
37. Ruppert Beer for that smile of pleasure / same
38. Adam Scheidt Brewing Co., Norristown, Pa. / same
39. Schmidt's City Club Beer
40. Simon Pure Beer Ale, the best taste in town
41. Weber Waukesha Brewing Co., Waukesha, Wisconsin / Weber in "W"
42. Weber in "W" trademark only / same
43. Wiedemann's Fine Beer / same
44. Wieland's Beer / same

I-7

1. Acme Beer and Ale, Acme Brewing Co., Los Angeles
2. For opening Acme Beer Keglet
3. American Brewing Co., Rochester, N.Y., Tam O'Shanter Ale, Apollo Beer
4. Anheuser Busch, Budweiser, King of canned beers
5. Atlas Prager Beer
6. Ballantine's Ales Beer (3 rings)
7. Handy way to order Ballantine's Ale Beer (hand & 3 rings)
8. Best Brewing Co., Hapsburg Beer Quality Lager
9. For opening Brown Derby Beer cans or bottles
10. Coors Beer, Golden, Colo.
11. Croft Ale
12. Drewrys, Canada Pride since 1877
13. Esslinger's Beer and Ale (waiter)
14. Feigenspan P.O.N. Beer & Ale
15. Fort Pitt Brewing Co., Pittsburgh, Pa.
16. Fox DeLuxe Beer
17. Genesee Brewing Inc., Rochester, N.Y., Genesee Beer and 12 Horse Ale
18. Haberle Congress Brewing Co., Syracuse, N.Y., Congress Light Beer
19. Hamm's smooth mellow beer
20. Hampden Mild Ale
21. Peter Hand Brewing Co., Meister Brau "The Beer"
22. Harvard has what it takes
23. Kings Brewery, Inc., Brooklyn, N.Y., Kings Beer and Ale
24. Enjoy Krueger's on draught, where not available, drink it from keglined cans
25. Liebmann Breweries, Rheingold Beer, Scotch Ale
26. Miller Select Beer
27. The Famous Old Narragansett Banquet Ale
28. Drink the famous New England Ale in double-lined cans
29. Northampton Brewery Corp., Northampton, Pa., Tru-Blu Beer and Ale
30. For opening Nu-Globe Beer
31. Pabst Blue Ribbon / same
32. For opening Pabst Tapa Can
33. For opening Pabst Tapa Can, made in the United States of America
34. Pilser's Original Extra Dry Beer, N.Y.
35. Red Top Brewing Co., Cincinnati, Ohio / same
36. Jacob Ruppert Brewery, New York
37. Schaefer America's Oldest Lager Beer
38. For opening Schmidt's City Club Beer
39. Schultz Quality Beer-Ale
40. Stroudsburg Brewing Co., Stroudsburg, Pa., Stroud-Beer
41. Waldorf Lager, Champagne of beer
42. Drink Won-up

I-8

1. Peter Fox Brewing Co., Chicago
2. Northampton Brewery Corp., Northampton, Pa., Tru-Blu Beer and Ale

I-9

1. Waldorf / Ale & Lager

I-10

1. Northampton Brewery Corporation, Northampton, Pa., Tru-Blu Beer and Ale

I-11

1. Alps Brau Beer / Old Crown Ale Beer
2. Ambassador Beer — Export Brewed
3. Enjoy Diamond Bright American Beer / same
4. Make friends with American Beer
5. Thirsty? Drink! American Beer / same
6. Anheuser Busch (A & eagle) / same
7. Atlas Prager Bohemian Light Beer / Got it? Get it!
8. Atlas Prager Bohemian Light Lager / Got it? Get it!
9. Atlas Prager Extra Dry Beer / Got it? Get it!
10. Augustiner Gam Beers
11. Ballantine Ale & Beer (3 rings) / same
12. Blatz Milwaukee's finest beer / same
13. Boh — Bohemian Lager Beer
14. Bosch Brewing Co., Houghton, Mich. / Bosch Beer (tuba player)
15. Bosch Brewing Co., Houghton, Mich. / Bosch Beer, bright bold flavor
16. Braumeister Milwaukee's choicest beer
17. Breunig's Lager / same
18. Buckeye Brewing Co., Toledo, Ohio / Buckeye Beer
19. Budweiser King of Beers / same
20. Budweiser King of Beers / (Eagle in A) Anheuser-Busch, Inc.
21. The Burger Brewing Co., Cincinnati & Akron, Ohio / Have fun, have a Burger Beer
22. Burgermeister Beer / Burgie
23. Burgermeister Brewing Co., San Francisco-Los Angeles, Calif., a division of Jos. Schlitz Brewing Co. / BURGIE!
24. Burgermeister Pilsner Beer
25. Busch Bavarian Beer / same
26. Calumet Breweries, Inc., Calumet, Ind.
27. Carling, Hey Mabel!
28. Carling
29. Always buy Carling
30. C.V. for me, Champagne Velvet Beer / Champagne Velvet Beer
31. For the good life Champagne Velvet
32. Champagne Velvet for the good life / Champagne Velvet Beer
33. Champale
34. Columbia Preferred Beer
35. Columbia Preferred Beer / same
36. Coors America's Fine Light Beer / same
37. Time out for Dawson Gold Crown Beer / Time out for Dawson Diamond Ale
38. Dixie Beer for a bright cheerful tomorrow / same
39. Drewrys Extra Dry Beer (mountie) / same
40. Duquesne / same
41. E & B Brewing Co., Inc., Detroit 7, Michigan / E & B Beer and Ale
42. Eastside Old Tap Lager
43. Esquire Premium Beer / Stoney's Pilsener Beer
44. Esslinger Extra Dry Beer / same
45. Premium F & S Beer
46. F & S Beer, Porter and Ale, Fuhrmann & Schmidt Brewing Co.
47. Falls City Beer it's pasturized, it's bitter free / same
48. Falstaff Brewing Corp., St. Louis, Mo. / Falstaff America's Premium Beer
49. Falstaff Brewing Corp., St. Louis, Mo. / Falstaff The choicest product of the brewer's art
50. Falstaff Brewing Corp., St. Louis, Mo., Omaha, Nebr., New Orleans, La., San Jose, Cal., Fort Wayne, Ind. / Premium Quality Falstaff Beer
51. Falstaff Brewing Corp., St. Louis, Mo. / Premium Quality Falstaff Beer
52. Fechtels
53. Fehr's X/L Beer
54. Fesenmeier Brewing Co., Huntington, W. Va. / Fesenmeier Beer "Brings you good cheer"
55. Fisher Beer / Sparkle brewed to the altitude
56. Fitgers Beer, naturally brewed / Fitgers Beer, naturally better
57. Fitzgerald Beer-Ale / same
58. Peter Fox Brewing Co., Waukesha, Wisc., Brewed with Wisconsin's world famous Waukesha water / Fox DeLuxe Beer
59. Peter Fox Brewing Co., Waukesha, Wisc., Brewed with Wisconsin's world famous Waukesha water / Fox Head "400" Beer
60. Gamecock Ale / Old Export Pilsner
61. Gettelman Milwaukee Beer / Gettelman $1,000 Beer
62. The Globe Brewing Co., Baltimore 1, Md. / Arrow 77, The Globe's finest brew
63. Gluek, Minneapolis, Minn. (lion) / same
64. M.K. Goetz division of Pearl Brewing Co., St. Joseph, Missouri / Country Club
65. Gretz
66. Griesedieck Bros. Beer — St. Louis
67. G/B Griesedieck Bros. Beer — St. Louis
68. Gunther Brewing Company, Baltimore, Maryland / Real Beer Gunthers
69. Theo. Hamm Brg. Co., St. Paul, Minn. & San Francisco, Calif. / Hamm's Beer refreshing as the land of sky blue waters
70. Hampden Beer Ale
71. Hampden Harvard Beer-Ale
72. Hampden Harvard Breweries, Inc., Willimansett, Mass. / Dobler Beer-Ale
73. Harvard Ale or Export Beer
74. Hanley Pilsener Beer / same
75. Hanley Lager Beer / same
76. House of Heileman / Heileman's Old Style, Kingsbury Beer, Fox Head
77. Holihan's Pilsener Beer
78. Holihan's Pilsener Beer / same
79. Horlacher Pilsner Beer (Penguin) / same
80. 14K Hudepohl Beer saves the day / same
81. Independent Milwaukee Brewery, Milwaukee, Wis., Braumeister / Braumeister Milwaukee's choicest beer
82. Products of International Breweries, Inc., Detroit Mich., Buffalo, N.Y., Tampa, Fla., Findlay, O. / Frankenmuth Beer & Ale, Iroquois Beer & Ale, Silver Bar Beer & Ale, Old Dutch Beer
83. Iron City Beer, it's real beer / Beat 'em Bucs!
84. Iron City Beer, it's real beer / Boost the Pirates — sponsored on radio and television by the Iron City Brewery, Pittsburgh, Pennsylvania
85. Iron City Beer, it's real beer / A friend of mine from the Iron City Brewery in Pittsburgh gave me this
86. Kings Ale / Original Old German Lager Beer
87. Kingsbury, swing to king / same
88. Knickerbocker Beer / same (town crier)
89. Koch's Beer Ale
90. G. Krueger Brg. Co., Newark, N.J. / Ambassador Export Brewed Beer
91. G. Krueger Brg. Co., Newark, N.J. / Krueger Beer Ale (K man)
92. Leinenkugel's Beer / Made with Chippewa Water from The Big Eddy Spring

93. Lone Star Beer makes the most of nature's best
94. Lone Star Beer, have fun with your thirst / same
95. Lone Star Beer, have fun with your thirst / Lone Star Beer, it's certified
96. Lone Star Beer, Texas fine light beer / same
97. Manns Export Ale / Old Export Pilsner
98. Miller Brewing Co., Milwaukee, Wis. / Miller High Life Beer
99. Narragansett Lager Beer / Hi Neighbor
100. Narragansett Lager Beer / Hi Neighbor from one of America's great breweries
101. National Brewing Co., Baltimore, Md. / Drink National Beer
102. National Brewing Co., Baltimore, Md. / National Beer from Chesapeake Bay land of pleasant living
103. National Brewing Co., Baltimore, Md. / National Beer quality so good you can taste it
104. The National Brewing Co., Balt., Md., Orlando, Fla., The National Brewing Co., Detroit, Mich. / National Bohemian Beer, wet, cold and delicious
105. Oconto Premium Beer / same
106. Oertel Brewing Co., Oertel's 92 Beer / Oertel's Real Draft (on glass), Louisville, Kentucky
107. Oertel Brewing Co., Incorporated, Louisville, Kentucky / Oertels 92 Beer, cheer up with Oertels' '92 Beer
108. Old Crown Ale Beer / same
109. Old Crown Brewing Corporation, Fort Wayne, Indiana / Old Crown Ale Beer
110. Old Dutch Beer / Old Dutch Beer, International Brys, Inc., Findlay, Ohio
111. Old Dutch Premium Beer
112. Old Reading best tasting beer in town / same
113. Original Old German Lager Beer / Queen's Brau Select Beer
114. Oshkosh Brewing Co., Oshkosh, Wis. / Chief Oshkosh Beer B'Gosh it's good
115. Oshkosh Brewing Co., Oshkosh, Wis. / Chief Oshkosh Beer custom brewed for all Wisconsin
116. Oshkosh Brewing Co., Oshkosh, Wis. / Chief Oshkosh Beer brewed on the shores of Lake Winnebago
117. Peoples Brewing Co., Oshkosh, Wis., Beverly 1-2020 / Peoples Beer hits the spot
118. Pfeiffer Brewing Co. / Pfeiffer, the real beer from Great Lakes Country
119. Piel's Beer, Piel Bros., Brooklyn, N.Y. / same
120. Pilsener Brewing Company, Cleveland, Ohio / P.O.C. Pilsener Beer
121. Potosi Brewing Co., Potosi, Wisconsin / Good old Potosi Beer
122. Potosi Brewing Co., Potosi, Wisconsin / It's Holiday Beer Time
123. Rahr's Beer / same
124. Rainier Ale / Old Stock
125. Reading Premium, the friendly beer for modern people / same
126. Reading Premium Beer for friendly flavor / same
127. Regal Beer
128. Regal Pale / Now for that Regal feeling
129. Regal Select / Now for that Regal feeling
130. Regent Premium Ale-Beer / same
131. Rhinelander Brewing Co., Rhinelander, Wis.
132. Rolling Rock Premium Beer / same
133. Make a date with...Royal 58 Beer / Treat yourself royally
134. Ruppert Knickerbocker / same
135. Adam Scheidt Brewing Co., Norristown, Pa., The Aristocrat of Ales, Ram's Head Ale / Headed for pleasure, Valley Forge Beer
136. Schlitz, Jos. Schlitz Brewing Co., Milwaukee, Brooklyn, Los Angeles, San Francisco, Kansas City, Tampa / Schlitz the beer that made Milwaukee famous
137. Jos. Schlitz Brewing Co., Milwaukee, Wis. and Tampa, Fla., Milwaukee Beer / Old Milwaukee Beer
138. Schmidt's of Philadelphia, brewers since 1860 / same
139. Schoenhofen Edelweiss Co., Chicago, Illinois / Cheery Beery Edelweiss Light Beer
140. Schoenhofen Edelweiss Co., Chicago, Illinois / Edelweiss a case of good judgement
141. Schoenling Brewing Co., Cincinnati, Oh., Phone Cherry 4344 / Schoenling Beer, Cincinnati's finest
142. Spearman Beer-Ale
143. Stag Beer
144. Stag Beer / same
145. Stegmaier Brewing Co., Wilkes Barre, Pa. / Stegmaier Gold Medal Beer
146. Storz Brewing Co., Omaha, Nebraska / Storz America's light refreshing beer
147. Enjoy Sunshine Premium Beer / same
148. Tivoli Colorado's First Beer / Brewers of Hi•En Brau
149. Tropical Ale and Beer / same
150. Geo. Walter Brewing Co., Appleton, Wis., your friendly local brewery / Adler Brau, Appleton Beer
151. Walters, Colorado's light refreshing beer / same
152. Walters, Eau Claire, Wis. / same
153. Weber Special Premium Beer / same
154. West Virginia Beer-Ale, That'll win Ya!
155. Wilson's since 1875
156. Van Merritt Brewing Co., Chicago, Ill., world's most honored beer / Van Merritt
157. Yuengling Premium Beer / Yuengling America's oldest brewing family
158. Yusay Pilsen Premium Beer

I-12

1. Arizona Brewing Co., Inc., Phoenix, Arizona, A-1 Pilsner Beer / A-1 brewed with crystal pure water
2. Arizona Brewing Co., Inc., Phoenix, Arizona, True Pilsner flavor / A-1 Pilsner Beer
3. Anheuser Busch, Inc. (Eagle in A) / same
4. Augustiner Gam Beer / same
5. Ballantine Ale & Beer (3 rings) / same
6. Bartels Beer / same
7. Bavarian Beer
8. Blatz Milwaukee's favorite premium beer / same
9. Bosch Brewing Co., Houghton, Mich. / Bosch Beer bright bold flavor
10. The Burger Brewing Co.. Cincinnati, Ohio / Burger a finer beer
11. Burgermeister Beer / Burgermeister a truly fine pale beer
12. Burgie / (Burgie man — happy face)
13. Burgie / (Burgie man — sad face)
14. Carling / same
15. From the New Carling Brewery, Atlanta, Ga. / Carling
16. Cleveland-Sandusky Brewing Corp., Cleveland, Ohio / G/B Lager Beer
17. Dixie 45 Beer / same
18. Dobler Beer-Ale / same
19. Duquesne / same
20. Eastside Old Tap Lager / same
21. Esquire Premium Beer / Stoney's Pilsener Beer

22. Fitgers naturally brewed / same
23. Fitzgerald Beer — Ale / same
24. Fort Pitt Brewing Co., Baltimore, Maryland
25. Genesee Beer — Ale / same
26. Gluek, Mineapolis, Minn. (lion)
27. Goebel Beer / same
28. Goebel Beer / There's a wonderful difference
29. Goebel 22 Beer / You can taste the difference only Goebel its crystilled for true beer flavor (rooster head)
30. Grain Belt...from perfect brewing water / Grain Belt Premium, been a long time a brewing
31. Grain Belt Beer; diamond clear / Grain Belt Premium been a long time a brewing
32. Grand Prize Beer / same
33. Great Falls Select / same
34. Gretz Philadelphia's only extra premium beer (man on high wheeler)
35. Hamm's Beer / (Hamm's bear)
36. Hamm's Beer / Born in the land of sky blue waters
37. Hamm's Beer / From the land of sky blue waters
38. Hamm's Beer / Specially designed for Hamm's new easy-open aluminum tops
39. Hamm's Beer, Bursting with freshness / Pour yourself some freshness...have yourself a Hamm's
40. Hedrick Beer-Ale / Still the best
41. Heileman's Old Style, America's quality beer/same
42. Heileman's Old Style, Bright rich flavor lager / same
43. Hensler Light Beer
44. Highlander Beer / same
45. It's Holiday Beer time / same
46. Holihan's Ale-Pilsener / same
47. Jos. Huber Brewing Co., Monroe, Wis. / Huber Premium Beer
48. 14K Hudepohl / same
49. International Breweries, Inc., Detroit, Mich., Buffalo, N.Y., Tampa, Fla., Findlay, Ohio, Covington, Ky. If it's International, you know it's better / IBI (in shield), Iroquois, Frankenmuth, Old Dutch, Bavarian's, Silver Bar
50. International Breweries, Inc., Detroit, Mich., Buffalo, N.Y., Tampa, Fla., Findlay, O. International family of fine beers / IBI (in shield + 4 shields)
51. Kaier's Beer / same
52. Kingsbury Breweries Co., Manitowoc, Sheboygan, Wisconsin, Kingsbury Sioux City Brg. Co., Sioux City, Iowa / Kingsbury Pale Beer fit for a king
53. Kingsbury Pale Beer / Kingsbury fit for a king, Manitowoc, Sheboygan, Wis.
54. Kingsbury, swing to King (crown) / same
55. Pour a Koehler Collar / same
56. Koehler three fine brews / same
57. G. Krueger Brg. Co., Newark, N.J. / Ambassador Export Brewed Beer
58. Lebanon Valley Brewing Company, Lebanon, Pa.
59. Leinenkugel Beer, famous since 1867
60. Lucky Lager Age-dated Beer / It's Lucky when you live in America
61. Lucky Lager, the real lager beer / This is your Lucky opener
62. Lucky Light / Remarkably non-filling
63. Mann's Export Ale / Old Export Pilsner
64. Miller Brewing Co., Milwaukee, Wis. / Miller High Life Beer
65. Oertels 92 Beer, Oertel Brewing Co. / Oertel's real draft beer, Louisville, Kentucky
66. Oland's Export India Pale Ale / Oland's Schooner Beer
67. Old Dutch modern light beer
68. Pabst Blue Ribbon / same
69. Pfeiffer Brewing Company / Pfeiffer, the real beer from the Great Lakes Country
70. Pfeiffer Premium Beer / (Pfeiffer)
71. Piel Bros., Brooklyn, N.Y., Piels Light Beer / same
72. Point Special Beer / same
73. Potosi Brewing Co., Potosi, Wisconsin / Good old Potosi Beer
74. Regal Beer / same
75. Regal Pale / One of America's 2 great beers
76. Regal Select Beer / same
77. Reisch Brewing Co., Springfield, Ill. / Reisch Beer
78. Rheingold Extra Dry Lager Beer / same
79. Richbrau Beer / same
80. Rolling Rock Premium Beer / same
81. Schaefer, America's oldest lager beer / same
82. Adam Scheidt Brewing Co., Norristown, Pa., The Aristocrat of Ales, Ram's Head Ale / Headed for pleasure Valley Forge Beer
83. August Schell Brg. Co., New Ulm, Minn. / Schell's pleasure packed beer
84. Schmidt, St. Paul, Minn. / The brew that grew with the great Northwest
85. Remember Sebewaing Beer
86. Standard / Standard Dry
87. The Standard Brewing Co., Cleveland, Ohio / Standard Beer
88. Standard Rochester Brewing Co., Inc., Rochester, New York / Topper Pilsner
89. Stegmaier Brewing Co., Wilkes Barre, Pa. / Stegmaier Gold Medal Beer
90. Sterling
91. Sterling aged that extra month / (rooster on weather vane)
92. Storz Brewing Company, Omaha, Nebraska, U.S.A. / Storz, America's light refreshing beer
93. Enjoy Sunshine Premium / same
94. Topper / Topper Beer
95. Topper / Topper Pilsener
96. Utica Club "U.C. for me" Pilsener Beer and Cream Ale / same
97. Walter's Colorado's light refreshing beer
98. Wiedemann's Fine Beer / same
99. Yuengling Premium Beer / Yuengling, America's oldest brewing family
100. Yusay Pilsen Beer / same

I-13

1. Drink all-grain American Beer
2. Bartels Extra Light Beer / same
3. Becker's Mellow Beer / same
4. The Burger Brewing Co., Cincinnati, Ohio / Burger, a finer beer
5. Burgermeister Beer / A truly fine pale beer
6. Butte Special Beer is better beer / same
7. Canadian Ace Brewing Co., Chicago, Ill., Canadian Ace / Canadian Ace Brand Beer and Ale, Made in U.S.A.
8. Coors America's fine light beer / same
9. Dixie 45 (45 in circle) Beer / same
10. Falls City Beer, It's pasturized, it's bitter free / same
11. Falstaff Brewing Corp., St. Louis, Mo. / Falstaff America's Premium quality beer
12. Fesenmeier Brewing Co., Huntington, W. Va. / Fesenmeier Beer brings you good cheer
13. Fitger Beer, natural brewed / same
14. If it's Gibbons, it's good / same
15. M.K. Goetz Brewing Co., St. Joseph & Kansas City, Missouri / Country Club Malt Liquor

16. Great Falls Select / same
17. Gretz Beer
18. Theo. Hamm Brg. Co., St. Paul, Minn., Hamm's Beer from the land of sky blue waters / Hamm's Beer from the land of sky blue waters
19. Hampden Ale-Beer
20. Peter Hand Bry. Co., Chgo., Ill., over 250 million glasses enjoyed by Midwesterners every year / Meister Brau the custom brew
21. Peter Hand Bry. Co., Chgo., Ill., enjoyed by Midwesterners at the rate of over a million glasses daily / Real Draft Beer, Meister Brau the custom brew
22. same as above except — 300 million glasses yearly
23. same as above except — 450 million glasses yearly
24. Hensler Light Beer
25. Holihan's Ale—Beer
26. Hudepohl 14K / same
27. International Breweries, Inc., Detroit, Mich., Buffalo, N.Y., Tampa, Fla., Findlay, O., International family of fine beers / IBI (plus four shields)
28. Kaier's Beer / same
29. Kingsbury Breweries Co., Manitowoc, Sheboygan, Wis., Kingsbury Sioux City Brg. Co., Sioux City, Iowa / Kingsbury Pale Beer fit for a king
30. Lancers
31. Lebanon Valley Brewing Co., Lebanon, Pa.
32. Meister Brau Premium Beer / same
33. Meister Brau — we're expecting you / same
34. National Bohemian Beer (Mr. Boh) / same
35. Olympia Beer "It's the water" / same
36. Pearl — it's lighter / same
37. Pfeiffer famous beer / (Pfeiffer)
38. Pfeiffer Premium Beer / (Pfeiffer)
39. Piel Bros., Brooklyn, N.Y., Piel's Light Beer / same
40. Pilsener Brewing Company, Cleveland, Ohio / P.O.C. Pilsener Beer
41. Rainier Ale, Old Stock / same
42. Rheingold Extra Dry Lager Beer / By George, that's Beer!
43. Sterling
44. Sterling — aged that extra month / same
45. Storz Brewing Co., Omaha, Nebraska, U.S.A. / Storz America's light refreshing beer
46. Enjoy Sunshine Premium Beer / same
47. Tavern Pale, Chgo., Ill.
48. Topper Beer / Topper
49. Tropical Ale and Beer
50. Valley Forge Beer / Rams Head Ale
51. West Bend Lithia Co., West Bend, Wis.
52. Wiedemann's Fine Beer / same
53. Yusay Pilsen Beer / same

I-14

1. Quick! Quick! My Beverwyck / same
2. Canadian Ace Brewing Co., Chicago, Ill., Canadian Ace / Canadian Ace Brand Beer and Ale
3. Coor's America's fine light beer / same
4. Duke and Duquesne are one and the same
5. Duquesne / same
6. Drink Esslinger's Beer-Ale
7. Falls City Beer, It's pasturized, its bitter free / same
8. Fuhrmann & Schmidt Brewing Co., F & S Beer, Porter, and Ale
9. Gibbons is good / same
10. M.K. Goetz Brewing Co., St. Joseph & Kansas City, Mo. / Country Club Malt Liquor
11. Gretz, Philadelphia's only extra premium beer / (man on high wheeler)
12. Haberle Congress Brewing Co., Inc., Syracuse, N.Y. / Congress Light Beer
13. 14K Hudepohl / same
14. Drink Jax Beer / same
15. Lebanon Valley Brewing Co. / same
16. Leisy's Fine Beer / same
17. Lone Star America's certified quality beer / same
18. Miller Brewing Co., Milwaukee, Wis. / Miller High Life Beer
19. Drink Muehlebach Beer / same
20. Olympia Beer "It's the water" / same
21. Henry F. Ortlieb Brewing Co., Phila., Pa., Ortlieb's Premium Beer / same
22. Premium Quality Pearl / same
23. Pilsener Brewing Company, Cleveland, Ohio / P.O.C. Pilsener Beer
24. Rainier Ale, Old Stock / same
25. Rainier Beer / same
26. Rheingold Extra Dry Lager Beer / same
27. Schaefer America's Oldest Lager Beer / same
28. Southern Select Beer / same

I-15

1. A-1 Pilsner Beer
2. Ballantine Ale-Beer (3 rings) / same
3. Blatz Beer / same
4. Brewers Association of America Convention 1957 / Emro Mfg. Co., Inc., St. Louis, Mo.
5. Drewry's Limited, U.S.A., Inc., Hampden / Harvard Division / Fitzgerald Beer-Ale
6. Duquesne / Silver Top special premium lager beer
7. Edelbrew grows it's own flavor
8. Erin Brew / same
9. Esslinger's Beer-Ale
10. Esslinger's Beer-Ale, Little man (waiter) / same
11. Esslinger's Premium Beer, just right / same
12. Falls City Beer / same
13. Fox DeLuxe
14. Gunther Brewing Co., Inc., Baltimore, Md. / Gunther Premium Dry Beer
15. Heileman's Old Style Lager, Wisconsin's finest beer / same
16. Drink Jax Beer
17. Take a break for a Lone Star Beer / same
18. Lucky Lager Age-dated Beer / It's Lucky when you live in America
19. Lucky Lager Beer / No finer beer made East or West
20. Maier Brewing Company, Los Angeles, Calif. / Brew "102"
21. Meister Brau / same
22. Narragansett Lager Beer
23. Famous Narragansett Ale & Lager / Hi Neighbor, have a Gansett
24. National Brewing Co., Baltimore, Md. / Drink National Beer
25. Piel Bros., Brooklyn, N.Y., Piels Jumbo Opener /Taste what's happened to Piels
26. Piel Bros., Brooklyn, N.Y., The beer with the "all beer" taste / Piels jumbo opener
27. Piel's Light Beer / same
28. R & H Beer & Ale / same
29. Rams Head Ale / Valley Forge Beer
30. Schaefer America's Oldest Lager Beer / same
31. Schaefer Fine Beer / same
32. The William Simon Brewery, Buffalo, N.Y., Simon Pure Beer-Ale / same
33. Stegmaier Brewing Co., Wilkes Barre, Pa. / Stegmaier Gold Medal Beer
34. Stroh's Beer, it's lighter (shield)

I-16

1. A-1 brewed with Christal pure water / A-1 the Western way to say welcome
2. Bavarian Beer / same
3. Black Label Beer
4. Peter Bub Brewing, Inc., Winona, Minn. / Bub's Beer makes it fun to be thirsty!
5. Coors America's fine light beer / same
6. Esslinger Extra Dry Beer / same
7. Falls City Beer, It's pasturized, it's bitter free / same
8. Great Falls Select / Great Falls Select Fine Beer
9. Holihan's Ale-Pilsner / same
10. 14K Hudepohl
11. Lancer's Beer / same
12. A million a day say Lone Star Beer / same
13. Lone Star Beer, Have fun with your thirst / Lone Star Beer, certified quality
14. Lone Star Beer makes the most of nature's best / same
15. Louis F. Neuweiler's Sons, Allentown, Penna. /Neuweiler Beer & Ale
16. Olympia Beer "It's the water" / same
17. Point Special Beer
18. Rahr's Beer / same
19. Schmidt's of Philadelphia, brewers since 1860 / same
20. Utica Club Beer for natural beer, one punch / same
21. West Bend Lithia Co., West Bend, Wis. / same

I-17

1. A-1, The Western way to say welcome / A-1 brewed with crystal pure water
2. Acme Beer / Acme Light Dry Beer
3. Acme Beer-Ale / same
4. Acme Gold Label / Bulldog Beer-Ale
5. Ambrosia Brewing Co., Nectar Beer / same
6. Arizona Brewing Co., Inc., Phoenix, Ariz., A-1 Pilsner Beer / same
7. Imperial Lagered Arrow Beer, it hits the spot / same
8. Atlantic Beer "The beer of the South"
9. Atlas Brewing Company, Chicago, Illinois, America's most imitated beer / Atlas Prager Extra Dry Beer
10. Atlas Brewing Company, Chicago, Illinois, Got it? Get it! / Atlas Prager Extra Dry Beer
11. Ballantine Ale & Beer (3 rings) / same
12. Blatz Beer / same
13. Blatz Milwaukee's favorite premium beer / same
14. Blatz Milwaukee's finest beer / same
15. Blatz Milwaukee's famous premium beer
16. Bohemian Club / Old Fashion lager beer
17. Burgermeister Beer / Burgermeister, a truly fine pale beer
18. California Gold Label Beer (covered wagon) / The flavor of the West
19. Camden Beer, none better
20. Canadian Ace Brewing Co., Chicago, Ill., Canadian Ace / Canadian Ace Brand Beer and Ale, Made in U.S.A.
21. Carling / same
22. Carling's Red Cap Ale / same
23. Champagne Velvet Gold Label Beer / same
24. Cooks Gold Blume Beer—500 Ale/same
25. Time out for Dawson's Gold Crown Beer / same
26. Dawson's is calorie controlled / same
27. Diamond State 100% Pure Grain Beer / same
28. Dobler Beer-Ale / same
29. Drewrys Extra Dry Beer (mountie) / same
30. (Drewrys mountie only)
31. Eastern Beverage Corp., Hammonton, N.J. / Holland Premium Beer
32. Esslinger's Premium Beer, just right / same
33. Falls City Beer / same
34. Falstaff / Falstaff Beer
35. Fehr's X/L Beer / same
36. Fiesta Meister Brau / same
37. Fitzgerald Beer-Ale / same
38. Fox DeLuxe / same
39. Fox DeLuxe the great Chicago Beer / same
40. Fox Head "400" Beer, brewed with Waukesha water
41. Frankenmuth Melodry Beer and Ale / same
42. Genesee Beer-Ale / same
43. Gettelman $1,000 Milwaukee Beer / same
44. If it's Gibbons, it's good, Gibbons Premium Beer / same
45. M.K. Goetz Brewing Co., St. Joseph & Kansas City, Mo. / Country Club Stout Malt Liquor
46. M.K. Goetz Brewing Co., St. Joseph & Kansas City, Mo. / Country Club the bright beer
47. (Goebel's Brewster the Rooster only) / same
48. Goebel Beer Private Stock 22 / Brewster the Goebel Rooster (2 roosters)
49. Compliments of Goebel Brewing Co. of California, Oakland, Calif. / Goebel Beer
50. Compliments of Goebel Brewing Co. of California, Oakland, Calif. / If it's Goebel, it's good!
51. Grain Belt from perfect brewing water / Grain Belt been a long time a brewing
52. Grand Prize Pale Dry Beer / same
53. Grand Prize Pale Dry Beer / Real beer flavor
54. Great Falls Select / same
55. Griesedieck Bros., Beer, St. Louis / same
56. Gunther Brewing Company, Baltimore, Md. / Get in the golden mood, Gunther Beer
57. Gunther Brewing Co., Baltimore, Md. / Gunther Premium Dry Beer
58. Theo. Hamm Brewing Co., St. Paul, Minn., San Francisco, Los Angeles, Baltimore / Hamm's Beer from the land of sky blue waters
59. Theo. Hamm Brg. Co., St. Paul, Minn. / Hamm's Beer from the land of sky blue waters
60. Hamm's Beer, bursting with freshness / Pour yourself some freshness, have yourself a Hamm's
61. Peter Hand Bry. Co., Chgo., Ill., Meister Brau the custom brew / Meister Brau the custom brew
62. Heileman's Old Style Lager, America's quality beer / same
63. Heineken's Beer / same
64. Hensler (whale in water), it's a whale of a beer
65. For opening Highlander Beer / same
66. Horlacher Pilsner Beer (Penguin) / same
67. Independent Milwaukee Brewery, Milwaukee, Wis., Braumeister / Braumeister, Milwaukee's choicest beer
68. Product of International Breweries, Inc. / Frankenmuth Beer & Ale, Iroquois Ale & beer
69. Iroquois Ale and Beer (Indian head) / same
70. Drink Jax Beer / same
71. Kaier's beer over 100 years / same
72. Kings Ale / Original Old German Lager Beer
73. Kingsbury Pale Beer / Kingsbury, brewed to please you, Manitowoc-Sheboygan, Wis.
74. Kingsbury Pale Beer / Kingsbury, fit for a king, Manitowoc-Sheboygan, Wis.
75. Krantz Brewing Corp., Findlay, Ohio / Old Dutch Beer
76. G. Krueger Brewing Co., Newark, N.J., Krueger Beer, Ale (K man) / same
77. Thirsty?? Leinenkugel Beer / same
78. Leisy's Fine Beer / same

79. Lone Star America's certified quality beer / same
80. Menominee Marinette Brewing Co., Menominee, Mich. / Silver Cream Beer, Old Craft Brew
81. Miller Brewing Co., Milwaukee, Wis. / Miller High Life Beer
82. Molson / same
83. Monarch Beer / Fun for the money
84. Mt. Carbon Beer / same
85. Muehlebach / same
86. Muehlebach Beer / same
87. Famous Narragansett Ale & Lager / Hi Neighbor! Have a 'Gansett
88. National Bohemian Beer / (Mr. Boh)
89. National Brewing Co., Baltimore, Md. / Drink National Beer
90. Louis F. Neuweiler's Sons, Allentown, Pa. /Neuweilers Ale & Beer
91. Old Georgetown Premium Quality Beer / same
92. Old Milwaukee America's Light Beer / same
93. Old Reading Beer, it's wonderful good / same
94. Olympia Beer "It's the water" / same
95. Henry F. Ortlieb Brewing Co., Phila., Pa., Ortlieb's Premium Beer / same
96. Oshkosh Brewing Co., Oshkosh, Wis. / Chief Oshkosh Beer, B'Gosh it's good
97. Pabst Blue Ribbon / same
98. (Pfeiffer only)
99. Pfeiffer's Famous Beer / (Pfeiffer)
100. Pfeiffer's Famous Beer / (Pfeiffer) St. Paul, Minn.
101. Piel Bros., Brooklyn, N.Y., Piel's Light Beer / same
102. Piel Bros., N.Y., Piel's Beer, less N.F.S. / same
103. Pilsener Brewing Company, Cleveland, Ohio / P.O.C. Pilsener Beer
104. Point Special Beer / same
105. Regal Pale / One of America's 2 great beers
106. Rheingold Extra Dry / same
107. Rheingold Extra Dry Lager Beer / same
108. Rubsam & Horrmann Brewing Co., New York, N.Y. /Crown Premium Beer
109. Ruppert Knickerbocker Beer / same
110. Schaefer America's oldest lager beer / same
111. Adam Scheidt Brg. Co., Norristown, Pa. / Prior Beer, liquid luxury
112. Adam Scheidt Brg. Co., Norristown, Pa., Rams Head (ram's head), The Aristocrat of Ales / Valley Forge, A beer worthy of its name
113. Jos. Schlitz Brewing Co., Milwaukee, Wis., Old Milwaukee Genuine Draft Beer / Old Milwaukee Genuine Draft Beer
114. Schlitz, Jos. Schlitz Brewing Company, breweries at Milwaukee, Wis., Brooklyn, N.Y., Kansas City, Mo., Tampa, Fla., Los Angeles and San Francisco, Calif. / Schlitz the beer that made Milwaukee famous.
115. Schlitz, Jos. Schlitz Brewing Company, breweries at Milwaukee, Wis., Brooklyn, N.Y., Los Angeles, Calif. / Schlitz the beer that made Milwaukee famous
116. Jacob Schmidt Brewing Co., St. Paul, Minnesota / Schmidt's Beer, draft beer flavor
117. Schmidt, St. Paul, Minn. / Schmidt, The brew that grew with the great Northwest
118. Schmidt's of Philadelphia, brewers since 1860 / same
119. Schmidt, St. Paul / Pfeiffer Premium Beer
120. Schoenhofen Edelweiss Co., Chicago, Illinois / Edelweiss a case of good judgement
121. The William Simon Brewery, Buffalo, N.Y. Simon Pure Beer Ale / same
122. Stag Beer
123. Stag Beer / same
124. Standard Brewing Co., Cleveland, Ohio / Erin Brew
125. Standard Brewing Co., Rochester, N.Y., Old Ox Cart Dry Beer / Standard Dry Ale
126. Star Union Brewing Company, Peru, Illinois / Star Model Beer
127. Stegmaier Brewing Co., Wilkes Barre, Pa. / Stegmaier Gold Medal Beer
128. Say Stein's everytime / same
129. Storz Beer / same
130. Storz Brewing Company, Omaha, Nebraska, U.S.A. / Storz, America's light refreshing beer
131. The Stroh Brewery Co., Detroit 26, Michigan / You'll like Stroh's Beer, it's lighter
132. The Stroh Brewery Co., Detroit, Michigan / You'll like Stroh's Beer, it's lighter
133. The Stroh Brewery Co., Detroit, Michigan / A quality opener for a quality product
134. The Stroh Brewery Co., Detroit 26, Michigan, Stroh's Beer / A quality opener for a quality product
135. Enjoy Sunshine Beer / same
136. Enjoy Sunshine Premium Beer / same
137. Tavern Pale / Free gifts — save those coupons (hand removing neck label from bottle)
138. Tech Premium Beer / same
139. Tivoli Beer brewed for Western taste / same
140. Topper Beer / same
141. United States Brewing Co., Chicago's oldest brewery /Rheingold super dry
142. Utica Club "U.C. for me" Pilsener Beer and Cream Ale / same
143. Valley Brew Premium Beer
144. Wausau Brewing Co., Wausau, Wis. / Schoen's Old Lager
145. Weber Waukesha Brewing Co., Waukesha, Wisconsin / (Weber in W)
146. Yusay Pilsen Beer / same

I-18

1. Acme Gold Label / Acme Bull Dog Ale
2. Ballantine Ale-Beer (3 rings) / same
3. Blatz Beer / same
4. Burgermeister Beer / Burgermeister, a truly fine pale beer
5. Carling's Red Cap Ale
6. Dobler Beer — Ale
7. Esslinger's Premium Beer, just right / same
8. Fehr's X/L Beer / same
9. Fitzgerald Beer—Ale / same
10. Fox DeLuxe, The great Chicago Beer / same
11. Frankenmuth Beer & Ale, Iroquois Beer & Ale /Product of International Breweries, Inc.
12. Compliments of Goebel Brewing Co. of California, Oakland, Calif. / If it's Goebel, it's good
13. Gunther Brewing Co., Inc., Baltimore, Md. / Gunther Premium Dry Beer
14. Heileman's Old Style Lager, America's quality beer / same
15. G. Krueger Brewing Co., Newark, N.J., Krueger Beer-Ale / same
16. Leisy's Fine Beer / same
17. Take a break for a Lone Star Beer / same
18. Lucky Lager Beer / No finer beer made East or West
19. Maier Brewing Co., Los Angeles, Calif. / Brew "102"
20. Meister Brau
21. National Brewing Co., Baltimore, Md. / Drink National Beer
22. Louis F. Neuweiler Sons, Allentown, Pa. / Neuweiler Beer & Ale
23. Oertel Brewing Co., Inc., Louisville, Kentucky / Oertels 92 Beer, cheer up with 92

24. R & H Beer & Ale / same
25. Rheingold Extra Dry Lager Beer / same
26. Ruppert Knickerbocker Beer / same
27. Schaefer America's oldest lager beer
28. Schaefer Fine Beer / same
29. Adam Scheidt Brg. Co., Norristown, Pa., Ram's Head, Aristocrat of Ales / Valley Forge, a beer worthy of it's name

I-19

1. Blatz
2. Coors
3. Esslingers (little man)
4. Genesee the bright taste in beer
5. M.K. Goetz Brewing Co., St. Joseph, Mo. / Country Club
6. M.K. Goetz Brewing Co., St. Joseph, Mo. / Goetz Beer
7. Miller High Life / same
8. Neuweiler Beer Ale / same
9. Original Pabst Blue Ribbon / same
10. Drink Pearl Beer / same
11. Schaefer Beer / America's Oldest lager beer

I-20

1. Adler Brau, Appleton Beer
2. Blatz
3. Coors
4. Genesee naturally more refreshing
5. Genesee the beer more people like
6. Hamm's Beer / From the land of sky blue waters
7. Leinenkugel Beer / Chippewa Falls, Wis.
8. Storz Brewing Co. / Storzette

I-21

1. Stegmaier Gold Medal Beer / Stegmaier Brewing Co., Wilkes Barre, Pa.

I-22

1. Arizona Brewing Co., Inc., Phoenix, Ariz., A-1 Pilsner Beer
2. Camden Beer, none better
3. Canadian Ace
4. Duquesne
5. E & B Brewing Co., Inc., Detroit 7, Mich.
6. Erin Brew
7. Esslinger's Premium Beer, Phila., Pa.
8. Falls City Beer
9. Fisher Beer
10. Grand Prize Beer
11. Hanley Export Lager Beer
12. Miller Brewing Co., Milwaukee, Wis., Miller High Life Beer
13. Rahr's Beer
14. Regal Beer
15. Schlitz
16. Silver Bar
17. Standard Dry Ale
18. Tavern Pale, Chgo., Ill.
19. Topper Beer

J-1

1. Bohemian Lager Beer — Boh
2. Gluek's First Prize Beer
3. Gluek's First Prize Beer, Minneapolis, Minn.
4. Haffenreffer Malt Liquor
5. Jax Ale Beer
6. Old Dutch Premium Beer
7. Jos. Schlitz Brewing Co., Milwaukee, Wis., U.S.A. / Schlitz the beer that made Milwaukee famous
8. Schmidt Beer
9. Schmidt's City Club Beer

J-2

1. Hanley Beer Ale
2. Sterling

J-3

1. Coors America's fine light beer
2. Duquesne Pilsener "The finest beer in town"
3. Falstaff, The choicest product of the brewer's art / Falstaff Beer, St. Louis-Omaha-New Orleans-San Jose
4. Griesedieck Bros. Beer — St. Louis / same
5. For opening Highlander Beer
6. Drink Muehlebach Beer
7. Old Crown Ale Beer
8. Pickwick Beer — Light Ale — Ale
9. Premium quality Pearl
10. Regal Pale Beer / same
11. Schmidt's City Club Beer
12. Southern Select Beer
13. Sterling
14. Utica Club Pilsner Beer and Cream Ale "U.C. for me" / same

J-4

1. Arrow Beer — it hits the spot / same
2. Best Brewing Co., Chicago, Embassy Club Beer / same
3. Quick! Quick! My Beverwyck / same
4. Dawson's Brewery, Inc., New Bedford, Mass. / Time out for Dawson's Ale & Beer
5. Esslinger's Premium Beer, just right / same
6. Falstaff, The choicest product of the brewer's art / Falstaff Beer, St. Louis-Omaha-New Orleans-San Jose
7. Falstaff Brewing Corp., St. Louis, Mo.-Omaha, Nebr., New Orleans, La. / Premium quality Falstaff Beer
8. Hornung Beer / same
9. G. Krueger Brewing Co., Newark, N.J. (K man), Krueger Beer-Ale / same
10. Pabst Blue Ribbon / same

J-5

1. Ambrosia Brewing Co., Nectar Beer / same
2. Atlas Brewing Co., Chicago, Illinois, Got it? Get it! / Atlas Prager Beer
3. Ballantine Ale Beer (3 rings) / same
4. Berghoff Brewing Corp., Fort Wayne, Indiana / Berghoff Beer
5. Quick! Quick! My Beverwyck / same
6. Coors America's fine light beer / same
7. Dawson's Brewery, Inc., New Bedford, Mass. / Time out for Dawson's Ale & Beer
8. Diamond State 100% Pure Grain Beer / same
9. Brew 103 by E & B, it's beer as beer should taste / same
10. Erin Brew / same
11. Falstaff Brewing Corp., St. Louis, Omaha, New Orleans, San Jose, Fort Wayne / Premium quality Falstaff Beer
12. (Goebel's Brewster the rooster only)
13. Griesedieck Bros. Beer, St. Louis / same
14. Hamm's Beer / same
15. Theo. Hamm Brg. Co., St. Paul, Mn. / Hamm's Preferred, America's most refreshing beer
16. For opening Highlander Beer / same
17. Horlacher Pilsner Beer (Penguin) / same

18. Hornung Beer-Ale / same
19. Iron City Beer / Tech Golden Beer
20. Drink Jax Beer / same
21. Krantz Brewing Corp., Findlay, Ohio / Old Dutch Beer
22. G. Krueger Brewing Co., Newark, N.J., Krueger Beer-Ale (K Man) / same
23. Maier Brewing Co., Los Angeles, Calif. / Maier Beer since 1875
24. Miller Brewing Co., Milwaukee, Wis. / Miller High Life Beer
25. Mitchell's Premium Beer / same
26. Drink Muehlebach Beer / same
27. Famous Narragansett Ale & Beer / same
28. Old Crown Ale Beer / same
29. Premium quality Pearl / same
30. Ram's Head Ale (Ram's head) / Valley Forge Beer
31. Red Top Brewing Co., Cincinnati, Ohio / same
32. Regal Pale Beer
33. Rheingold Extra Dry / same
34. Ruppert for that smile of pleasure / same
35. Schaefer America's oldest lager beer / same
36. Schmidt's City Club Beer
37. Schmidt's of Philadelphia, brewers since 1860 / same
38. Schoenhofen Edelweiss Co., Chicago, Illinois / Edelweiss a case of good judgement
39. Stag Beer
40. Sterling
41. Storz Beer / same
42. Tech Golden Beer / same
43. Terre Haute Brewing Co., Terre Haute, Ind. / CV the beer with the million dollar flavor
44. Tivoli Beer brewed for Western tastes / same
45. Utica Club Pilsener Beer and Cream Ale "U.C. for me" / same
46. Walter's Beer tastes better / same

J-6

1. Acme Beer
2. Arrow Beer — it hits the spot
3. Atlas Prager Beer
4. Atlas Prager Beer / same
5. Ballantine Ale Beer (3 rings)
6. Blatz Beer
7. Canadian Ace Brand Beer and Ale
8. Diamond State 100% Pure Grain Beer
9. Embassy Club Beer, Chicago
10. Falls City Beer
11. Krueger Beer Ale (K man)
12. Meister Brau
13. Old Crown Ale Beer
14. Pabst Blue Ribbon
15. R & H Beer-Ale
16. Rheingold Extra Dry
17. Schlitz Beer, Clinton L. Grey
18. Sterling
19. Storz
20. Trommer's Beer

J-7

1. For beer in cans marked Keglined (no beer advertisers noted)

J-8

1. Time out for Dawson's calorie controlled Beer & Ale
2. Duquesne Pilsener, the finest beer in town
3. Fox Head Brewing Co., Waukesha, Wis., Fox Head 400 Beer (fox head), brewed with Waukesha water
4. Gretz Beer (man on high wheeler)
5. Famous Narragansett Ale & Lager
6. Good Old Reading Beer, traditionally Pennsylvania Dutch
7. Piel's Light Beer (man)
8. Stegmaier Brewing Co., Wilkes Barre, Pa., Stegmaier Gold Medal Beer

J-9

1. Coors America's fine light beer, Adolph Coors Company, Golden, Colo. U.S.A.

K-1

1. Old Milwaukee, America's Light Beer

K-2

1. Blatz
2. Falstaff
3. Jax Beer, Jackson Brewing Co., New Orleans, La.

K-3

1. Rheingold Extra Dry Lager Beer

K-4

1. Tapster (no beer advertising)

L-1

1. Blatz
2. Budweiser
3. Coors
4. Miller High Life
5. Pabst Blue Ribbon
6. Ruppert Knickerbocker
7. Schlitz

L-2

1. Anheuser Busch (corkscrew inside)
2. Anheuser Busch Malt Nutrine (corkscrew inside)
3. Grand Prize Pale Dry Beer (lighter inside)

L-3

1. Michelob Beer

L-4

1. Atlas Prager Beer
2. Ballantine Extra Fine Beer
3. Barbarosa
4. Blatz Pilsner Beer
5. Canadian Brand Cream Ale
6. Canandaigua Premium Lager Beer
7. Canandaigua Extra Dry Lager Beer, George F. Stein Brewery, Inc., Buffalo, N.Y.
8. Citizen's Beer
9. Fehr's X/L the beer that xcels, Frank Fehr Brewing Co., Louisville, Ky.
10. Fleck's Beer, Ernest Fleckenstein Brewing Co., Faribault, Minn.
11. Fleck's Cave Aged Beer
12. Gluek Brewing Co., Minneapolis, Minn., Gluek's Beer
13. Iron City Lager
14. Koppitz Silver Star
15. Miller
16. Miller High Life
17. Pittsburgh Brewing Co., Pitts., Pa., Iron City Lager
18. Jacob Ruppert, New York, Ruppert Knickerbocker Beer
19. Schlitz Beer
20. Schlitz Export Beer
21. Schlitz Export Vitamin D
22. Tech Beer

23. Terre Haute Brewing Co., Terre Haute, Ind., CV Champagne Velvet Brand Beer

M-1

1. Canandaigua High Hopped Ale
2. Ask for Pickwick Ale, Haffenreffer, Boston Ale that is ale / same
3. Pickwick Ale, Haffenreffer, Inc. & Co., brewers since 1870, America's finest ale / Pickwick Stout, Haffenreffer, Inc. & Co., Boston, brewers since 1870
4. Haffenreffer in brown bottles
5. Harvard Brewing Co., Lowell, Mass., Harvard Ale / Harvard Brewing Co., Lowell, Mass., Harvard Beer
6. The Hudepohl Brewing Co., Cincinnati, Ohio, fine Hudepohl Beer / same
7. King's Bohemian Vienna Type Brew, Malt, King's Pure Malt Co., Boston / King's Chremal, King's Pure Malt Co.
8. Good Old Scotch Brew made under formula of James Aitkin & Company, Falkirk, Scotland by Liebmann Breweries, Inc., New York / Good Old Scotch Brew for real refreshment
9. Old Colony Brews, compliments of Old Colony Brewing Co., Boston, Mass. / same
10. Pickwick Beer in brown bottles / same

M-2

1. Amber Ale, Lyon & Sons Brewing Co., Newark, N.J.
2. Kent Ale, Lyon & Sons Brewing Co., Newark, N.J.
3. Goebel Beer — Pure food Goebel Beer, Detroit
4. Harvard Beer / same

M-3

1. Famous Beverwyck Beers, Ales, Beverwyck Breweries, Inc., Albany, New York
2. Bismarck Beer Deep cellar lagered
3. City Club, Toronto, Canada
4. Drink Daufer's Beer, since 1848, Allentown's favorite, Daeufer-Lieberman Brewery
5. Edelweiss Beer
6. Erin Brew, The Standard Brewing Co., Cleveland, Ohio
7. Gunther's the word for quality beer, brewers since 1881, Baltimore, Md.
8. Koehler's Beer, The Erie Brewing Co., Old Dobbin Ale
9. Old Anchor Beer, Brackenridge Brewing Co., Brackenridge, Pa.
10. Old Carnegie "The beer with character" Phone 550 Carnegie, Chartiers Valley Brewery, Carnegie, Pa.
11. Old Export Beer, Cumberland Brewing Co., Cumberland, Md.
12. The Original Old German Beer, The German Brewing Co., Cumberland, Md.
13. Old Stock, Brown Glow, Philadelphia Brewing Co., Philadelphia, Pa.
14. Piel's Fine lager beers, established 1883, Brooklyn, N.Y.
15. Shea's Select Beer
16. Sunshine Beers, Ales, Porter, Have Sunshine in your home, Healthful as Sunshine, Barbey's, Inc., Reading, Pa., Established 1861
17. S-K Lager Beer, healthful and refreshing, Schorr-Kolkschneider Brewing Co.
18. Stegmaier's Beer, the original Gold Medal Beer, The Stegmaier Brewing Co., Wilkes Barre, Penna.
19. Zett's Sparkling Ale

M-4

1. Blatz Milwaukee (Print)
2. Blatz Milwaukee (Script)

M-5

1. Tivoli Beer, Tivoli Brewing Company, Denver, Colorado

M-6

1. Gibbons Beer, ring for it
2. Hamm's Preferred Stock Beer fully aged, Happy New Year, Saliman Bros., Denver
3. Ring for Hopfheiser Beer
4. Ring for Pennsy Select Pilsener by brewers of Old Shay Ale
5. Signal Beer, Signal for a taste sensation
6. Ring for Wagner Beer, Wagner Brewing Co., Miami, Fla.

M-7

1. Silver Top Beer, Old Nut Brown Ale, Duquesne Pilsener, the finest beers in town, Duquesne Brewing Co., Pittsburgh, Pa.

M-8

1. Stoney's Beer

M-9

1. Ballantine Beer

M-10

1. Handy Way to Order Ballantine's

M-11

1. P. Ballantine & Sons, Newark, N.J., Drink Ballantine Ale-Beer — Purity, Body, Flavor

M-12

1. P. Ballantine & Sons, Newark, N.J., Drink Ballantine Ale-Beer — Purity, Body, Flavor

M-13

1. Ballantine's — Purity, Body, Flavor

M-14

1. Schmidt's of Philadelphia

M-15

1. Miller — 100 years in America, 1855-1955, Miller High Life / High Life

M-16

1. Budweiser / Beechwood

M-17

1. Budweiser King of Beers

M-18

1. Honorary Budweiser Brewmaster, 7 Golden Keys / This calls for Bud — 7 Golden Keys

M-19

1. Burger Beer
2. Miller / High Life
3. Narragansett Lager — Ale / Narragansett Brewing Co., Cranston, R.I.
4. Schlitz

M-20

1. The Gutsch Brewing Co.

M-21

1. Rainier

M-22

1. Edelweiss / Green River

M-23

1. Coors, America's fine light beer
2. Stag

M-24

1. Coors

M-25

1. Lemp, St. Louis

M-26

1. Coors—Golden

M-27

1. Lone Star Beer — Long Live Long Necks

M-28

1. Coors

N-1

1. Pabst Blue Ribbon

N-2

1. Drink Dixie Beer

N-3

1. Schmidt's Light Beer

N-4

1. Congress Beer / Haberle Congress Brewing Co., Inc.
2. The Star Beverage Co., Minster, Ohio / Wooden Shoe Lager Beer

N-5

1. Compt's West End Brg. Co. / Utica Club, it's in the Taste, Pilsener — Wuerzburger — Cream Ale

N-6

1. Drink American Club Beer made by / Lembeck & Betz, Eagle Brewing Co., Jersey City, N.J.

N-7

1. Hoster-Schlee's & Columbus, delightful beers

N-8

1. Compliments of Schuster Brewing Co., Rochester, Minn.

N-9

1. Camden Beer, Lord Camden Ale, Lager, Pilsner
2. Drink Fox Head Beverages made with Waukesha Spring Water
3. Fox Head Waukesha Sparkling Beverages, carbonated beverages
4. Mathie Ruder Brew. Co., Wausau, Wis., Red Ribbon Beer
5. Drink Muehlebachs Pilsener Beer
6. Neuweiler Beer-Ale "Nix Besser"
7. Trenton Old Stock Beer
8. Vienna Style Beer, Vienna Brewing Co., Cincinnati

N-10

1. Drink Krueger's Beverages

N-11

1. Fort Pitt Beer
2. Stoney's America's Best Beer

N-12

1. Beck's Buffalo's Best Beer

O-1

1. Hamm's Beer

O-2

1. Simon Pure Beer, Old Abbey Ale, Extra Pale Ale, William Simon Brewery, Buffalo, N.Y.

O-3

1. Valley Forge Beer

O-4

1. Coors, America's fine light beer

O-5

1. Braumeister
2. Burgermeister
3. Dixie 45 Beer
4. Falstaff Beer
5. Grand Prize Lager Beer
6. Jax Beer
7. Lucky Lager
8. Pearl
9. Premium Quality Falstaff Beer
10. Southern Select

O-6

1. Drink Esslinger's Premium Beer

O-7

1. Drewrys Beer

P-1

1. Anthony & Kuhn Brewing Co.

P-2

1. Compliments of The Greenway Brew'g Co., Syracuse, N.Y.

P-3

1. Pabst Milwaukee

P-4

1. Sequoia Beer

P-5

1. Anheuser Busch

P-6

1. Drink F and S Beer, Shamokin, Pa.

P-7

1. Burkhardt's, the Genuine Beer, Ale, and Porter
2. Compliments of Christian Atz Brewery, Egg Harbor City, N.J.
3. Birkenhauer's Old Fashioned Brewery, Newark, N.J., American Brew-Old Fashioned-Medium-German Brew-Dark-Brewery Bottling
4. C & J Michel, LaCrosse, Wis.
5. Drink Stegmaier Gold Medal
6. If you want the best, Drink Stegmaier's Wilkes Barre Beer, bottled at the brewery, established 1867, incorporated 1897

P-8

1. American Brewing Co., Brewers and bottlers of fine Beers, Macon, Ga., U.S.A., American Queen
2. The American Brewing Co., St. Louis, Mo., U.S.A., A-B-C Bohemian Beers
3. Anheuser Busch
4. Anthony & Kuhn, St. Louis

5. John F. Betz & Son, Ltd., Philadelphia, Pa.
6. Blatz Milwaukee, fine table beers
7. Buffalo Brewing Co., Sacramento, Cal., New Brew, Bohemian, and other famous brands
8. Buffalo Co-op Brewing Co., Buffalo, New York, Superior Stock Ale
9. Dick Bros., Quincy, Illinois
10. The Joseph Fallert Brewing Co., Limited, 52-66 Meserole St., Borough of Brooklyn, City of New York
11. The Fecker Brewing Co., Tiger Head & Export Beer
12. John Gund Brewing, LaCrosse, Wis.
13. Gund's Peerless Beer, LaCrosse, Wis.
14. Hamm's Beer
15. Hamm's Brewery, St. Paul, Minn.
16. A. Hupfel's Son's Brewery, New York, U.S.A.
17. Indianapolis Brewing Co., Dusseldorfer-Grand Prize, Cross of Honor, Gold Medal
18. Keeley Brg. Co., Pale High Three
19. The Koppitz Melchers Brewing Co., Detroit, U.S.A. Pale Select
20. Leisy Brewing Co.
21. Wm. J. Lemp Brewing Co., St. Louis, Mo., St. Louis-Lemp
22. Lion Brewery, Cincinnati, O.
23. Lutz Brewing Co., Allegheny
24. McAvoy Brewing Co., Chicago, Malt Marrow
25. A & J Michel Brw'g Co., LaCrosse, Wis., Perfection
26. Minneapolis Brewing Co., Drink Golden Grain Belt Beer
27. Mobile Brewery, Mobile, Ala., Phones 624 and 45
28. Moerlein, Cincinnati, U.S.A.
29. Narragansett Brewing Co., Providence, R.I.
30. National Brewery Co., St. Louis, Mo., Griesedieck Bros., Props.
31. The Neef Bros. Brewing Co., Denver, Colo., Compliments of NBBCo.
32. Pabst Milwaukee
33. Pittsburg Pure Beer Brg. Co.
34. Savannah Brewing Co., Brewers of pure beer
35. Peter Schoenhofen Brewing Company's Edelweiss
36. The Peter Schoenhofen Brg. Co., Eddmalt makes flesh and blood
37. P. Schoenhofen Brewing Co., Chicago, Edelweiss
38. Stroh's Beer, Detroit
39. Tennessee Brewing Co., Memphis, Tenn.
40. Texas Brewing Co., Fort Worth, Texas
41. Van Nostrand's PB Ale, Bunker Hill Lager
42. Wacker & Birk, Chicago, Brewers of fine beer
43. Wainwright Brewing Co., Pittsburgh

P-9

1. Heim Beer F.H.B. Co., Kansas City, Mo.
2. Winona Brewery, Wm. Shellhas, Proprietor
3. The Best Yuengling's Porter-Ale and Beer, Pottsville, Pa.

P-10

1. Anheuser Busch
2. Genesee Brew Co., Rochester, N.Y.
3. Schlitz, Milwaukee, U.S.A., Schlitz Beer

P-11

1. Monterey Beer, Salinas Brewing Company

P-12

1. J.C. Helb, wholesaler and bottler, 420-422 E. Market St., East York, Pa.

SECTION III

MORE ....

The National Beer Belaying Pin Opener was designed by John Schneider of the National Brewing Co. in conjunction with an advertising campaign for the Chesapeake Bay area, "Land of Pleasant Living." The handle is in the shape of a belaying pin which was used on the Clipper Ships to hang and release ships' lines and ropes. Distributor cost was 85 cents per opener with a minimum order of 12. Approximately 100,000 of these openers were sold between 1960 and 1963. (Opener from the collection of Don Reed.)

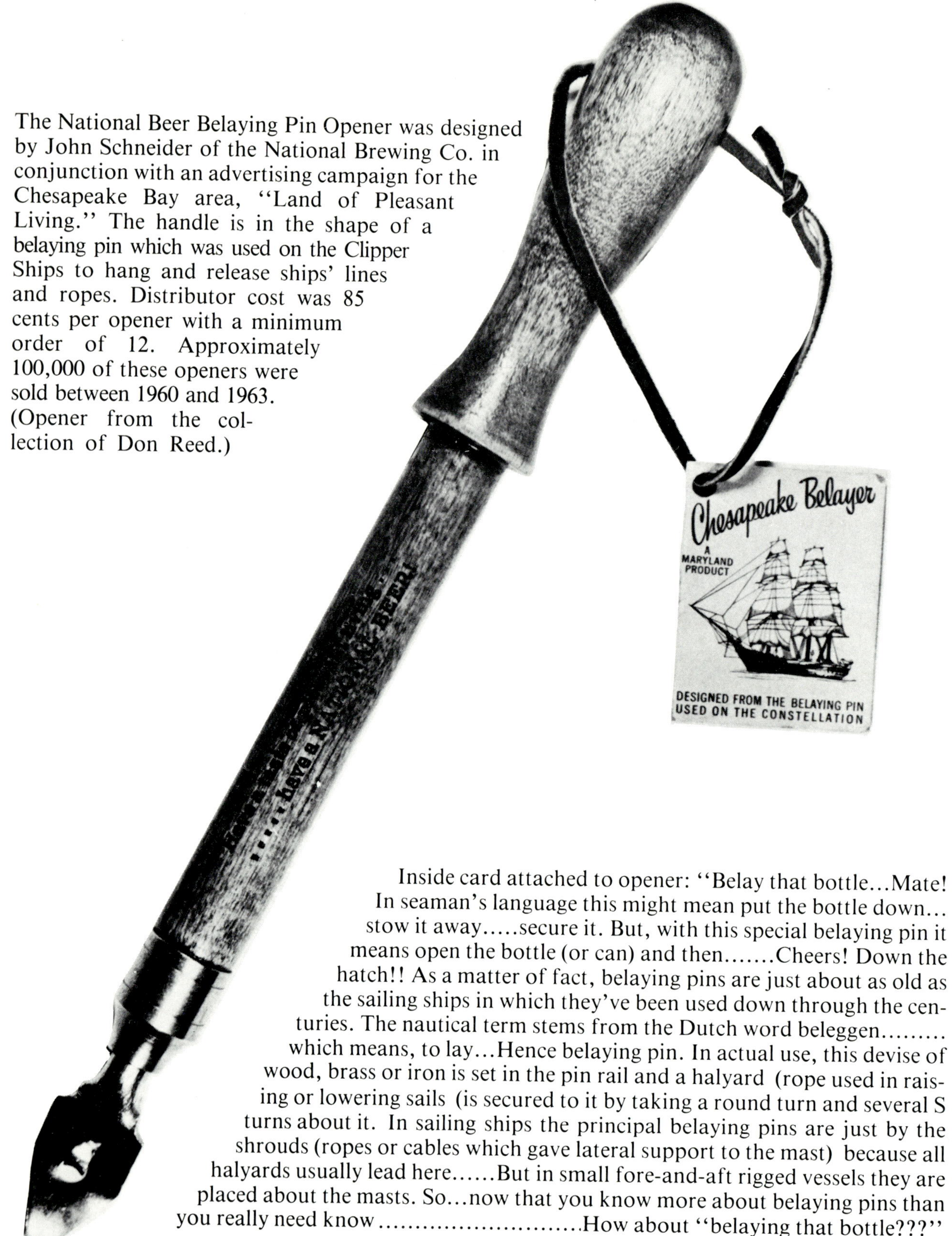

Inside card attached to opener: "Belay that bottle...Mate! In seaman's language this might mean put the bottle down... stow it away.....secure it. But, with this special belaying pin it means open the bottle (or can) and then.......Cheers! Down the hatch!! As a matter of fact, belaying pins are just about as old as the sailing ships in which they've been used down through the centuries. The nautical term stems from the Dutch word beleggen......... which means, to lay...Hence belaying pin. In actual use, this devise of wood, brass or iron is set in the pin rail and a halyard (rope used in raising or lowering sails (is secured to it by taking a round turn and several S turns about it. In sailing ships the principal belaying pins are just by the shrouds (ropes or cables which gave lateral support to the mast) because all halyards usually lead here......But in small fore-and-aft rigged vessels they are placed about the masts. So...now that you know more about belaying pins than you really need know ....How about "belaying that bottle???"

The inscription on this opener is "Return these keys to Olympia Brewing Co., Olympia, Washington and receive reward." On the reverse is the number 2757. An estimated 10,000 of these openers were handed out by Olympia personnel between the years 1906 and 1912. Number 2757 was sent to the Olympia Brewing Company agency in San Francisco in 1909. (Pictured larger than actual size)

(Opener from the collection of Harry Horn. Information supplied by Don M. Lee, Manager of Communications Services, Olympia Brewing Co.)

The openers shown below were collected by the author while putting this book together!

Opener manufacturing machinery at the Handy Walden Co. in Woodside, Queens, New York.

The handsome display case below shows a few sample openers made by the Handy Walden Co. in 1963 using the "Ro-Loc Process." This process would allow the manufacture of millions of openers without need to change blanks for various customer runs. The logo in color could then be added as orders were received. It was at this time, however, that twist off caps and pull tabs began to boom. As a result, no orders were taken for these openers and only the samples were manufactured.

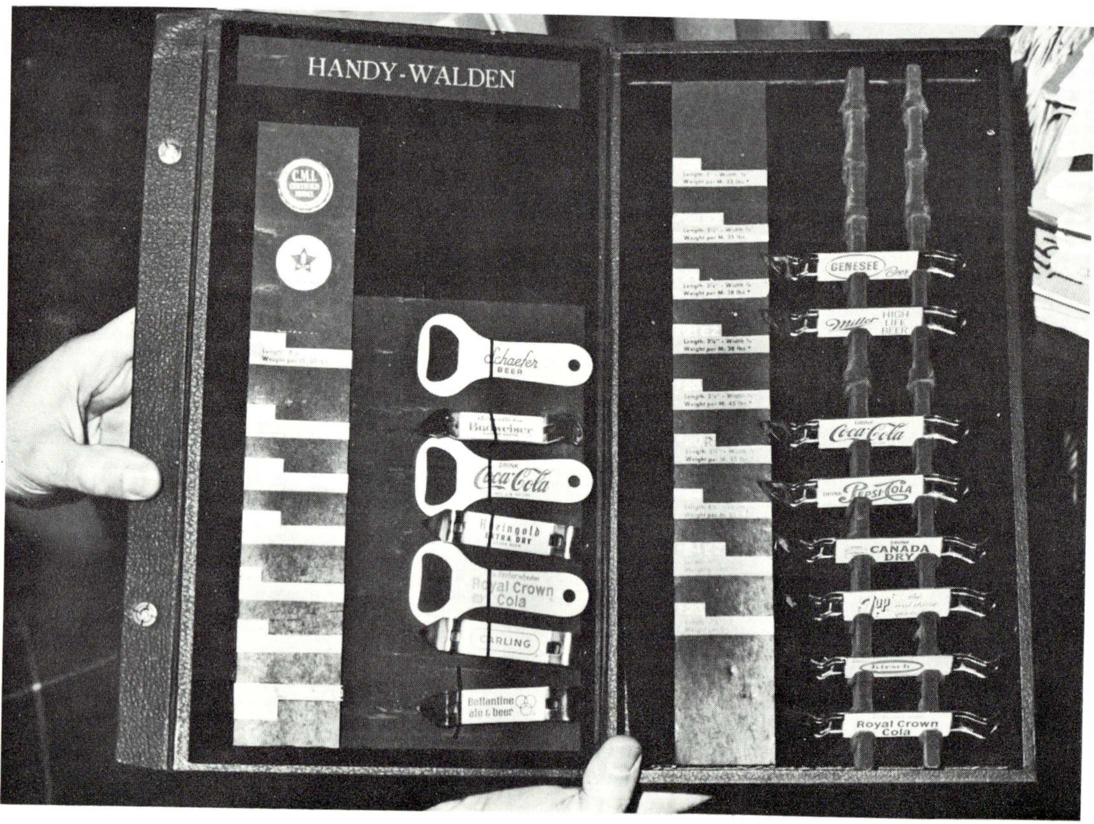

ADVERTISING SPECIALTIES

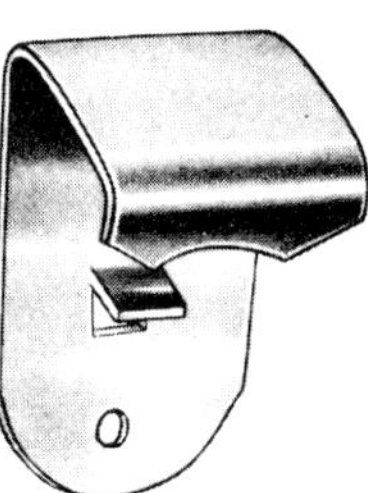

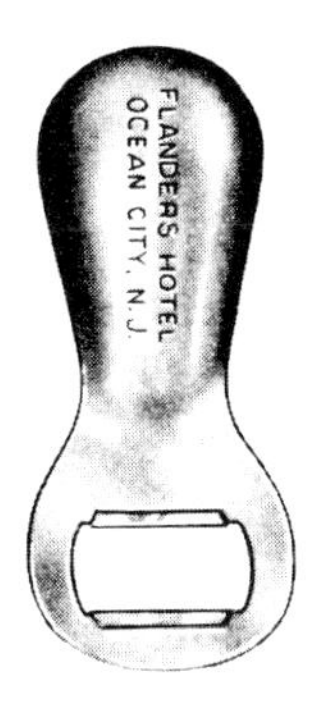

Handy Walden, Inc., a member of the Handy Group of companies, is happy to send you this catalogue. Pictured within are the many variations of openers which we can supply – from large to small, with adaptions for special requirements. Featured also are our patented "Canhandles," the first real answer to the old problem of using the can as a drinking container.

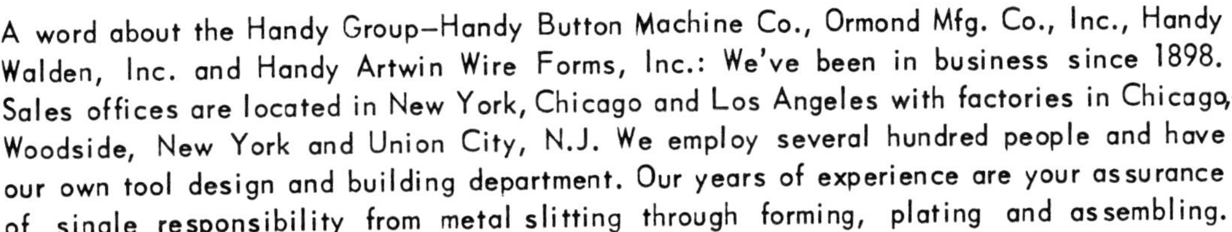

A word about the Handy Group–Handy Button Machine Co., Ormond Mfg. Co., Inc., Handy Walden, Inc. and Handy Artwin Wire Forms, Inc.: We've been in business since 1898. Sales offices are located in New York, Chicago and Los Angeles with factories in Chicago, Woodside, New York and Union City, N.J. We employ several hundred people and have our own tool design and building department. Our years of experience are your assurance of single responsibility from metal slitting through forming, plating and assembling.

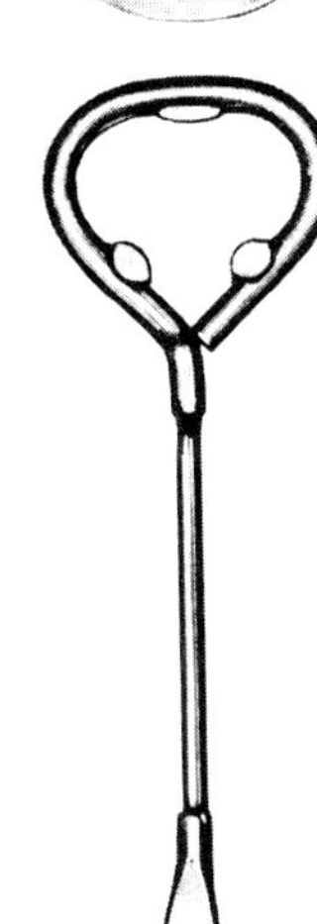

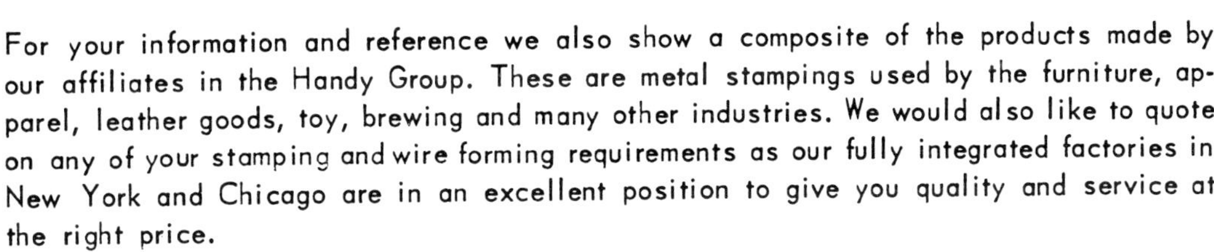

For your information and reference we also show a composite of the products made by our affiliates in the Handy Group. These are metal stampings used by the furniture, apparel, leather goods, toy, brewing and many other industries. We would also like to quote on any of your stamping and wire forming requirements as our fully integrated factories in New York and Chicago are in an excellent position to give you quality and service at the right price.

ASSOCIATE MEMBER

HANDY-WALDEN, Inc.

Division of HANDY BUTTON MACHINE CO. of N. Y., Inc.

313 W. 37th St. NEW YORK 18, N. Y. OXford 5-1880

the DOUBLE HEADERS

by

HANDY-WALDEN, Inc.

Division of HANDY BUTTON MACHINE CO. of N. Y., Inc.

Made of Hardened Tool Steel, Nickel, Copper or N.T.C. (Non-Tarnish Chromate) Plated.

#24

Length: 4-3/8" – Width: ¾"
Weight per M: 53 Lbs. *

#26R

Length: 3-½". Width 5/8"
Weight Per M: 37 Lbs.
With Bottle and Can Ends Reversed

#26RH

Length: 3-½". Width: 11/16"
Weight per M: 37 Lbs.
With Bottle End Angled for easy use with the popular Handy Bottle.

#26RHW

Length: 3-½". Width: 11/16"
Weight per M: 37 Lbs.
With widening ears and bottle end angled for easy use with the popular Handy Bottle.

*

OPENERS FOR EVERY NEED IN EVERY STYLE—

#20

Length: 3-7/8". Width: ¾"
Weight per M: 50 Lbs. *

#22

Length: 3-¼". Width: 5/8"
Weight per M: 35 Lbs.

#22W

Length: 3-¼". Width: 11/16"
Weight per M: 35 Lbs.
With ears added to increase width and prevent dropping opener into a bottle.

#22H

Length: 3-¼". Width: 5/8"
Weight per M: 35 Lbs.
With Bottle End Angled for easy use with the popular Handy Bottle.

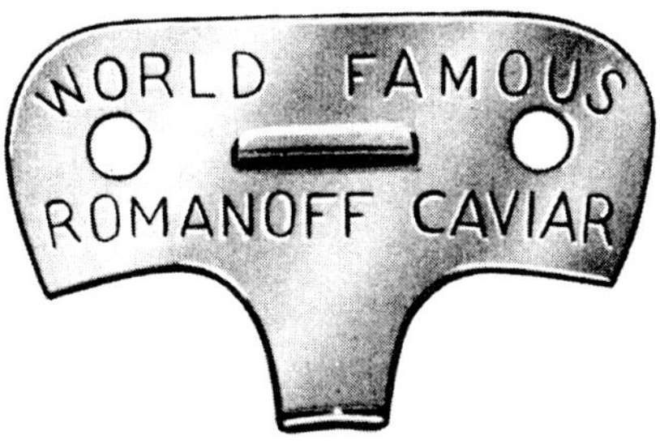

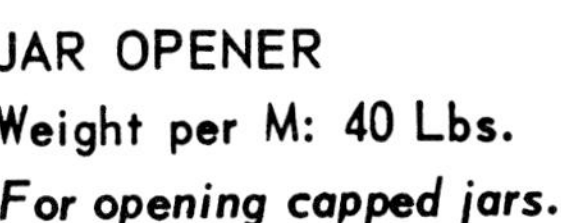

JAR OPENER
Weight per M: 40 Lbs.
For opening capped jars.

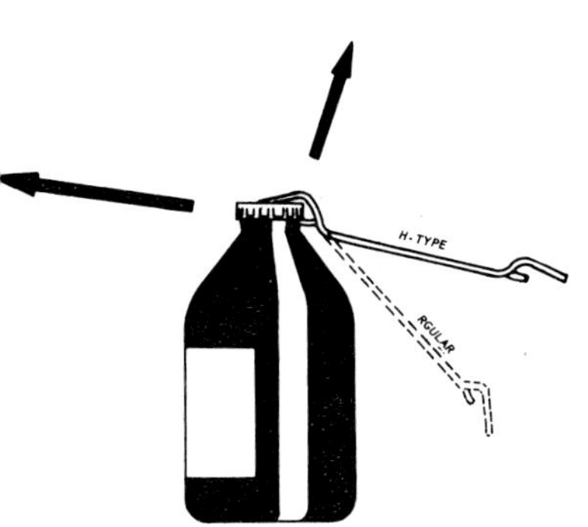

Note added clearance of H type opener. This gives added finger room and leverage.

SAMPLES, PRICES AND FURTHER INFORMATION ON REQUEST
We will welcome your inquiries regarding any special stampings which you may require, and we'll be happy to help you develop them.

Presenting the new look

HANDY WALDEN'S PATENTED CANHANDLES

Feels like a stein
Hands stay dry
Drinks stay cold
No glasses needed
Fits any 12 oz. can

Perfect for picnics, barbecues, home parties, boating, camping, hunting and fishing, reunions, fraternal meetings, conventions and just plain every day drinking.

#CH - 1
Handle only
Weight per M:
50 lbs.

#CH - 2
Combination Opener
and Handle
Weight per M:
70 lbs.

IMPRINTED AS DESIRED

CH - 2 made of hardened tool steel

Finishes: nickel (standard), gilt, copper, black

#101

Length: 3½"
Weight per M: 50 lbs.

WAL-OPE

Your Trade Mark Goes Here

Height: 2". Width: 1½"
Fits every bottle cap – Easily attached to wall.

#21 EZ

Length: 3-7/8", Width: 5/8"
Weight per M: 41 lbs.

#105

Length: 4-1/8". Width 3/4"
Weight per M: 50 lbs.

#108

Length: 3". Width 5/8"
Weight per M: 32 lbs.
Available with either flat or contoured handle. Specify when ordering.

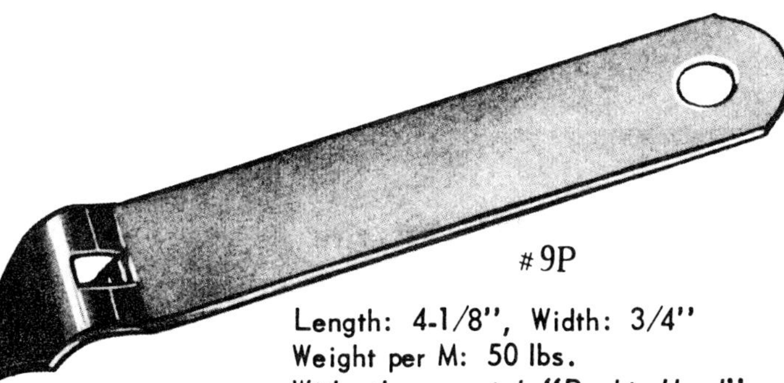

#9P

Length: 4-1/8", Width: 3/4"
Weight per M: 50 lbs.
With the special "Packie-Head" engineered so that cutting head does not protrude beyond the falcrum. Can't pierce cans when packed in a carton.

#25

Length: 3". Width: 5/8"
Weight per M: 32 lbs.

#23

Length: 4-5/8". Width: 3/4"
Weight per M: 60 lbs.

All made of hardened tool steel, nickel, copper or N.T.C. (non-tarnish chromate) plated.

OTHER ADVERTISING SPECIALTIES

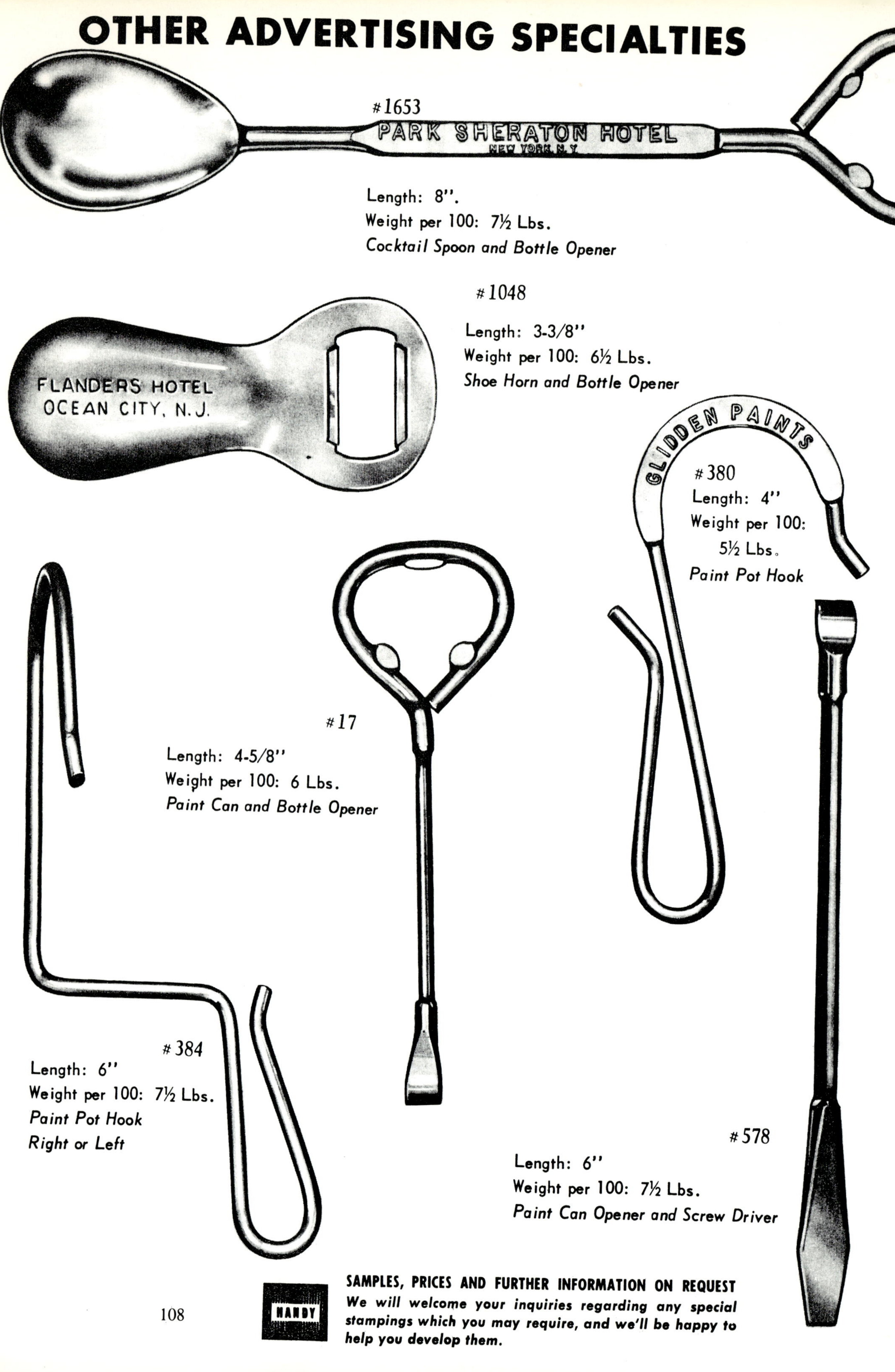

#1653

Length: 8".
Weight per 100: 7½ Lbs.
Cocktail Spoon and Bottle Opener

#1048

Length: 3-3/8"
Weight per 100: 6½ Lbs.
Shoe Horn and Bottle Opener

#380
Length: 4"
Weight per 100:
5½ Lbs.
Paint Pot Hook

#17

Length: 4-5/8"
Weight per 100: 6 Lbs.
Paint Can and Bottle Opener

#384
Length: 6"
Weight per 100: 7½ Lbs.
Paint Pot Hook
Right or Left

#578

Length: 6"
Weight per 100: 7½ Lbs.
Paint Can Opener and Screw Driver

HANDY

SAMPLES, PRICES AND FURTHER INFORMATION ON REQUEST
We will welcome your inquiries regarding any special stampings which you may require, and we'll be happy to help you develop them.

LOWEST COST ADVERTISING!

"HANDY" OPENERS

LOWEST COST ADVERTISING
A fraction of a penny buys a **"BILLBOARD MESSAGE"** that gets **REPEATED EXPOSURE** in the hands of a **CAPTIVE AUDIENCE.**

Get **VALUE** from your opener purchases Go **"COLOR LOGO"**!

Ro-loc
LOGO IN COLOR
Process

"Tops in Taste"

Hardened surface **RESISTS WEAR,** and is **ALCOHOL PROOF.**

FULL RANGE of colors is available in **2** or **1 COLOR FORMAT** on white or other **COLOR BACKGROUND,** on all popular styles of openers.

"HANDY" openers are finished in bright nickel plate and engineered to pierce cans and open bottles with ease and safety.

Ro-loc Process by

HANDY WALDEN, INC.
Manufacturers of Can and Bottle Openers
313 WEST 37th STREET NEW YORK 18, N. Y. OXFORD 5-1880
Factories and Warehouses • NEW YORK • CHICAGO • LOS ANGELES

"Quick and Easy Opener"
by
JOHN BURROUGHS

This particular punch type of opener was developed and patented by personnel of the American Can Company's Research Department at Maywood, Illinois. The first model was devised on August 15, 1932, with the patent applied for on April 13, 1933, and then granted on April 2, 1935.

The original model was developed primarily for opening containers with liquid and not for the beer can which was introduced in January, 1935. The length of the earlier openers was approximately 134 mm and then later shortened to 122 mm to simulate the height of a beer can for inclusion in beer cases. Commercial production started at the American Can Machine Shop in Newark, New Jersey and then continued at the Essex Factory, also in Newark, until sometime prior to 1942. Although American held the patent, a license was granted sometime in 1935-1936 to the Vaughan Manufacturing Company of Chicago to also produce the opener. Vaughan continued production after American ceased.

The public was first introduced to this opener when it was given away at the Chicago World's Fair in 1933, at which time about a million were distributed. Production by August 1935 reached 4 million and by January, 1937, 31 million. The popularity was such that a Boston jewelry store produced a sterling silver model in 1938 which sold for $6.00.

The indications are that Pabst beer was the first advertising on this opener as it was originally shown to their representatives as early as October, 1932. The Pabst Export Beer Tapa Can appeared in 1935 and on the label of this container it showed how to use the Quick and Easy Opener.

The term of Quick and Easy Opener apparently appeared only on those openers without or prior to the addition of the Keglined trade mark. However, more recent models produced by Vaughan do show the Quick and Easy Opener statement.

A possible sequential breakdown of the openers is as follows: (Notes — 1. Patent pending April, 1933 to 1935, 2. Keglined registered in 1934, 3. Pre-"Keglined" opener printing included a. Quick and Easy Opener, b. Pats. Pend. or Patent 1996550, c. Canco in oval, d. Made in USA and e. American Can Company and 4. "Keglined" opener printing included a. For beer in cans marked, b. Keglined, c. Canco in oval, d. Patent 1996550 and 5. Trade mark American Can Company).

1. 134 mm — Pre-Keglined patent pending information on obverse and plain on reverse side.
2. 122 mm — Pre-Keglined same as number 1.
3. 122 mm — Pre-Keglined with patent number and same as number 1.
4. 122 mm — Pre-Keglined with information on reverse and advertising on obverse side (for opening Pabst Tapa Can).
5. 122 mm — Keglined on obverse and plain on reverse side.
6. 122 mm — Keglined reverse and advertising on obverse side — Prager.
7. Same as 6 — Pabst.
8. Same as 6 — Miller.

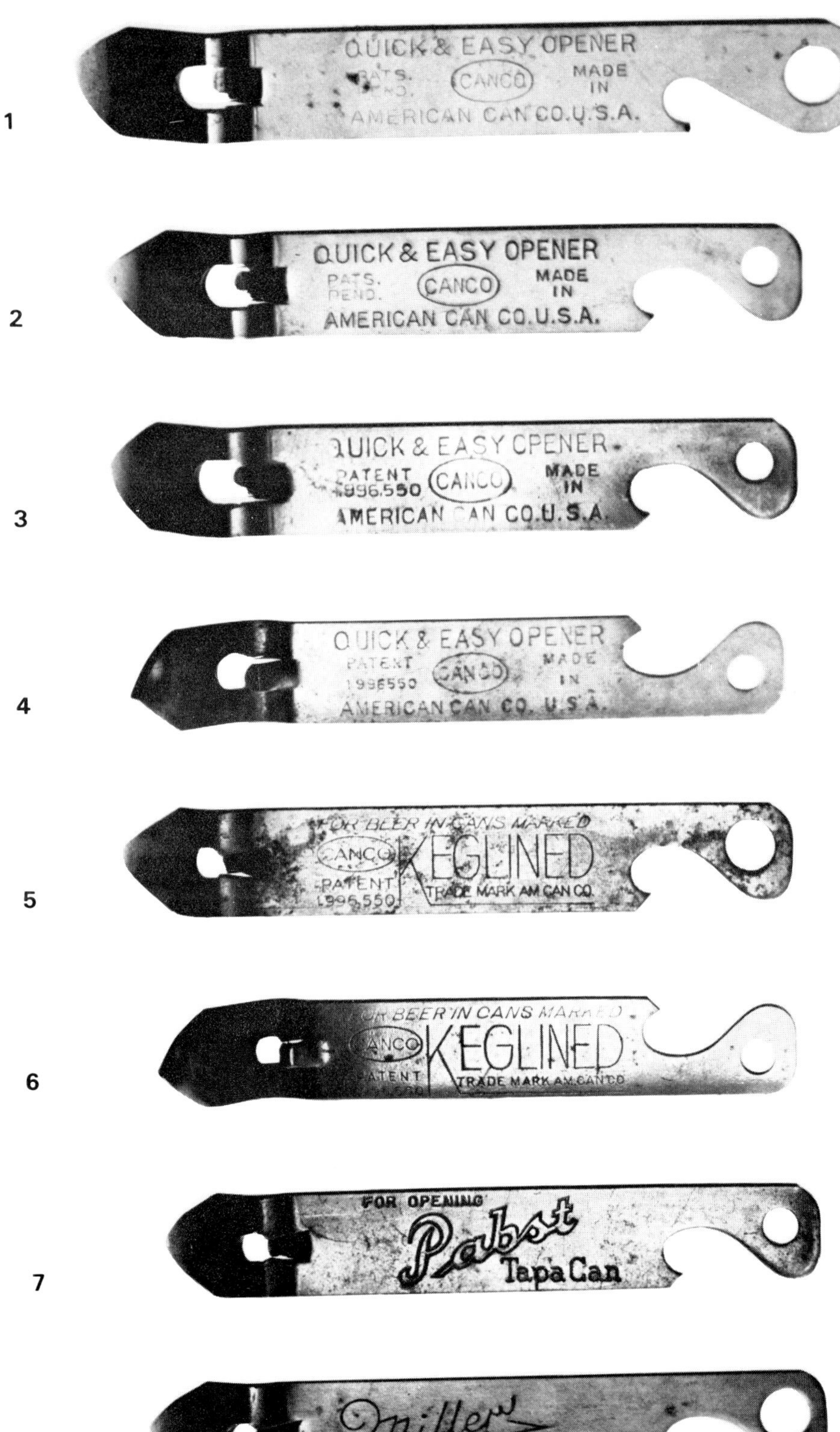
1
QUICK & EASY OPENER
PATS. PEND.
CANCO
MADE IN
AMERICAN CAN CO. U.S.A.
2
QUICK & EASY OPENER
PATS. PEND.
CANCO
MADE IN
AMERICAN CAN CO. U.S.A.
3
QUICK & EASY OPENER
PATENT 1996550
CANCO
MADE IN
AMERICAN CAN CO. U.S.A.
4
QUICK & EASY OPENER
PATENT 1996550
CANCO
MADE IN
AMERICAN CAN CO. U.S.A.
5
FOR BEER IN CANS MARKED
CANCO
PATENT 1996550
KEGLINED
TRADE MARK AM CAN CO
6
FOR BEER IN CANS MARKED
CANCO
KEGLINED
TRADE MARK AM CAN CO
7
FOR OPENING
Pabst
Tapa Can
8
Miller
SELECT BEER

ADVERTISING OPENERS OF THE CLEVELAND & SANDUSKY BREWING COMPANY

by
Glenn C. Kuebeler

The Cleveland & Sandusky Brewing Company (CSBC) was formed in 1898 through a consolidation of seven Cleveland, Ohio breweries and two Sandusky, Ohio breweries. The Cleveland breweries were: Baehr (founded in 1866), Bohemian (1850's), Cleveland (1852), Columbia (ca 1860), Gehring (1857), Phoenix (ca 1870), and Star (1869). The Sandusky breweries were Kuebeler (1867) and Stang (1850). Five additional breweries were added to the conglomerate later: Barrett (1890) in 1898, Union (ca 1875) in 1899, Schlather (1857) in 1902, Fishel (ca 1900) in 1907, and Lorain (unknown).

In 1902, CSBC had a combined plant capacity of over 800,000 barrels annually with a total capitalization of $10,546,000. The annual output of over 600,000 barrels represented over 60% of all the beer sold in Northern Ohio and 75% of all that sold in the city of Cleveland. Total sales revenue in 1910 was $1,030,336.

Only the Stang Brewery remained in operation during prohibition, producing near beer and carbonated soda beverages in a wide variety of flavors. Business was conducted under the name of The Cleveland-Sandusky Company, which was formed in 1929 as a wholly owned subsidiary of CSBC.

The first CSBC plant to begin production of real beer in 1933, following the repeal of prohibition, was the Stang Brewery. The Fishel Brewery in Cleveland was reopened soon afterwards, and following the final shutdown of the Stang plant in 1935, it became the only CSBC operating plant until business ceased in 1962. The company name was changed in 1936 to The Cleveland-Sandusky Brewing Corporation.

CSBC brands were Crystal Rock, Gold Bond, and Old Timers Ale. A premium beer, Our Brewmaster's Special, and a non-alcoholic malt beverage, New York Special, were marketed during the 1950's.

As with other breweries, CSBC made use of bottle and can openers as an advertising media. On the following pages are descriptions and photographs of varieties of CSBC openers known to the author.

GUIDE TO CSBC OPENERS

1. Picture of a woman clothed in an old style bathing suit and wading in water. The outside edge of the opener is the outline of the woman. Lettering on the reverse is "That Good Crystal Rock Beer." The opener is 73mm long and is patented by C.T. & O. Co. of Chicago.
2. Same as # 1 except woman wading in water is nude. An old-time CSBC brewery employee claims it was called "September Morn."
3. Clothed woman. 73mm long. Patented by C.T. & O. Co. of Chicago. Reverse of openers says "Crystal Rock Beer, Sandusky, O." The round hole in the opener was for attaching it to a key ring. The square hole was to allow the opener to be used as a wrench for opening a valve on carbide gas tanks used to supply gas to the headlights on early automobiles. The small tanks were attached to the running board on the auto and contained solid carbide in one section and water in another.
4. 61mm opener. Obverse says "Drink Crystal Rock Brew" — reverse is blank. The small "V" at the top is a cutting edge used for cutting cigar tips.
5. 73mm opener. Obverse says "Crystal Rock Beer" — reverse "The Cleveland & Sandusky Brewing Co."
6. 76mm key shaped opener. Obverse: "Drink Crystal Rock Beer." Reverse: "The Cleveland & Sandusky Brewing Co., Sandusky, Ohio."
7. 82mm. "Drink Crystal Rock Beer" on one side only. (Also known — same opener with "Drink Gold Bond Beer")
8. 81mm. "Gold Bond Beer" on both sides.
9. 81 mm with head bent up at about 45°. The obverse says "Drink Brewed Crystal Rock." The reverse says "The Cleveland-Sandusky Co., Cleveland, O.—Sandusky, O." which is the name used during prohibition.
10. 116mm. One side only: "Crystal Rock Beer." (Also known — same opener with "Old Timers Ale.")
11. 98mm combination bottle cap lifter and can piercer. "G/B Lager Beer" on obverse and "Cleveland-Sandusky Brewing Corp., Cleveland, Ohio" on reverse. Also: "CM/APP.—Vaughan U.S.A. — Pat. Pend." (Another variety includes the number "59" after U.S.A. denoting the year 1959).
12. Wall-mounted opener with four attachment screw holes. The opener portion is curved up 90° to the base. Overall size is 51mm by 64mm. Front side of the base says "Drink Gold Bond Brew."
13. 273mm combination bottle cap lifter and spatula. On obverse is raised lettering: "Cleveland & Sandusky Brewing Co., Gold Bond Beer, Harvard 1400, Central 3933."
14. Combination bottle cap lifter and slotted ladle. Same wording as number 13. Patented 2-23-15.
15. 200mm heavy handle ice pick with bottle opener hook. The handle has four flat sides with raised lettering on each: "Cleveland & Sandusky Brewing Co. / Gold Bond Beer / Cleveland, Ohio / Sixth City."

1
2
3
4
CRYSTAL ROCK
BREW
5
Crystal Rock
BEER
6
DRINK
CRYSTAL ROCK
BEER.
7
DRINK
Crystal Rock
Beer
8
Gold Bond Beer
9
BREWED
DRINK
CRYSTAL ROCK
10
Crystal Rock Beer
11
G. B

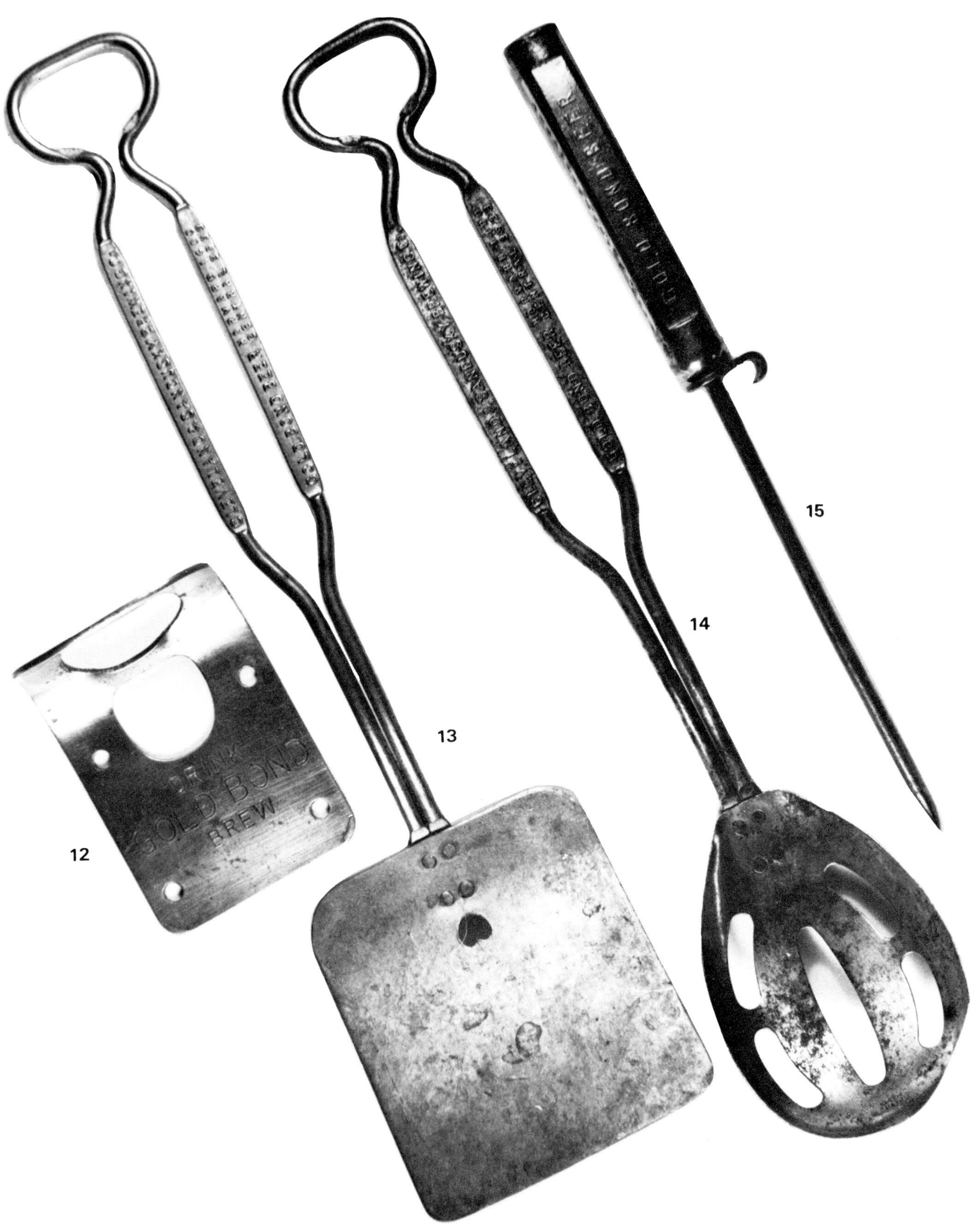
DRINK
GOLD BOND
BREW
12
13
14
15

FOREIGN OPENERS

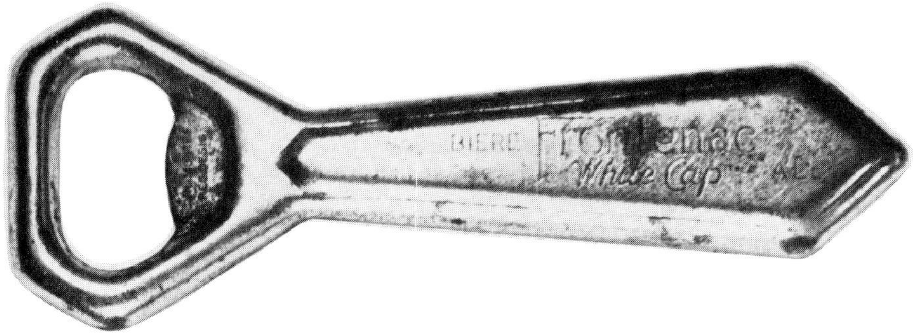
BIERE
White Cap

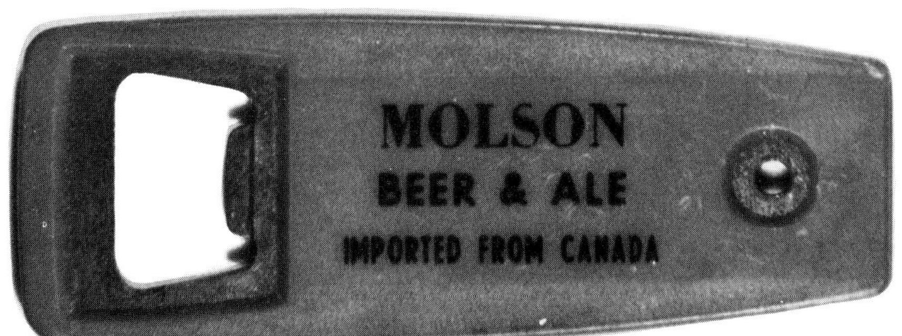

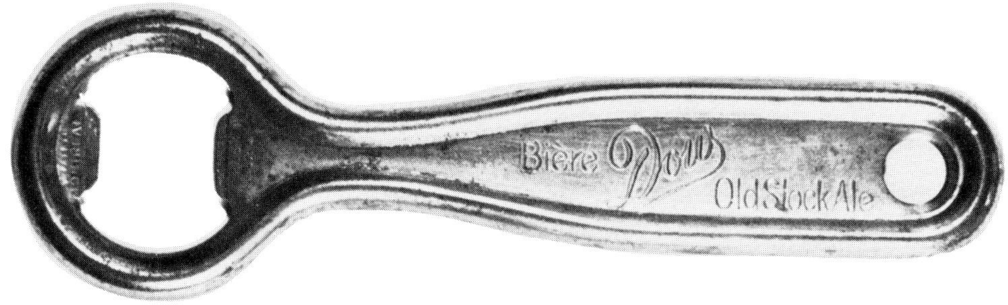
Biere Dow
Old Stock Ale

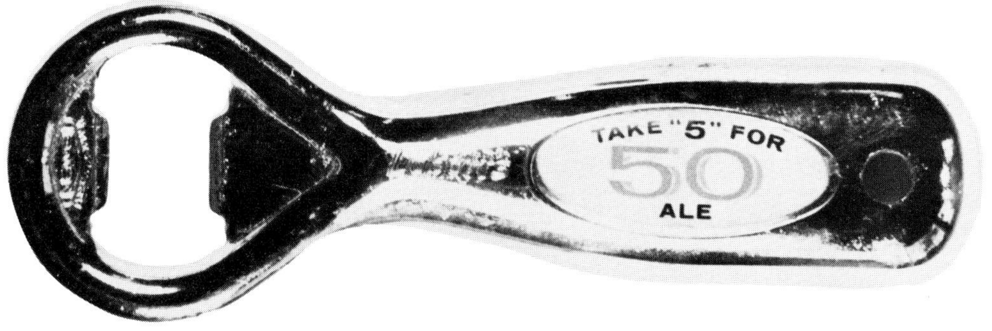
TAKE "5" FOR
50
ALE

MOLSON
BEER & ALE
IMPORTED FROM CANADA

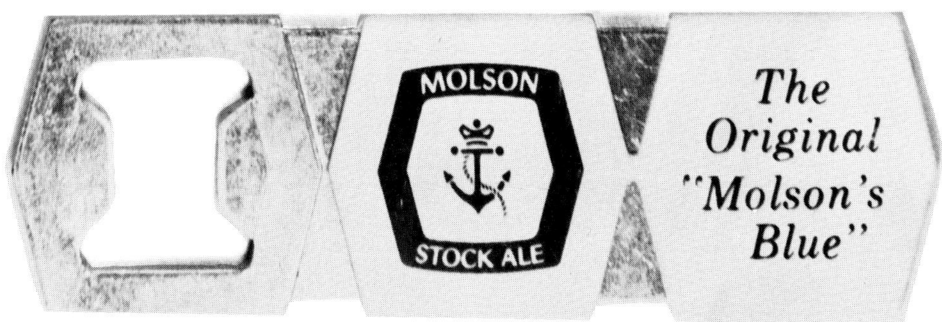

MOLSON
STOCK ALE
The Original "Molson's Blue"

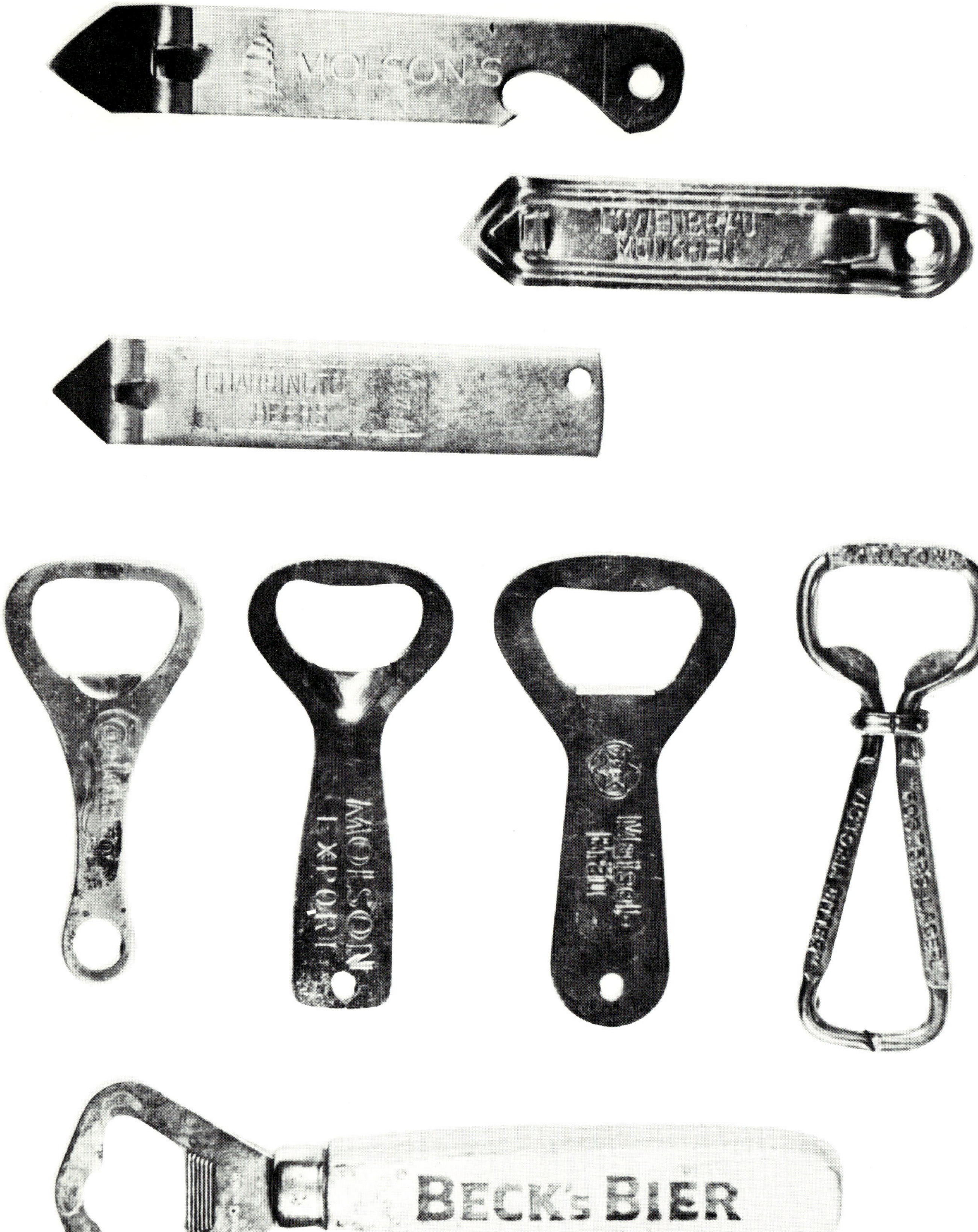
MOLSON'S
MOLSON
EXPORT
BECK's BIER

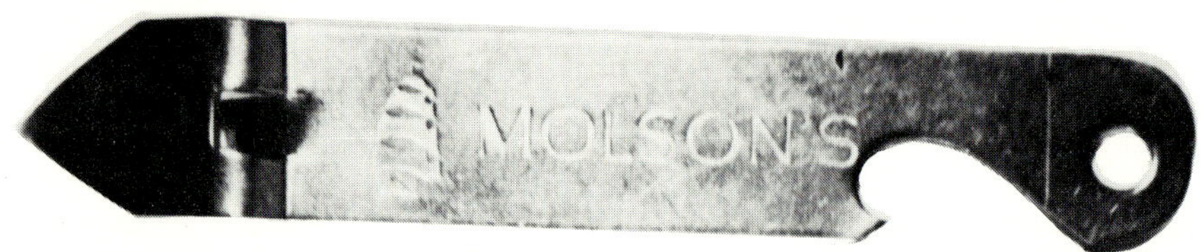

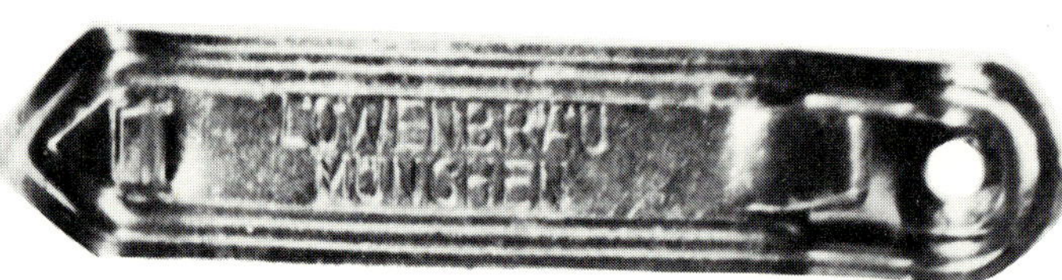

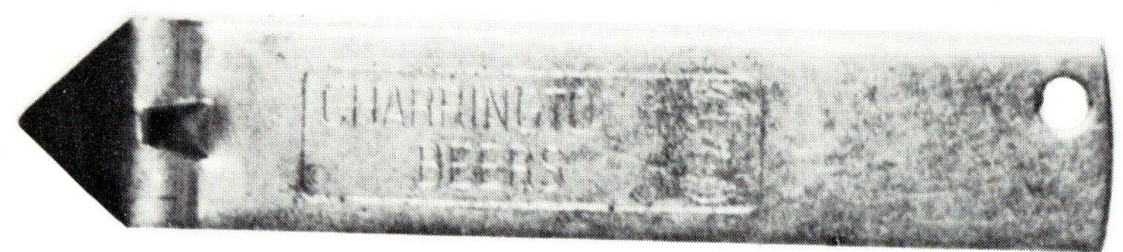

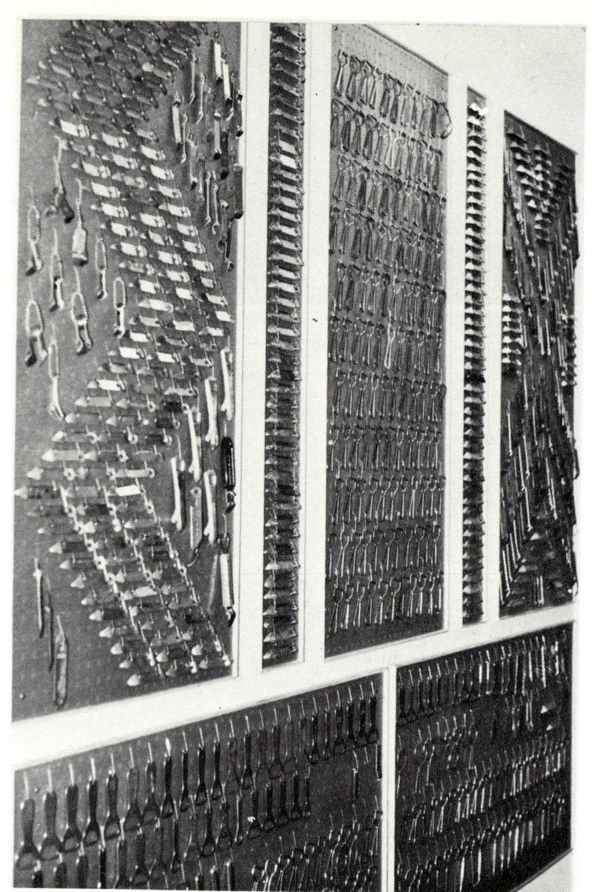

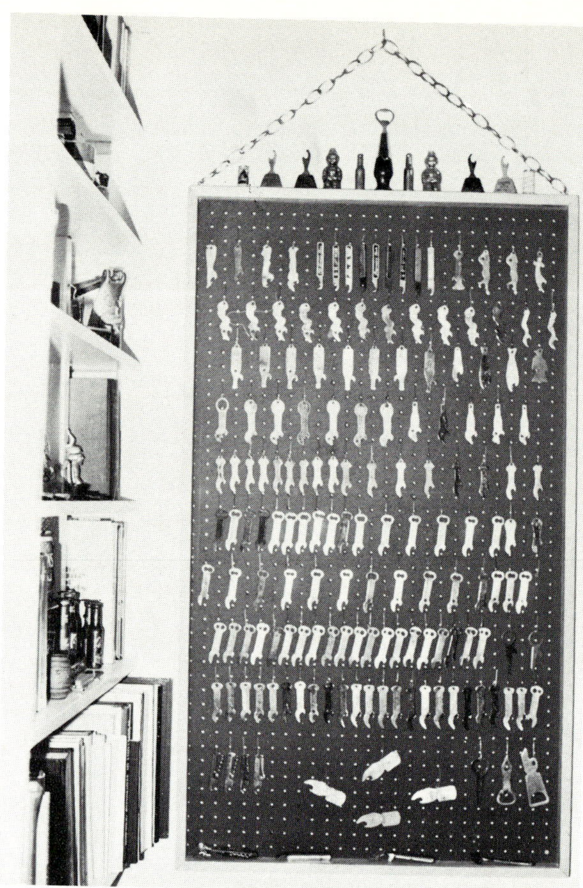

Part of the author's collection.